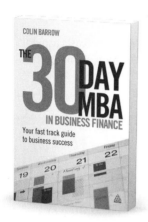

The 30 Day MBA in Business Finance

For many of the topics in the book there are direct links to the **free** teaching resources of the world's best business schools.

There are also links to hundreds of hours of **free** video lectures given by other distinguished Business School professors, from top schools including Cranfield, Wharton, Chicago, Harvard and CEIBS (China Europe International Business School).

From the Yale University School of Management (http://opa.yale.edu/netcasts.aspx) you can access Netcasts on such topics as the State of Private Equity, Banking, Early Stage Investing and How to Write a Business Plan.

You can download Duke University's top ranking Fuqua School of Business's lecture material on forecasting; a vital aid to anyone preparing financial projections.

Link into Cranfield's School of Management's Research Paper Series and see the latest insights in global supply chain logistics, or watch Harvard's Professor Michael Porter – a leading world proponent of international business strategy methodology – outline his ideas.

You can find a list of all these online resources and more at the back of the book and interspersed within the chapters. Visit **http://www.koganpage.com/ editions/the-30-day-mba-in-business-finance/9780749462154**.

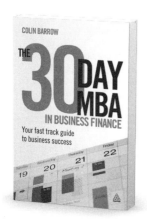

The 30 Day MBA in Business Finance

Colin Barrow

KoganPage

LONDON PHILADELPHIA NEW DELHI

Publisher's note

Every possible effort has been made to ensure that the information contained in this book is accurate at the time of going to press, and the publishers and author cannot accept responsibility for any errors or omissions, however caused. No responsibility for loss or damage occasioned to any person acting, or refraining from action, as a result of the material in this publication can be accepted by the editor, the publishers or the author.

First published in Great Britain and the United States in 2011 by Kogan Page Limited

120 Pentonville Road	1518 Walnut Street, Suite 1100	4737/23 Ansari Road
London N1 9JN	Philadelphia PA 19102	Daryaganj
United Kingdom	USA	New Delhi 110002
www.koganpage.com		India

© Colin Barrow, 2011

The right of Colin Barrow to be identified as the author of this work has been asserted by him in accordance with the Copyright, Designs and Patents Act 1988.

ISBN   978 0 7494 6215 4
E-ISBN   978 0 7494 6216 1

British Library Cataloguing-in-Publication Data

A CIP record for this book is available from the British Library.

Library of Congress Cataloging-in-Publication Data

Barrow, Colin.
   The 30 day MBA in business finance : your fast track guide to business success / Colin Barrow.
– 1st ed.
      p. cm.
   ISBN 978-0-7494-6215-4 – ISBN 978-0-7494-6216-1   1. Business enterprises–Finance–Study and teaching.   2. Risk management.   3. Decision making.   4. Master of business administration degree.   I. Title.   II. Title: Thirty-day MBA in business finance.
   HG4014.B37 2011
   658.15–dc22
                                                                                        2011008558

Typeset by Graphicraft Ltd, Hong Kong
Printed and bound in India by Replika Press Pvt Ltd

CONTENTS

List of figures   viii
List of tables   ix

Introduction   1

PART ONE   The fundamentals of business finance   7

01   Financial business reports   9

Who uses financial information and why   10
Accounting branches   11
Bookkeeping – the way transactions are recorded   13
Cash flow   16
The profit and loss account (income statement)   21
The balance sheet   24

02   The rules of the game   31

Fundamental conventions   31
Accounting conventions   35
The rule makers   36
International accounting standards   37
Protecting investors   37

03   Analysing financial reports   38

Analysing accounts   40
Accounting ratios   41
Some problems in using ratios   49
Getting company accounts   51
Using financial data to improve performance   56

04   Finance as a value creator   66

Cost, volume, pricing and profit decisions   68
Profit maximization vs shareholder value   78

The cost of capital   79
Future investment decisions   83
Outsourcing   86
Shares and markets   89

PART TWO Corporate capital structures   91

05   The role of business structures in financing
      business   93

Corporate structures   94
Help and advice on business corporate structure   99

06   Debt finance   100

Bank lending   101
Local financing initiatives   105
Bonds, debentures and mortgages   106
Asset usage financing   111

07   Equity   115

Private equity   117
Public capital   125
What investors want   135
Hybrids   138
Money for free   138

PART THREE Financial strategies and
special topics   141

08   Risk management   143

Gearing – leverage   144
Customer default   147
Online and distance trading   156
Foreign exchange   156

09   Business tax and reporting procedures   159

Principles of taxation   160
Tax types   161

Auditors – the gatekeepers 164
Filing accounts 168
Directors' responsibilities and duties 169
Values and the accounting reports 171

10   Mergers and acquisitions 174

Going on the acquisition trail 176
Valuing a target 179
Limit the risks 184
City code on takeovers and mergers 186

11   Business plans and budgets 187

Forecasting 188
Economic cycles 190
Business plans 193
Budgets and variances 197

12   The core 201

Marketing 202
Organizational behaviour 208
Motivation 214
Strategy 217
Shaping strategy – tools and techniques 222

LIST OF FIGURES

FIGURE 1.1   A simple system of keeping business records 15

FIGURE 4.1   Amazon: The more it lost the more it was worth! 67

FIGURE 4.2   Cost model: 1 showing fixed costs 70

FIGURE 4.3   Variation on cost model 1: showing a 'step up' in fixed costs 70

FIGURE 4.4   Cost model 2: showing behaviour of variable costs as volume changes 71

FIGURE 4.5   Cost model showing total costs and fixed costs 72

FIGURE 4.6   Cost model showing a break-even point 73

FIGURE 4.7   Break-even chart for special deals 76

FIGURE 6.1   Cobra Beer's financing strategy 110

FIGURE 7.1   Funding appetite 136

FIGURE 8.1   The truth about the risk of failure 144

FIGURE 8.2   Risk and gearing 146

FIGURE 8.3   Part of a credit report 149

FIGURE 8.4   EAT Ltd profit and loss accounts for the years to June 2008 and June 2009 150

FIGURE 8.5   EAT Ltd balance sheets for June 2008 and June 2009 151

FIGURE 8.6   Age analysis of debtors' invoices 154

FIGURE 8.7   Foreign exchange translation exposure in millions 158

FIGURE 11.1   Scatter diagram example 189

FIGURE 11.2   Scatter diagram – the line of best fit 190

FIGURE 11.3   Textbook economic cycle 192

FIGURE 12.1   Example SWOT chart for a hypothetical Cobra Beer competitor 204

FIGURE 12.2   A framework for understanding organizational behaviour 209

FIGURE 12.3   Basic hierarchical organization chart 210

FIGURE 12.4   Line and staff organization chart 212

FIGURE 12.5   Functional organization chart 212

FIGURE 12.6   Matrix organization chart 213

FIGURE 12.7   Strategic business unit organization chart 214

FIGURE 12.8   The experience curve 219

FIGURE 12.9   Ansoff's Growth Matrix 222

FIGURE 12.10   The Boston Matrix 224

FIGURE 12.11   The purpose pyramid 224

FIGURE 12.12   The balanced scorecard 227

LIST OF TABLES

TABLE 1.1   An example of a double-entry ledger   14

TABLE 1.2   High Note six-month cash flow forecast   18

TABLE 1.3   Un-audited condensed cash flow statement for Straight plc (for the six months ended 30 June 2007)   20

TABLE 1.4   Profit and loss account for High Note for the six months, April–September   22

TABLE 1.5   High Note extended profit and loss account   23

TABLE 1.6   High Note balance sheet at 30 September   25

TABLE 1.7   Equivalent balance sheet for a US corporation   26

TABLE 1.8   Part of the balance sheet for Liverpool Football Club and Athletic Grounds plc   27

TABLE 1.9   A package of accounts   30

TABLE 2.1   Example of the changing 'worth' of an asset   32

TABLE 2.2   Example of a badly matched profit and loss account   35

TABLE 3.1   Factors that affect profit performance   39

TABLE 3.2   High Note extended profit and loss account   42

TABLE 3.3   High Note balance sheet at 30 September   44

TABLE 3.4   Tesco's 'Steering Wheel' ratios   48

TABLE 3.5   Difficult comparisons   49

TABLE 3.6   Google Inc company accounts   53

TABLE 3.7   Tesco company accounts – group income statement   56

TABLE 3.8   High Note's profit and loss account and balance sheet   57

TABLE 3.9   Evaluating a discount offer   60

TABLE 3.10   Product profitability (1)   63

TABLE 3.11   Product profitability (2)   63

TABLE 3.12   Fixed costs allocated by contribution level   64

TABLE 3.13   Product profitability using contribution   64

TABLE 4.1   Calculating a margin of safety   74

TABLE 4.2   The payback method   84

TABLE 4.3   Using discounted cash flow (DCF)   85

TABLE 8.1   The effect of gearing on shareholders' returns   145

TABLE 10.1   Discounting a stream of future earnings   181

TABLE 11.1   Executive summary – history and projections   195

TABLE 11.2   The fixed budget   198

TABLE 11.3   The flexed budget   199

Introduction

- What an MBA in Business Finance knows
- Why *you* need that knowledge too
- How to use this book
- Planning your learning programme

The honour of being the world's first business school is usually said to go to Wharton, founded in 1881 by Joseph Wharton, a self-taught businessman. A miner, he made his fortune through the American Nickel Company and the Bethlehem Steel Corporation, later to become the subject of the earliest business case studies. Harvard Business School, a comparative latecomer, opened in 1908 with a faculty of 15 but it wasn't until the late 1950s that the first business schools opened their doors in the UK – LBS (London Business School), Cranfield, and the Manchester Business School in the vanguard. In mainland Europe it took a further two decades for business schools to establish a niche in the market.

The MBA was launched as an answer to the apparent lack of both professionalism and a recognized qualification for business managers. Accountants, engineers, scientists, actuaries, chemists, psychologists and a host of others in and around the organizational world had a body of knowledge and an accrediting association that ensured those practising in the field met at least some minimum criteria. The MBA to some extent addressed that problem and now over 2,000 institutions around the world turn out hundreds of thousands of MBAs each year. With the growing complexity of business it rapidly became apparent that there was a need for a more specialized business degree rather than the all-singing all-dancing general MBA. While that was fine for giving an overview, anyone wanting to get into the bowels of a particular disciplinary area as a management practitioner needed something with a bit more substance. And so the specialized MBAs were born.

The MBA in Business Finance, the subject of this book, goes under various titles. Initially the subject started out as a specialization within the general MBA. Edinburgh runs an MBA with a 'Specialism in Finance', as does Wharton which, as well as being the first business school, was first with a specialist finance Master's programme in 1881. The University of Chicago Booth School of Business runs a finance programme with a strong focus on understanding the behaviour of securities, drawn from its Center for Research in Security Prices – the leading provider of historical stock market data. At the LBS its pre-eminent programme is its Master's in Finance, and Cranfield, MIT (Massachusetts Institute of Technology) and Stanford use that title also. However, at Liverpool and Northeastern Universities, as with many others, the subject goes by the title 'MBA in Finance'. Even the MBAs in the financial arena are being subjected to further specialization. Bangor Business School in North Wales offers an MBA in Islamic Banking and Finance.

What is the content of an MBA in Financial Management and what use will that be to me?

Anyone who wants to play a more rounded role in shaping and implementing the direction of the organization he or she works in but is inhibited by his or her lack of financial and accounting knowledge will find that reading this book will equip him or her to take part in the strategic decision making on an equal footing with MBA graduates, while feeling at ease in the process. It places MBA finance and accounting skills within reach of all professionals in large and small organizations in both the public and private sectors, providing them with a competitive edge over less knowledgeable colleagues.

Business finance comprises a number of disciplinary areas, each with a number of components. The disciplines contain the tools with which you can effectively analyse a business's financial situation, drawing on both internal information relevant to the business and external information on its markets, competitors and general business environment as a prelude to deciding what to do.

The emphasis in this book is on the terms 'concepts' and 'tools'. The business world is full of conflicting theories and ideas on how organizations could or should work, or how they could be made to work better. They come in and out of fashion, get embellished or replaced over time. A good analogy would be the difference between the limited number of tools a carpenter, for example, has in his or her toolbox, and the infinite number of products that could be made from those same tools. The ultimate success of the product the carpenter makes is partly down to his or her skills in using those tools and partly down to the world he or she is operating in at a particular time. A glance in a carpenter's toolbox will reveal an enduring range of common robust implements – screwdrivers, pliers, spanners, smoothing planes, saws and hammers.

In business, for example, there is no such thing as an optimal capital structure, or the right number of new products to bring to market, or whether or not going for an acquisition is a winning strategy. What's best in terms of, say, a debt to equity ratio varies with the type of organization and the prevailing conditions in the money market. That ratio will be different for the same organization at different times and when it is pursuing different strategies. Layering an inherently risky marketing strategy, say diversifying, with a risky financing strategy, using borrowed rather than shareholders' money, creates a potentially more risky situation than any one of those actions in isolation. But whichever of the choices a business makes, the tools used to assess financial and marketing strengths and weaknesses are much the same. It is the concepts and tools to be used in those disciplines that this book explains, and it shows you how to use both individually to comprehensively assess a business situation.

The MBA Business Finance core disciplines

There are a small number of core subject areas that comprise the subject matter of an MBA Business Finance programme. Many business schools eschew some vital elements within these disciplines as they are considered either too practical, un-sexy from a research/career prospective or more skill- or art-oriented than academic. So, for example, some schools assume a high degree of basic accounting knowledge as a prerequisite or simply provide an online learning resource to cover the subject. In some cases there may well be unique content in specialized electives, say on Financial Analysis of Mergers, Acquisitions and Other Complex Corporate Restructurings as taught at the London Business School, or Dealing with Financial Crime on offer at Cass Business School. At Copenhagen, MBA students will be given a thorough grounding in Norwegian, Swedish and Danish banking in the interwar years, but may well skip over the world banking crisis of 2008–10.

The irreducible core MBA Business Finance syllabus is as follows.

The fundamentals of business finance

- Business reports: cash flow, profit and loss (income statements) and balance sheets – their structures, purpose and limitations.

- The rules of the game: accounting concepts, principles and procedures. What accounts do and don't reveal about performance.

- Analysing financial reports: sources of financial information. Using ratios to measure and compare business performance.

- The role of finance in creating value: profit maximization vs shareholder value, calculating the cost of various types of capital, capital investment appraisal techniques.

Corporate capital structures

- The role of business structures in financing business: sole traders, partnerships, limited partnerships, companies private and public.

- Debt finance: the role of banks, loans, overdrafts, bonds, syndicated loans, commercial paper, government support schemes.
- Asset financing: leasing finance, hire purchase, sale and leaseback.
- Working capital funding: factoring, invoice discounting, bills of exchange, acceptance credit, supplier finance.
- Equity: an overview, equity investors – criteria and rewards, valuing businesses, shares – ordinary, preference and convertible, business angels and seed corn funding, business incubators, venture capital – private, venture capital – publicly funded, corporate venture funding, stock markets.
- Mezzanine finance: a hybrid of debt and equity financing that is typically used to finance the expansion of existing companies. Mezzanine financing is basically debt capital that gives the lender the rights to convert to an ownership or equity interest.

Financial strategies and special topics

- Risk management: an overview of financial risk, gearing and leverage, credit scoring and rating, options and derivatives, futures, forwards and swops, exchange rate risks – possible impact – options – covering in forward markets, financial due diligence, directors' responsibilities in financing, warranties and indemnities, risk and the business cycle.
- Business tax and reporting procedures: tax treatment of sources of finance, accounting for investors, the role and responsibilities of the auditor, debt covenants – legal reason for foreclosing on loans, options for business closure, financial pecking order in the event of failure.
- Mergers and acquisition: business valuation methods, search methods, choosing and using corporate finance advisers, negotiation parameters, dealing with earn outs, the human side of M&A, accounting for merged businesses.
- Business plans and budgets: forecasting methods and causal relationships, budgeting guidelines, building a budget model, setting and flexing the budget, cash and capital budgets, monitoring performance through variance analysis, preparing plans.

The main uses of MBA Business Finance knowledge

Specialist business finance knowledge as covered in this book or in a business school equips the student with a thorough understanding of financial theory and practice and helps him or her master the skills needed to use accounting and finance tools essential to interpreting and influencing financial performance. With these skills you can:

- Gain the financial analysis and strategic perspective you need to interact effectively with top management as a partner in making key business decisions.
- Play a full role in financial planning and control, financial analyses, foreign exchange risk management and capital budgeting.
- Take part effectively in acquisition strategies – buying, selling and joint ventures.
- Understand how businesses are financed and the criteria used by financial institutions when making funding decisions, and play a role in helping a business raise funds.
- Prepare business plans and financial projections.
- Understand how equity markets operate and how businesses can use such markets effectively.

MBA Business Finance knowledge can also open up opportunities for career development and change in a wide variety of areas including business analyst, mergers and acquisitions. investment, banking, trading, investment management, hedge funds, security analysis, institutional sales, security brokerage, capital markets, risk management, the finance function for companies or non-profits as well as regulatory and trade bodies, and investor relations. Even quite dramatic career changes may be possible once you have a sound grasp of this subject area. The LBS quotes the case of a part-time student on its programme who within the three years, from 2008 to 2010, made the transition from broadcast financial journalism to boutique investment management in the emerging markets fixed income field.

How this book is organized and how to use it

Each of chapters in the book covers the essential elements of each of the core disciplines in a top MBA Business Finance programme. For many of the topics there are web addresses for *free* teaching resources of the world's best business schools. There are also web addresses for hundreds of hours of *free* video lectures given by distinguished business school professors from top schools including LBS, Imperial, Oxford and Aston. You will find the address to download Duke University's top-ranking Fuqua School of Business's lecture material on forecasting, and the link for Cranfield School of Management's Research Paper Series, where you can see the latest insights into business finance.

Depending on your knowledge of basic finance you should plan to spend about eight days on each of the three sections. You should draw up a time-table spread over, say, 12, 24 or 36 weeks. You will need to build in a couple of days for revision before you take your final exam.

The subject areas within each chapter correspond to what you would find in the syllabus at major business schools in terms of theoretical under-pinning and the practical application of that theory that you would pick up from fellow students.

The final chapter, The Core, contains the basic tools that an MBA will use or need to refer to more or less every working day. All MBA students, whether they take a general programme or one that specializes in a parti-cular disciple, as this book does, will be required to study the four core disciples: Finance and Accounting (the subject of this book), Marketing, Organizational Behaviour and Strategy.

There are two online appendices for this book. One contains a financial information resource directory listing all the key areas for uncovering key financial and related business facts that will help you stay on top of the subject. The second covers all aspects of personal development; using it will ensure you keep abreast of current thinking in business finance. You should visit this on a regular basis to ensure you have all the advantages that some-one with an MBA in Business Finance would hope for in terms of career progression. Here you will find how to update your skills and knowledge by taking short courses at top business schools around the globe. By attending you can usually get onto the school's alumni list, plugging into a valuable business network in the process.

PART ONE
The fundamentals of business finance

Financial statements are like the tip of an iceberg: underneath the visible part are a lot of record-keeping, accounting methods and reporting decisions. The managers of a business, the investors in a business and the lenders to a business need a firm grasp on these accounting reports so they will know how to recognize both the good and bad signals.

Accountants prepare three primary financial statements. The *profit and loss account* (*income statement* in the United States) reports the profit-making activities of the business and how much profit or loss the business made. The *balance sheet* reports the financial situation and position of the business in terms of its assets and liabilities at a point in time and usually the last day of the profit period. The *cash flow statement* reports how much cash was actually realized from profit and other sources of cash, and what the business did with this money. In short, the financial life of a business and its prospects for success or danger of failing are all revealed in its financial statements.

The way in which accounting information is recorded and reported is regulated by statutory bodies and the accounting profession. Auditors, amongst other responsibilities, have a duty to ensure these rules are followed and the accounts represent a *true and fair* picture of the enterprise for the period under consideration. The way in which accounting information is analysed involves the use of a standard range of business tools and ratios that can be applied across all types of venture, so providing some common yardstick.

The final section of this part is concerned with the specific ways in which accounting information can help managers add value to the business by, amongst other things, ensuring profitability is achieved quickly and that all investments are at least planned so as to improve the venture's profitability.

Financial business reports

01

- The bookkeeping process
- Cash flow forecasts and statements
- Calculating profit
- Balancing the books

Accounting is the process of recording and analysing transactions that involve events that can be assigned a monetary value. By definition financial information can only be a partial picture of the performance of an enterprise. People, arguably a business's most valuable asset, don't appear anywhere in the accounts, except for football clubs and the like where people are the subject of a transaction.

Although accounting has become more complex, involving ever more regulations, and has moved from visible records written in books to key stokes in a software program, the purpose is the same; to establish:

- what a business owns by way of assets;
- what a business owes by way of liabilities;
- the profitability, or otherwise, at certain time intervals, and how that profit was achieved.

An MBA in Finance is unlikely to be required to perform the recording side of the accounting process, except in the very smallest of organizations, or if the venture is his or her own. But it is only by knowing how accounts are prepared and the rules governing the categorizing of assets and liabilities (more on this in Chapter 2) that they can gain a good understanding of what the figures really mean. For example, it is not obvious to the uninitiated that a company's shares are classed as a liability and it is extremely unlikely that the assets as recorded will realize anything like the figures shown in the accounts, audited or not. Bear Stearns, an 85-year-old investment bank, was sold for $2 (£1.25/€1.50) a share to J P Morgan Chase in

2008, roughly a total of $236 (£151/€177) million for a business that was worth $20 (£12.5/€15) billion only a few weeks previously. This provides a vivid insight into the gap between reported and realizable figures in the accounting world. Nevertheless, accounting reports do provide a valuable insight into business performance and in any event are a basic requirement for shareholders and regulators alike.

Who uses financial information and why

The aim of all accounting information is to provide the particular user with relevant and timely data to make decisions. Who are these users of accounting information and what decisions do they need to take? Possible users are an extensive group, who require the information to be impartial, accurate and timely. They include:

- *Shareholders* of limited companies will be influenced in their decision to remain investors or to increase/decrease their holding by receiving information about the financial performance and financial position of the company. This usually occurs twice a year in the form of a profit and loss account and a balance sheet relating to the first half-year and, later on, the full year.

- *Owner-managers* of non-incorporated businesses will require the above information but they will also be privy to more detailed and more frequent information about the business's financial affairs.

- *Management* in companies range from director level down to supervisor level. Each person requires accounting information to help him or her in his or her role. Supervisors may be concerned with operating costs for a very small part of the undertaking. Directors need to control the overall performance of the company and make strategic financing and investment decisions. Middle managers need feedback on whether they are meeting their financial targets.

- *Suppliers* need to assess the creditworthiness of potential and existing customers when setting the amount and period of credit allowed. This will partly, if not mainly, be based on the financial history of each customer, so the supplier's accountants will assess the latest profit and loss account and balance sheet. Other data on payment history may be obtained from credit agencies, for example, Dun & Bradstreet, to assist in this decision.

- *Customers* also need to be reassured, in this case to minimize the risk of their supplies drying up and disrupting their own output. Firms entering into a joint venture will also need mutual reassurance. Similar checks to those outlined above for suppliers will need to be carried out.

- *Employees* and their representatives have a vested interest in the financial health and future prospects of their employer. They rely on an assessment of the published accounts by experts for this.

- *Government* levies tax on the profits earned by businesses and Value Added Tax (or sales tax) on the sales value of most industries. Tax authorities rely on the information provided by companies for these purposes.

- *Competitors* can make some comparisons, for example, sales, profit or asset utilization per employee, from published accounting data in a process known as 'benchmarking'. This may provide clues to areas where performance may be improved particularly if explanations of differences in operating systems can be obtained.

- *Lenders* need to be confident that their capital is safe and that the borrowing company can service the loan or overdraft adequately, so again the financial statements of profit and loss account and balance sheet will be examined from this viewpoint.

- *Partners* need to keep track of business performance in much the same way as shareholders and to ensure appropriate and fair treatment by their fellow partners.

Accounting branches

Different users of accounting information will require different information and use it for different purposes. Accounting can be broken down into three main branches, with some overlap between, particularly in smaller enterprises where in effect all three areas will be the responsibility of a single person or department:

1 financial accounting;

2 management accounting; and

3 financial management.

1. *Financial accounting* is concerned with preparing financial statements summarizing past events, usually in the form of profit and loss accounts and balance sheets. These historic statements are mainly of interest to outside parties such as investors, loan providers and suppliers.

2. *Management accounting* involves assembling much more detailed information about current and future planned events to allow managers to carry out their roles of planning, control and decision making. Examples of management accounting information are product costs and cost data relevant to a particular decision, say, a choice between make or buy. Also included in management accounting are preparing and monitoring budgeted costs relating to a product, activity or service. Management accounting

information is rarely disclosed to outside parties, though bankers and private equity providers often ask for monthly management accounts as a condition of funding.

3. *Financial management* covers all matters concerning raising finance and ensuring it is used in the most efficient way. For example, it would be financially inefficient to raise a long-term loan or sell shares just to finance a short-term increase in sales. It would be the role of financial management to select and use a more cost-effective funding source such as an overdraft. The cost of capital is influenced by both the capital structure adopted and the riskiness of the investments undertaken.

Within these three broad areas of accounting there may be further subsets of accounting relating either to one specific activity, or across the whole spectrum. Examples of these are:

1 treasury;

2 taxation; and

3 audit.

1. *Treasury* is a finance function usually only found in a very large company or group of companies. For example, managing bank balances to get the maximum interest on positive balances or minimize the payment of interest on negative balances would be a typical treasury task. This might involve lending money overnight on the money markets. Treasury activity would also be concerned with managing exchange risk where financial transactions in foreign currencies are involved.

2. *Taxation* in a small company will be included in the duties of the financial accountant who may need to call on outside professional advice from time to time. Corporation tax on company profits is not straightforward and the system of capital allowances can be complex for some large companies, groups of companies, or multinational companies. The ramifications of VAT or sales tax where it applies, employee tax and other related deductions such as National Insurance and director benefits in kind, often call for the services of a specialist accountant, or team of accountants. Large companies usually use the services of such firms to minimize the pain and maximize the gain from such taxes and allowances.

3. *Audit* is another accounting function mainly found in larger organizations. Internal auditors monitor that accounting procedures, documents and computerized transactions are carried out correctly. This work is additional or complementary to that undertaken by external auditors who take a broader approach in providing an independent report to shareholders in the annual report.

Bookkeeping – the way transactions are recorded

The business world, except for the very smallest of one-man-bands, has moved away from single-entry bookkeeping. Even the elegance of the double-entry variety of bookkeeping with its assorted ledgers has been supplanted by the myriad checks and balances inherent in the software programs that now underpin much of the world's accounting records. Nevertheless, an MBA is expected to have some insight into how we arrived at the system of recording financial data used today.

Single-entry bookkeeping

Sometime before 3,000 BC the people of Uruk and other sister-cities of Mesopotamia began to use pictographic tablets of clay to record economic transactions. The script for the tablets evolved from symbols and provides evidence of an ancient financial system that was growing to accommodate the needs of the Uruk economy. The Mesopotamian equivalent of today's bookkeeper was the scribe. His duties were similar, but even more extensive. In addition to writing up the transaction, he ensured that the agreements complied with the detailed code requirements for commercial transactions. Temples, palaces and private firms employed hundreds of scribes, and much as with the accounting profession today it was considered a prestigious profession. In a typical transaction of the time, the parties might seek out the scribe at the gates to the city. They would describe their agreement to the scribe, who would take from his supply a small quantity of specially prepared clay on which to record the transaction.

Governmental bookkeeping in ancient Egypt developed in a fashion similar to the Mesopotamians. The use of papyrus rather than clay tablets allowed more detailed records to be made more easily. Extensive records were kept, particularly for the network of royal storehouses within which the 'in kind' tax payments such as sheep or cattle were kept, as coinage had not yet been developed. Egyptian bookkeepers associated with each storehouse kept meticulous records, which were checked by an elaborate internal verification system. These early accountants had good reason to be honest and accurate, because irregularities disclosed by royal audits were punishable by fine, mutilation or death. Although such records were important, ancient Egyptian accounting never progressed beyond simple list-making in its thousands of years of existence. The almost 1 million accounting records in tablet form survive in museum collections around the world.

China, during the Chao Dynasty (1122–256 BC), used bookkeeping chiefly as a means of evaluating the efficiency of governmental programmes and the civil servants who administered them. A level of sophistication was achieved that was not surpassed in China until after the introduction of the double-entry system a thousand years later.

Accounts in ancient Rome evolved from records traditionally kept by the heads of families, where daily entry of household receipts and payments were kept in an *adversaria* or daybook, and monthly postings were made to a cashbook known as a *codex accepti et expensi*.

Up to medieval times this single-entry system of bookkeeping, divided into two general parts, Income and Outgo, with a statement at the end showing the balance due to the lord of the manor, prevailed in England, as elsewhere. Although these accounts were fairly basic they were sufficient to handle the needs of the very simple business structures that prevailed. Businessmen operated for the most part on their own account, or in single venture partnerships that dissolved at the end of a relatively short period of time. This, incidentally, was still the essence of the structure of Lloyd's insurance market into the 21st century. Judging by the uniformity of the way that single-entry bookkeeping was practised it seems fairly certain that a model was worked out, written up and widely adopted.

Double-entry bookkeeping

Until Luca Paccioli wrote what was in essence the world's first accounting book, over 500 years ago, accounting records where maintained in single-entry format: one event merited one record. This meant that errors could only be prevented by a major duplication of effort, for example by having different people making and counting up parallel records. Paccioli, a mathematician who worked for the Doge of Venice, came up with a system of double-entry bookkeeping that required two entries for each transaction, thus providing built-in checks and balances to ensure accuracy. Each transaction requires an entry as a debit and as a credit.

To give an example, selling goods in a double-entry system might result in two separate journal entries – a debit reducing the stock by £250 and a corresponding credit of £250 of new cash in – a double entry (see Table 1.1). The debits in a double-entry system must always equal the credits. If they don't, you know there is an error somewhere. So, double entry allows you to balance your books, which you can't do with the single-entry method.

TABLE 1.1   An example of a double-entry ledger

General Journal of Andrew's Bookshop			
Date	Description of entry	Debit	Credit
10th July	Rent expense	£250	
	Cash		£250

Paccioli's genius lay in seeing that the ultimate balancing number in a company's accounts was the profit or loss for the owners of that enterprise. On the not unreasonable assumption that the business shown in Table 1.1 plans to make a profit from selling goods, the figures will look rather different. To keep the numbers simple, let's suppose the goods sold cost £125 (a 50 per cent margin), then the entries would be as follows. Goods in stock go down by £125, while cash goes up by £250. That net change of £125 is balanced by an increase in profits of £125, so the assets and liabilities are kept in balance. In this example, had the goods sold for less than was paid there would have been a loss, which would have reduced the value of the owners' stake in the business by a corresponding amount.

This is all an MBA Business Finance needs to know about bookkeeping; the main part of the knowledge he or she requires is how to interpret the figures once recorded.

Introducing record-keeping

If you find yourself in a small business without a full-time accountant and a less than satisfactory method of keeping accounting records, you may have to devise and implement one yourself. Accounting record systems, however complex, follow a similar model; see Figure 1.1.

All of the elements – sales invoices, purchase invoices and so forth – are in effect ledgers containing a record of the relevant events. A long time ago

FIGURE 1.1   A simple system of keeping business records

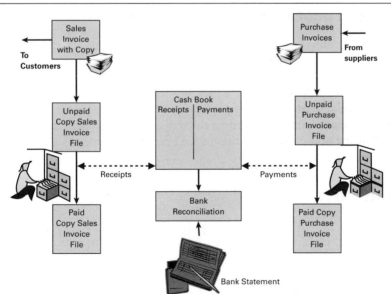

these actually were ledgers, but today they are entries in an accounting software package.

So that you don't get stuck doing work that is well below an MBA Business Finance's pay grade you need to buy an accounting package and get a bookkeeper to start entering the data and producing the standard business reports – profit and loss, balance sheets and performance comparisons.

Bookkeeping and accounting software

With the cost of basic bookkeeping and accounting software starting at barely $80 (£51/€60), and a reasonable package costing between $300 (£192/€225) and $800 (£510/€600), it makes good sense to plan to use such a system from the outset. There are dozens of perfectly satisfactory basic accounting and bookkeeping software packages on the market. The leading providers are:

Dosh (**www.dosh.co.uk)**

Microsoft Money (**www.microsoft.co.uk)**

MYOB (My Own Business) (**www.myob.co.uk)**

QuickBooks (**www.intuit.co.uk/store/en/quickbooks/index.jsp)**

Sage (**www.uk.sage.com)**

Simplex (**www.simplex.net)**

TAS (**www.tassoftware.co.uk)**

Getting a bookkeeper

These two professional associations, the International Association of Book-keepers (IAB) (**www.iab.org.uk**; Tel: 01732 458080) and the Institute of Certified Bookkeepers (**www.book-keepers.org**; Tel: 0845 060 2345), offer free matching services to help small businesses find a bookkeeper to suit their particular needs. Expect to pay upwards of £20 an hour for services that can be as basic as simply recording the transactions in your books, through to producing accounts, preparing the VAT return or doing the payroll.

Cash flow

There is a saying in business that profit is vanity and cash flow is sanity. Both are necessary, but in the short term, and often that is all that matters in business as it struggles to get a foothold in the shifting sands of trading, cash flow is life or death. The rules on what constitutes cash are very simple – it has to be just that, or negotiable securities designated as being as good as cash.

Cash flow is looked at in two distinct and important ways: as a projection of future expected cash flows, and as an analysis of where cash came from and went to in an accounting period and the resultant increase or decrease in cash available.

Cash flow forecasts

The future is impossible to predict with great accuracy but it is possible to anticipate likely outcomes and be prepared to deal with events by building in a margin of safety. The starting point for making a projection is to make some assumptions about what you want to achieve and testing those for reasonableness.

Take the situation of High Note, a business being established to sell sheet music, small instruments and music CDs to schools and colleges, which will expect trade credit and members of the public who will pay cash. The owner plans to invest £10,000 and to borrow £10,000 from a bank on a long-term basis. The business will require £11,500 for fixtures and fittings. A further £1,000 will be needed for a computer, software and a printer. That should leave around £7,500 to meet immediate trading expenses such as buying in stock and spending £1,500 on initial advertising. Hopefully customer's payments will start to come in quickly to cover other expenses such as some wages for bookkeeping, administration and fulfilling orders. Sales in the first six months are expected to be £60,000 based on negotiations already in hand, plus some cash sales that always seem to turn up. The rule of thumb in the industry seems to be that stock is marked up by 100 per cent, so £30,000 of bought in goods sell on for £60,000.

On the basis of these assumptions it is possible to make the cash flow forecast set out in Table 1.2. It has been simplified and some elements such as VAT (or sales tax) and tax on profits have been omitted for ease of understanding. The maths in the table is straightforward: the cash receipts from various sources are totalled, as are the payments. Taking one from the other leaves a cash surplus or deficit for the month in question. The bottom row shows the cumulative position. So for example while the business had £2,440 cash left at the end of April, taking the cash deficit of £1,500 in May into account, by the end of May only £950 (£2,450 − £1,500) cash remains.

Overtrading

In the example above the business looks like having insufficient cash, based on the assumptions made. An outsider, a banker perhaps, would look at the figures in August and see that the faster the sales grew the greater the cash flow deficit became. We know, using our crystal ball, that the position will improve from September and that if we can only hang on for a few more months we should eliminate our cash deficit and perhaps even have

TABLE 1.2 High Note six-month cash flow forecast

Month	April £	May £	June £	July £	Aug £	Sept £	Total £
Receipts							
Sales	4,000	5,000	5,000	7,000	12,000	15,000	48,000
Owners' cash	10,000						
Bank loan	10,000						
Total cash in	24,000	5,000	5,000	7,000	12,000	15,000	48,000
Payments							
Purchases	5,500	2,950	4,220	7,416	9,332	9,690	39,108
Rates, electricity, heat, telephone, internet, etc	1,000	1,000	1,000	1,000	1,000	1,000	
Wages	1,000	1,000	1,000	1,000	1,000	1,000	
Advertising	1,550	1,550	1,550	1,550	1,550	1,550	
Fixtures/fittings	11,500						
Computer, etc	1,000						
Total cash out	21,550	6,500	7,770	10,966	12,882	13,240	
Monthly cash							
Surplus/deficit(−)	2,450	(1,500)	(2,770)	(3,966)	(882)	1,760	
Cumulative cash balance	2,450	950	(1,820)	(5,786)	(6,668)	(4,908)	

a surplus. Had we made the cash flow projection at the outset and either raised more money, perhaps by way of an overdraft, spent less on fixtures and fittings, or set a more modest sales goal hence needing less stock and advertising, we would have had a sound business. The figures indicate a business that is trading beyond its financial resources, a condition known as 'overtrading' – anathema to bankers the world over.

You can do a number of 'what if' projections to fine-tune cash flow projections using a spreadsheet such as one from Business Link (**www.businesslink.gov.uk/Finance_files/Cash_Flow_Projection_Worksheet.xls**). It has a cash flow spreadsheet that you can copy and paste into an Excel file on your computer.

Statement of cash flows for the year

A cash flow statement summarizes exactly where cash came from and how it was spent during the year. At first glance it seems to draw on a mixture of transactions included in the profit and loss account and balance sheet for the same period end, but this is not the whole story. Because there is a time lag on many cash transactions, for example tax and dividend payments, the statement is a mixture of some previous year and some current year transactions; the remaining current year transactions go into the following year's cash flow statement during which the cash actually changes hands. Similarly, the realization and accrual conventions relating to sales and purchases respectively result in cash transactions having a different timing to when they were entered in the profit and loss account.

Example

A company had sales of $5 million this year and $4 million last year and these figures appeared in the profit and loss accounts of those years. Debtors at the end of this year were $1 million and at the end of the previous year were $0.8 million. The cash inflow arising from sales this year is $4.8 million ($0.8 million + $5 million – $1 million) whereas the sales figure in the profit and loss account is $5 million.

For these reasons it is not possible to look at just this year's profit and loss account and balance sheet to find all the cash flows; you need the previous year's accounts too. The balance sheet will show the cash balance at the period end but will not easily disclose all the ways in which it was achieved. Compiling a cash flow statement is quite a technical job and some training plus inside information is needed to complete the task. Nevertheless, the bulk of the items can be identified from an examination of the other two accounting statements for both the current and previous years.

From an MBA Business Finance's perspective it is understanding the requirement for a cash flow statement as well as the other two accounts that is important, and being able to interpret the significance of the cash movements themselves.

CASE STUDY Straight plc

Straight plc was established in 1993 as a supplier of container solutions for source-separated waste. Initially one man and a desk, the company grew to become the UK's leading supplier of kerbside recycling boxes as well as a key supplier of other types of waste and recycling containers. Turnover by 2008 was running at over £30 ($48/€35) million a year with operating profit in excess of £1 ($1.6/€1.18) million; see Table 1.3.

TABLE 1.3 Un-audited condensed cash flow statement for Straight plc (for the six months ended 30 June 2007)

	Half year to 30 June 2007 £'000	Half year to 30 June 2006 £'000	Year 31 Dec 2006 £'000
Net cash flows from operating activities	2,242	3,879	1,171
Cash flows from investing activities			
Purchases of property, plant and equipment	(603)	(464)	(701)
Proceeds from sale of property, plant and equip	345	–	–
Purchase of intangible assets	(55)	(87)	(193)
Purchase of investments	(35)	–	–
Interest received	28	58	107
Net cash used in investing activities	(320)	(493)	(787)
Cash flows from financing activities			
Dividends paid	(310)	(283)	(422)
Proceeds from issue of shares	13	–	128
Net cash used in financing activities	(297)	(283)	(294)
Net increase in cash and cash equivalents	1,625	3,103	90
Cash and cash equivalents at beginning of period	2,126	2,036	2,036
Cash and cash equivalents at the end of period	3,751	5,139	2,126

The three columns represent the cash activities for two equivalent six-month periods and for the whole of the preceding year. The cash of £2,126,000 generated to 31 December 2006 (bottom of the right-hand column) is carried over to the start of the June 2007 six-month period (second figure from bottom of left-hand column). By adding the net increase (or decrease) in cash generated in this period we arrive at the closing cash position.

The cash flow statement gives us a complete picture of how cash movements came about: from normal sales activities, the purchase or disposal of assets, or from financing activities. This is an expansion of the sparse single figure in the company's closing balance sheet stating that cash and cash equivalents is £3,751,000.

The profit and loss account (income statement)

If you look back to the financial situation in High Note, you will see a good example of the difference between cash and profit. The business has sold £60,000 worth of goods that it only paid £30,000 for, so it has a substantial profit margin to play with. While £39,108 has been paid to suppliers only £30,000 of goods at cost have been sold, meaning that £9,108 worth of instruments, sheet music and CDs are still in stock. A similar situation exists with sales. High Note has billed for £60,000 but only been paid for £48,000; the balance is owed by debtors. The bald figure at the end of the cash flow projection showing High Note to be in the red to the tune of £4,908 seems to be missing some important facts.

The difference between profit and cash

Cash is immediate and takes account of nothing else. Profit, however, is a measurement of economic activity that considers other factors that can be assigned a value or cost. The accounting principle that governs profit is known as the 'matching principle', which means that income and expenditure are matched to the time period in which they occur. (See Chapter 2 where the concepts that govern the treatment of costs and revenue – realization and accruals – are explained in more detail.) So for High Note the profit and loss account for the first six months would be as shown in Table 1.4.

TABLE 1.4   Profit and loss account for High Note for the six months, April–September

	£	£
Sales		60,000
Less cost of goods to be sold		30,000
Gross profit		30,000
Less expenses:		
Heat, electric, phone, internet, etc	6,000	
Wages	6,000	
Advertising	9,300	
Total expenses		21,300
Profit before tax, interest and depreciation charges		8,700

The structure of the profit and loss statement

This account is set out in more detail for a business to make it more useful when it comes to understanding how a business is performing. For example, though the profit shown in our worked example is £8,700 it would in fact be rather lower. As money has been borrowed to finance cash flow there would be interest due, as there would be on the longer-term loan of £10,000. In practice we have four levels of profit:

1 Gross profit is the profit left after all costs related to making what you sell are deducted from income.

2 Operating profit is what's left after you take away the operating expenses from the gross profit.

3 Profit before tax is what is left after deducting any financing costs.

4 Profit after tax is what is left for the owners to spend or reinvest in the business.

For High Note this could look much as set out in Table 1.5. A more substantial business than High Note will have taken on a wide range of commitments. For example, as well as the owner's money, there may be a long-term loan to be serviced (interest and capital repayments); parts of the workshop or offices may be sublet generating 'non-operating income'; and there will certainly we some depreciation expense to deduct. Like any accounting report it should be prepared in the best form for the user, bearing in mind the requirements of the regulatory authorities.

TABLE 1.5   High Note extended profit and loss account

	£s
Sales	60,000
Less the cost of goods to be sold	30,000
Gross profit	30,000
Less operating expenses	21,300
Operating profit	8,700
Less interest on bank loan and overdraft	600
Profit before tax	8,100
Less tax	1,827
Profit after tax	6,723

The elements to be included are:

- Sales (and any other revenues from operations).
- Cost of sales (or cost of goods sold).
- Gross profit – the difference between sales and cost of sales.
- Operating expenses – selling, administration, depreciation and other general costs.
- Operating profit – the difference between gross profit and operating expenses.
- Non-operating revenues – other revenues, including interest, rent, etc.
- Non-operating expenses – financial costs and other expenses not directly related to the running of the business.
- Profit before income tax.
- Provision for income tax.
- Net income (or profit or loss).

Profit and loss spreadsheet

There is an online spreadsheet at SCORE's website (**www.score.org**>Business Tools>Template Gallery>Profit and Loss). Download in Excel format and you have a profit and loss account with 30 lines of expenses, the headings of which you can change or delete to meet your particular needs.

The balance sheet

A balance sheet is a snapshot at a moment in time. On the one hand it shows the value of assets (possessions) owned by the business, and on the other it shows who provided the funds with which to finance those assets and to whom the business is ultimately liable.

Assets are of two main types and are classified under the headings of either fixed assets or current assets. *Fixed assets* come in three forms. First there is the hardware or physical things used by the business itself and which are not for sale to customers. Examples of fixed assets include buildings, plant, machinery, vehicles, furniture and fittings. Next come intangible fixed assets, such as goodwill, intellectual property, etc, and these are also shown under the general heading 'fixed assets'. Finally there are investments in other businesses. Other assets in the process of eventually being turned into cash from customers are called *current assets,* and include stocks, work-in-progress, money owed by customers and cash itself:

Total assets = Fixed assets + Current assets

Assets can only be bought with funds provided by the owners or borrowed from someone else, for example, bankers or creditors. Owners provide funds by directly investing in the business (say, when they buy shares issued by the company) or indirectly by allowing the company to retain some of the profits in reserves. These sources of money are known collectively as *liabilities*:

Total liabilities =
Share capital and reserves + Borrowings and other creditors

Borrowed capital can take the form of a long-term loan at a fixed rate of interest or a short-term loan, such as a bank overdraft, usually at a variable rate of interest. All short-term liabilities owed by a business and due for payment within 12 months are referred to as 'creditors falling due within one year', and long-term indebtedness is called 'creditors falling due after one year'.

So far in our High Note example the money spent on 'capital' items such as the £12,500 spent on a computer and fixtures and fittings have been ignored as has the £9,108 worth of sheet music, etc remaining in stock waiting to be sold and the £12,000 owed by customers who have yet to pay up. An assumption has to be made about where the cash deficit will be made up and the most logical short-term source is a bank overdraft.

For High Note at the end of September the balance sheet is set out in Table 1.6.

TABLE 1.6 High Note balance sheet at 30 September

	£	£
Assets		
Fixed assets		
Fixtures, fitting, equipment	11,500	
Computer	1,000	
Total fixed assets		12,500
Working capital		
Current assets		
Stock	9,108	
Debtors	12,000	
Cash	0	
	21,108	
Less current liabilities (creditors falling due within one year)		
Overdraft	4,908	
Creditors	0	
	4,908	
Net current assets [Working capital (CA-CL)]		16,200
Total assets less current liabilities		28,700
Less creditors falling due after one year		
Long-term bank loan		10,000
Net total assets		18,700
Capital and reserves		
Owner's capital introduced	10,000	
Profit retained (from P&L account)	8,700	
Total capital and reserves		18,700

Balance sheet structure

The layout of the balance sheet using UK accounting rules is something of a jumble, with assets and liabilities intermingled. In the United States the balance sheet traditionally separates assets and liabilities and sets the figures out either horizontally or vertically (see Table 1.7).

TABLE 1.7   Equivalent balance sheet for a US corporation

Assets (£)		Liabilities (£)	
Current		Current	
Cash	0	Overdraft	4,908
Accounts receivable	12,000	Accs Payable	0
Inventory	9,108	Loans longer than 1 year	10,000
Fixed assets	12,500	*Equity*	
		Owners capital	10,000
		Retained profit	8,700
Total assets	33,608	Total liabilities and equity	33,608

The most confusing aspect of the US balance sheet structure is that equities, that is the owners' stake in the venture, is lumped in with the liabilities. But when you consider that the accounts are prepared for the company or corporation, which has a separate legal identity from the various owners, this has as sort of pure logic to it. The profit and loss account (income statement) and cash flow layouts are broadly similar.

Other countries have their own variations and attempts are being made to harmonize accounting standards worldwide, with modest success.

Working capital

You will also have noticed in this example that the assets and liabilities have been jumbled together in the middle to net off the current assets and current liabilities and so end up with a figure for the working capital. 'Current' in accounting means within the trading cycle, usually taken to be one year. Stock will be used up and debtors will pay up within the year, and the overdraft, being repayable on demand, also appears as a short-term liability.

There are a number of other items not shown in the working capital section of the example balance sheet that should appear such as liability for tax and VAT (or sales tax) that have not yet been paid and should appear as current liability.

Intangible fixed assets

There are a number of seemingly invisible items that nevertheless have been acquired for a measurable money cost and so have to be accounted for. These are *goodwill*, where the price paid for an asset is above its fair market price. This is fairly common in the case of acquisitions where competition for a company can push prices higher. The other is *intellectual property* such as patents, copyright, designs and logos. These items too are amortized over their working life. So, for example, if patent is considered to have a 10-year life and cost £1 million to acquire it would be written down in the accounts by £100,000 a year.

Liverpool Football Club's accounts (see Table 1.8) show how a particular type of 'intellectual' property is dealt with. In this case it is footballer's being contracted in and out of the club. The same principles apply to any intangible asset.

TABLE 1.8 Part of the balance sheet for Liverpool Football Club and Athletic Grounds plc

	2006 £'000	2005 £'000
Fixed assets		
Intangible assets (see note 10)	81,350	80,105
Tangible assets	34,947	36,811
Investments	3	3
Total	116,300	116,919
Note 10. Intangible fixed assets		
Cost		
At 1 August 2005	134,706	
Additions in year	41,753	
Disposals in year	(36,868)	
At 31 July 2006	139,591	
Amortization		
At 1 August 2005	54,601	
Charge for year	24,636	
Impairments in year	5,250	
Disposals in year	(26,246)	
At 31 July 2006	58,241	
Net book amount		
At 31 July 2006	81,350	
At 31 July 2005	80,105	

The costs associated with the acquisition of players' registrations are capitalized as intangible fixed assets. These costs are fully amortized in equal instalments over the period of the players' initial contracts. Where a player's contract is extended beyond its initial period, amortization is calculated over the period of the extended contract from the date on which it is signed. Players' registrations are written down for impairment when the carrying amount exceeds the amount recoverable through use or sale.

Accounting for stock

Deciding on the stock figure to put into a balance sheet is a tricky calculation. Theoretically it is simple; after all you know what you paid for it. The rule that stock should be entered in the balance sheet at cost or market price, whichever is the lower, is also not too difficult to follow. But in the real world a business keeps on buying in stock so it has product to sell and the cost can vary every time a purchase is made.

Take the example of a business selling a breakfast cereal. Four pallets of cereal are bought in from various suppliers at prices of £1,000, £1,020, £1,040 and £1,060 respectively, a total of £4,120. At the end of the period three pallets have been sold, so logically the cost of goods sold in the profit and loss account will show a figure of £3,060 (£1,000 + £1,020 + £1,040). The last pallet costing £1,060 will be the figure to put into the balance sheet, thus ensuring that all £4,120 of total costs are accounted for.

This method of dealing with stock is known as FIFO (First in First Out), for obvious reason. There are two other popular costing methods that have their own merits. LIFO (Last in First Out) is based on the argument that if your are staying in business you will have to keep on replacing stock at the latest (higher) price, so you might just as well get used to that sooner by accounting for it in your profit and loss account. In this case the cost of goods sold would be £3,120 (£1,060 + £1,040 + £1,020), rather than the £3,060 that FIFO produces.

The third popular costing method is the average cost method, which does what it says on the box. In the above example this would produce a cost midway between that obtained by the other two methods; in this example £3,090.

All these methods have their merits, but FIFO usually wins the argument as it accommodates the realities that prices rise steadily and goods move in and out of a business in the order in which they are bought. It would be a very badly run shop that sold its last delivery of cereal before clearing out its existing stocks.

Methods of depreciation

Depreciation is how we show the asset being 'consumed' over its working life. It is simply a bookkeeping record to allow us to allocate some of the cost of an asset to the appropriate time period. The time period will be determined by such factors as how long the working life of the asset is. The principle methods of depreciation used in business are as follows.

The straight-line method

This assumes that the asset will be 'consumed' evenly throughout its life. If, for example, an asset is being bought for £1,200 and sold at the end of five years for £200, the amount of cost we have to write off is £1,000. Using 20 per cent per year so that the whole 100 per cent of cost is allocated we can work out the 'book value' for each year.

The declining balance method

This works in a similar way, but instead of an even depreciation each year we assume the drop will be less. Some assets, motor vehicles for example, will reduce sharply in their first year and less so later on. So while at the end of year one in both these methods of depreciation there is a £200 fall, in year two the picture starts to change. The straight-line method takes a further fall of £200, while the declining balance method reduces by 20 per cent (our agreed depreciation rate) of £800 (the balance of £1,000 minus the £200 depreciation so far), which is £160.

The sum of the digits method

This is more common in the United States than in the UK. While the declining balance method applies a constant percentage to a declining figure, this method applies a progressively smaller percentage to the initial cost. It involves adding up the individual numbers in the expected life span of the asset to arrive at the denominator of a fraction. The numerator is the year number concerned, but in reverse order.

For example, if our computer asset bought for $1,200 had an expected useful life of five years (unlikely) then the denominator in our sum would be 1+2+3+4+5 which equals 15. In the first year we would depreciate by 5/15 times the initial purchase price of $1,200, which equals $400. In year two we would depreciate by 4/15 and so on.

These are just three of the most common of many ways of depreciating fixed assets. In choosing which method of depreciation to use, and in practice you may have to use different methods with different types of asset, it is useful to remember what you are trying to do. You are aiming to allocate the *cost* of buying the asset as it should apply to each year of its working life.

Balance sheet and other online tools

SCORE (**www.score.org**>Business Tools>Template Gallery>Balance Sheet (projected)) is an Excel based spreadsheet you can use for constructing your own balance sheet. You can find guidance on depreciation, handling stock and on the layout of the balance sheet and profit and loss account as required by the Company's Act from the Accounting Standards Board (**www.frc.org**>ASB>Technical>FRSSE). Accounting Glossary (**www. accountingglossaty.net**) and Accounting for Everyone (**www.accountingfor everyone.com**>Accounting Glossary) have definitions of all the accounting terms you are every likely to come across in the accounting world.

Package of accounts

The cash flow statement, the profit and loss account and the balance sheet between them constitute a set of accounts, but conventionally two balance sheets, the opening and closing one, are provided to make a 'package'. By including these balance sheets we can see the full picture of what has happened to the owners' investment in the business.

Table 1.9 shows a simplified package of accounts. We can see from these that over the year the business has made £600 of profit after tax, invested that in £200 of additional fixed assets, £400 of working capital such as stock and debtors, balancing that off with the £600 put into reserves from the year's profits.

TABLE 1.9 A package of accounts

Balance sheet at 31 Dec 2010 (£)		P & L for year to 31 Dec 2011 (£)		Balance sheet at 2011 (£)	
Fixed assets	1,000	Sales	10,000	Fixed assets	1,200
Working capital	1,000	less cost of sales	6,000	Working capital	1,400
	2,000	Gross profit	4,000		2,600
		less expenses	3,000		
Financed by		Profit before tax	1,000	Financed by	
Owners' equity	2,000	Tax	400	Owners' equity	2,000
		Profit after tax	600	Reserves	600
					2,600

The rules of
the game

02

- Accounting conventions and principles
- Financial rule makers
- International accounting standards
- Protecting investors

Accounting is certainly not an exact science. Even the most enthusiastic member of the profession would not make that claim. There is considerable scope for interpretation and educated guesswork as all the facts are rarely available when the accounts are drawn up. For example we may not know for certain that a particular customer will actually pay up, yet unless we have firm evidence that they won't, for example if the business is failing, then the value of the money owed will appear in the accounts.

Obviously, if accountants and managers had compete freedom to interpret events as they will, no one inside or outside the business would place any reliance on the figures, so certain ground rules have been laid down by the profession to help get a level of consistency into accounting information.

Fundamental conventions

These are the enduring principles that govern the way in which the accounting profession assembles and presents financial information.

Money measurement

In accounting, a record is kept only of the facts that can be expressed in money terms. For example, the state of the managing director's health and the news that your main competitor is opening up right opposite in a more attractive outlet are important business facts. No accounting record of them is made, however, and they do not show up on the balance sheet, simply because no objective monetary value can be assigned to these facts.

Expressing business facts in money terms has the great advantage of providing a common denominator. Just imagine trying to add computer equipment and vehicles, together with a 4,000 sq m office, and then arriving at a total. You need a common term to be able to carry out the basic arithmetical functions, and to compare one set of accounts with another.

Business entity

The accounts are kept for the business itself, rather than for the owner(s), bankers, or anyone else associated with the firm. The concept states that assets and liabilities are always defined from the business's viewpoint. So, for example, were a business owner to lend his business money it would appear in the accounts as a liability, though in effect he might see it as his own money. Anything done with that money, say buying equipment, would appear in the accounts as an asset of the business. The owner's stake is accounted for only by the increase or decrease in net worth of the enterprise as a whole.

Cost concept

Assets are usually entered into the accounts at the cost on date of purchase. For a variety of reasons, the real 'worth' of an asset will probably change over time. The worth or value of an asset is a subjective estimate that no two people are likely to agree on. This is made even more complex, and artificial, because the assets themselves are usually not for sale.

So in the search for objectivity, the accountants have settled for cost as the figure to record. It does mean that a balance sheet does not show the current worth or value of a business. That is not its intention. Nor does it mean that the 'cost' figure remains unchanged forever. For example, the worth of a motor vehicle costing £6,000 may end up looking like Table 2.1 after two years.

TABLE 2.1   Example of the changing 'worth' of an asset

	Year 1	Year 2
Fixed assets	£	£
Vehicle	6,000	6,000
Less cumulative depreciation	1,500	3,000
Net asset	4,500	3,000

The depreciation is how we show the asset being 'consumed' over its working life. It is simply a bookkeeping record to allow us to allocate some of the cost of an asset to the appropriate time period. (See Chapter 1 for a more on depreciation methods.)

The time period will be determined by factors such as the working life of the asset. The tax authorities do not allow depreciation as a business expense, so this figure can't be manipulated to reduce tax liability, for example. A tax relief on the capital expenditure known as 'writing down' is allowed, using a formula set by government that varies from time to time depending on current economic goals, for example to stimulate capital expenditure.

Other assets, such as freehold land and buildings, will be re-valued from time to time, and stock will be entered at cost, or market value, whichever is the lower, in line with the principle of conservatism (see later in this chapter).

Other methods for recording assets

While cost at date of purchase is the norm for accounting for assets in conventional enterprises, there are certain types of businesses and certain situations when other methods of recording a monetary figure are used:

- *Market value:* this is usually used when an asset is actually to be sold and there is an established market for that particular type of asset. This could arise when a business or part of a business is to be closed down.

- *Fair value:* this is described as the estimated price at which an asset could be exchanged between knowledgeable but unrelated willing parties who have not and may not actual exchange. This basis is often used in the due diligence process where because of particular synergies a price higher than market value (resulting in goodwill) could reasonably be set.

- *Market to market:* this is where market value is calculated on a daily basis, usually by financial institutions such as banks and stockbrokers. This can result in dramatic changes in value in turbulent market conditions requiring additional assets, including cash, to be found to cover a fall in market price. This approach is blamed for helping to create liquidity 'black holes' by forcing banks to sell assets to meet liquidity targets, which in turn forces prices lower, requiring yet more assets to be sold.

Going concern

Accounting reports always assume that a business will continue trading indefinitely into the future – unless there is good evidence to the contrary. This means that the assets of the business are looked at simply as profit generators and not as being available for sale. Look again at the motor vehicle example above. In year two, the net asset figures in the accounts, prepared on a 'going concern' basis, is £3,000. If we knew that the business was to close down in a few weeks, then we would be more interested in the car's resale value than its 'book' value: the car might fetch only £2,000, which is quite a different figure.

Once a business stops trading, we cannot realistically look at the assets in the same way. They are no longer being used in the business to help generate sales and profits. The most objective figure is what they might realize in the marketplace.

In practice the directors and auditors have to believe a company will be viable for at least the next 12 months otherwise they have an obligation to draw attention to the danger that the company may not be a going concern, History shows that more companies experience going concern difficulties towards the end of a recession. In the early spring of 2010 for example, EMI, the holding company for the music group and Vantis, an AIM listed professional advisory group, were amongst a host of firms whose auditors raised such uncertainties. The general view is that a company has a better chance of survival if it is up-front about liquidity problems rather than let the market find out about difficulties and, in an atmosphere of mistrust, exaggerate the situation beyond what is warranted by the facts.

Dual aspect

To keep a complete record of any business transaction we need to know both where money came from and what has been done with it. It is not enough simply to say, for example, that a bank has lent a business €1 million; we have to show how that money has been used; for example to buy a property, increase stock levels, or in some other way. You can think of it as the accounting equivalent of Newton's third law: 'For every force there is an equal and opposite reaction.' Dual aspect is the basis of double-entry bookkeeping (see below).

The realization concept

A particularly prudent sales manager once said that an order was not an order until the customer's cheque had cleared, he or she had consumed the product, had not died as a result and, finally, had shown every indication of wanting to buy again. Most of us know quite different salespeople who can 'anticipate' the most unlikely volume of sales. In accounting, income is usually recognized as having been earned when the goods (or services) are dispatched and the invoice sent out. This has nothing to do with when an order is received, how firm an order is or how likely a customer is to pay up promptly. It is also possible that some of the products dispatched may be returned at some later date – perhaps for quality reasons. This means that income, and consequently profit, can be brought into the business in one period, and have to be removed later on.

Obviously, if these returns can be estimated accurately, then an adjustment can be made to income at the time. So the 'sales income' figure that is seen at the top of a profit and loss account is the value of the goods dispatched and invoiced to customers in the period in question.

The accrual concept

The profit and loss account sets out to 'match' income and expenditure to the appropriate time period. It is only in this way that the profit for the period can be realistically calculated. Suppose, for example, that you are calculating one month's profits when the quarterly telephone bill comes in. The picture might look like Table 2.2.

TABLE 2.2 Example of a badly matched profit and loss account

Profit and loss account for January, year 20XX	
	£
Sales income for January	4,000
Less telephone bill (last quarter)	800
Profit before other expenses	3,200

This is clearly wrong. In the first place, three months' telephone charges have been 'matched' against one month's sales. Equally wrong is charging anything other than January's telephone bill against January's income. Unfortunately, bills such as this are rarely to hand when you want the accounts, so in practice the telephone bill is 'accrued' for. The figure (which may even be absolutely correct if you have a meter) is put in as a provision to meet this liability when it becomes due.

Accounting conventions

These concepts provide a useful set of ground rules, but they are open to a range of possible interpretations. Over time, a generally accepted approach to how the concepts are applied has been arrived at. This approach hinges on the use of three conventions: conservatism, materiality and consistency.

Conservatism

Accountants are often viewed as merchants of gloom, always prone to taking a pessimistic point of view. The fact that a point of view has to be taken at all is the root of the problem. The convention of conservatism means that, given a choice, the accountant takes the figure that will result in a lower end profit. This might mean, for example, taking the higher of two possible expense figures. Few people are upset if the profit figure at the end of the day is higher than earlier estimates. The converse is never true.

Materiality

A strict interpretation of depreciation (see above) could lead to all sorts of trivial paperwork. For example, pencil sharpeners, staplers and paperclips, all theoretically items of fixed assets, should be depreciated over their working lives. This is obviously a useless exercise and in practice these items are written-off when they are bought.

Clearly, the level of 'materiality' is not the same for all businesses. A multinational may not keep meticulous records of every item of machinery under $1,000. For a small business this may represent all the machinery it has.

Consistency

Even with the help of those concepts and conventions, there is a fair degree of latitude in how you can record and interpret financial information. You should choose the methods that give the fairest picture of how the firm is performing and stick with them. It is very difficult to keep track of events in a business that is always changing its accounting methods. This does not mean that you are stuck with one method forever. Any change, however, is an important step.

The rule makers

The accounting professional bodies, with a little prodding from governments, are responsible for ensuring that accounting reports conform to what are known as Generally Accepted Accounting Practices (GAAP). A new entrant, International Accounting Standards, is challenging that term itself as GAAP rules have been interpreted differently on different continents and indeed largely ignored on others.

The rule book has to be adapted to accommodate changes in the way business is done. For example, international business across frontiers is now the norm, so rules on handling currency and reporting taxable profits in different countries have to be accommodated within a company's accounts in a consistent manner.

Although an MBA isn't usually expected to know all the rules, you should be able to get up to date before any meetings where the subject is likely to come up. You can keep track of changes in company reporting rules on the Institute of Chartered Accountants website (**www.icaew.com**>Accounting and corporate reporting>UK GAAP).

International accounting standards

In the UK there is a large degree of conformity of domestic standards with the international standards, and the Accounting Standards Board considers each new international standard carefully before deciding whether or not to include it in the domestic standard. Topics that have been the cause of disagreement in the recent past are the treatment of goodwill, deferred tax and pension costs.

The International Accounting Standards Board (IASB) announced on 22 November 2004 the membership of a new international working group, established jointly with the US Financial Accounting Standards Board (FASB). The aim was to complete their convergence project by June 2011. However, to say harmony has been achieved in the accounting standards world would be misleading. The battle has in some ways only just begun.

Protecting investors

When confidence in US businesses was rocked badly with a series of high profile financial frauds, Enron and Worldcom for example, the US government introduced the Sarbanes-Oxley Act, known less commonly but better understood as The Public Company Accounting Reforms and Investor Protection Act – 2002. The Act's purpose is to close the loopholes opened up by creative accountants who are always devising ways to overstate profits and understate liabilities and so make it easier for shareholders to see how profitable a business really is. The Act doesn't just apply to US companies; any businesses with shares listed on a US stock market that does business in the United States is swept into the net. Check out **www.sarbanes-oxley.com** for the low-down on that Act.

The UK version is The Companies (Audit, Investigations and Community Enterprise) Act. You can read up on the UK rules at the Office of the Public Sector Information (**www.opsi.gov.uk**>Legislation>UK>Acts>Public Acts 2004>Companies (Audit, Investigations and Community Enterprise) Act 2004.

03 Analysing financial reports

- The significance of accounting information
- Using business ratios
- Understanding the limitations of ratios
- Finding competitor accounts
- Improving business performance

In Chapter 1 the important financial statement of profit and loss (income statement), balance sheet and cash flow statement were explained. To recap – the trading performance of a company for a period of time is measured in the profit and loss account by deducting running costs from sales income. A balance sheet sets out the financial position of the company at a particular point in time, usually the end of the accounting period. It lists the assets owned by the company at that date matched by an equal list of the sources of finance. Cash flow measures the movement of money in and out of the organization at the time such events actually occur.

Reading company accounts, with practice, you can get some insight into a company's affairs. Comparing the current year's figure with the previous year's figure can identify changes in some of the key items and give insights into likely causes and remedies. Competitors' accounts can be studied to see their strengths and weaknesses from a financial perspective and perhaps also to give pointers as to how you own business's performance can be improved or modified.

However, just having the accounts of a business is not of much use if you can't analyse and interpret them. The tools for measuring the relationship between various elements of performance to see whether we are getting better or worse are known as ratios; simply put these involve expressing one thing as a proportion of another with a view to gaining an appreciation of what has happened. For example, miles per gallon is a measure of the efficiency of a motor vehicle. If that 'ratio' is 40 mpg in one period and 30 mpg in another it would be a cause for concern and investigation as to what had caused the drop in performance.

Ratios are used to compare performance in one period, say last month or year, with another – this month or year; they can also be used to see how well your business is performing compared with another, say a competitor. You can also use ratios to compare how well you have done against your target or budget. In the financial field the opportunity for calculating ratios is great, for computing useful ratios, not quite so great. These are the key ratios every business needs to keep track of.

You can see that Table 3.1 is nothing more than a simplified profit and loss account on the left and the assets section of the balance sheet on the right. Any change that increases net profit (more sales, lower expenses, less tax, etc), but does not increase the amount of assets employed (lower stocks, fewer debtors, etc), will increase the return on assets. Conversely, any change that increases capital employed without increasing profits in proportion will reduce the return on assets.

TABLE 3.1 Factors that affect profit performance

	£			£	£
Sales	100,000	Fixed assets			12,500
– Cost of sales	50,000				
= Gross profit	50,000	Working capital			
– Expenses	33,000	Current assets	23,100		
= Operating profit	17,000	– Current liabilities	6,690 = 16,410		
– Finance charges	8,090	Total net assets			28,910
= Net profit	8,910				

Now let us suppose that events occur to increase sales by £25,000 and profits by £1,000 to £9,910. Superficially that would look like an improved position. But if we then discover that to achieve that extra profit new equipment costing £5,000 and a further £2,500 had to be tied up in working capital (stock and debtors) the picture might not look so attractive. The return being made on assets employed has dropped from 31 per cent (£8,910/28,910 × 100) to 27 per cent (£9,910/[28,910 + 5,000 + 2,500] × 100).

Analysing accounts

The main analytical approach is to examine the relationship of pairs of figures extracted from the accounts. A pair may be taken from the same statement, or one figure from each of the profit and loss account and balance sheet statements. When brought together, the two figures are called ratios. Some financial ratios are meaningful in themselves, but their value mainly lies in their comparison with the equivalent ratio last year, a target ratio, or a competitor's ratio.

Before we can measure and analyse anything about a business's accounts we need some idea of what level or type of performance a business wants to achieve. All businesses have three fundamental objectives in common which allow us to see how well (or otherwise) they are doing.

Making a satisfactory return on investment

The first of these objectives is to make a satisfactory return (profit) on the money invested in the business. It is hard to think of a sound argument against this aim. To be satisfactory the return must meet four criteria:

1 It must give a fair return to shareholders, bearing in mind the risk they are taking. If the venture is highly speculative and the profits are less than bank interest rates, your shareholders (yourself included) will not be happy.

2 You must make enough profit to allow the company to grow.
If a business wants to expand sales it will need more working capital and eventually more space or equipment. The safest and surest source of new money for this is internally generated profits, retained in the business: reserves. (A business has three sources of new money: share capital or the owner's money; loan capital, put up by banks, etc; and retained profits, generated by the business.)

3 The return must be good enough to attract new investors or lenders. If investors can get a greater return on their money in some other comparable business, then that is where they will put it.

4 The return must provide enough reserves to keep the real capital intact. This means that you must recognize the impact inflation has on the business. A business retaining enough profits each year to make a 3 per cent growth is actually contracting by 1 per cent if inflation is running at 4 per cent.

Maintaining a sound financial position

As well as making a satisfactory return, investors, creditors and employees expect the business to be protected from unnecessary risks. Clearly, all businesses are exposed to market risks: competitors, new products and price changes are all part of a healthy commercial environment. The sorts of unnecessary risk that investors and lenders are particularly concerned about are high financial risks, such as overtrading.

Cash flow problems are not the only threat to a business's financial position. Heavy borrowing can bring a big interest burden to a small business, especially when interest rates rise unexpectedly. This may be acceptable when sales and profits are good; however, when times are bad, bankers, unlike shareholders, cannot be asked to tighten their belts – they expect to be paid all the time. So the position audit is not just about profitability, but about survival capabilities and the practice of sound financial disciplines.

Achieving growth

Making profit and surviving are insufficient achievements in themselves to satisfy shareholders, directors or ambitious MBAs – they want the business to grow too. But they do not just want the number of people they employ to increase or the sales turnover to rise, however nice that may be. They want the firm to become more efficient, to gain economies of scale and to improve the quality of profits.

Accounting ratios

Ratios used in analysing company accounts are clustered under five headings and are usually referred to as 'tests':

1 tests of profitability;
2 tests of liquidity;
3 tests of solvency;
4 tests of growth; and
5 market tests.

Tests of profitability

There are six ratios used to measure profit performance. The first four profit ratios are arrived at using only the profit and loss account and the other two use information from both that account and the balance sheet.

Gross profit

This is calculated by dividing the gross profit by sales and multiplying by 100. Using the example of High Note from Chapter 1 (see Table 3.2), the sum is £30,000/£60,000 × 100 = 50%. This is a measure of the value we are adding to the bought in materials and services we need to 'make' our product or service; the higher the figure the better.

TABLE 3.2   High Note extended profit and loss account

	£
Sales	60,000
Less the cost of goods to be sold	30,000
Gross profit	30,000
Less operating expenses	21,300
Operating profit	8,700
Less interest on bank loan and overdraft	600
Profit before tax	8,100
Less tax	1,827
Profit after tax	6,723

Operating profit

This is calculated by dividing the operating profit by sales and multiplying by 100. In this example the sum is £8,700/£60,000 × 100 = 14.5%. This is a measure of how efficiently we are running the business, before taking account of financing costs and tax. These are excluded as interest and tax rates change periodically and are outside our direct control. Excluding them makes it easier to compare one period with another or with another business. Once again the rule here is the higher the figure the better.

Net profit before and after tax

Dividing the net profit before and after tax by the sales and multiplying by 100 calculates these next two ratios. In this example the sums are £8,100/£60,000 × 100 = 13.5% and £6,723/£60,000 × 100 = 11.21%. This is a measure of how efficiently we are running the business, after taking account of financing costs and tax. The last figure shows how successful we are at creating additional money to either invest back in the business or distribute to the owner(s) as drawings or dividends. Once again the rule here is the higher the figure the better.

Return on equity

This ratio is usually expressed as a percentage in the way we might think of the return on any personal financial investment. Taking the owners' viewpoint, their concern is with the profit earned for them relative to the amount of funds they have invested in the business. The relevant profit here is *after* interest, tax (and any preference dividends) have been deducted. This is expressed as a percentage of the equity that comprises ordinary share capital and reserves. So in this example the sum is: return on equity = £6,723/£18,700 × 100 = 36%.

Return on capital employed

This takes a wider view of company performance than return on equity by expressing profit before interest, tax and dividend deductions as a percentage of the total capital employed, irrespective of whether this capital is borrowed or provided by the owners.

Capital employed is defined as share capital plus reserves plus long-term borrowings. Where, say, a bank overdraft is included in current liabilities every year and in effect becomes a source of capital, this may be regarded as part of capital employed. If the bank overdraft varies considerably from year to year, a more reliable ratio could be calculated by averaging the start- and end-year figures. There is no one precise definition used by companies for capital employed. In High Note's balance sheet (see Table 3.3) the sum is: return on capital employed = £8,700/£18,700 + £10,000 × 100 = 30%.

Tests of liquidity

In order to survive companies must also watch their liquidity position, by which is meant keeping enough short-term assets to pay short-term debts. Companies go out of business compulsorily when they fail to pay money due to employees, bankers or suppliers.

The liquid money tied up in day-to-day activities is known as working capital, the sum of which is arrived at by subtracting the current liabilities from the current assets. In the case of High Note we have £21,108 in current assets and £4,908 in current liabilities, so the working capital is £16,200.

Current ratio

As a figure the working capital doesn't tell us much. It is rather as if you knew your car had used 20 gallons of petrol but had no idea how far you had travelled. It would be more helpful to know how much larger the current assets are than the current liabilities. That would give us some idea whether the funds would be available to pay bills for stock, the tax liability and any other short-term liabilities that may arise. The current ratio, which is arrived at by dividing the current assets by the current liabilities, is the measure used. For High Note this is £21,108/£4,908 = 4.30. The convention is to express this as 4.30:1 and the aim is to have a ratio of between 1.5:1 and 2:1. Any lower and bills can't be met easily and much higher and money is being tied up unnecessarily.

TABLE 3.3   High Note balance sheet at 30 September

	£	£
Assets		
Fixed assets		
Fixtures, fitting, equipment	11,500	
Computer	1,000	
Total fixed assets		12,500
Working capital		
Current assets		
Stock	9,108	
Debtors	12,000	
Cash	0	
	21,108	
Less current liabilities (creditors falling due within one year)		
Overdraft	4,908	
Creditors	0	
	4,908	
Net current assets [Working capital (CA-CL)]		16,200
Total assets less current liabilities		28,700
Less creditors falling due after one year		
Long-term bank loan		10,000
Net total assets		18,700
Capital and reserves		
Owner's capital introduced	10,000	
Profit retained (from P&L account)	8,700	
Total capital and reserves		18,700

Quick ratio (acid test)

This is a belt and braces ratio used to ensure a business has sufficient ready cash or near-cash to meet all its current liabilities. Items such as stock are stripped out as although these are assets the money involved is not immediately available to pay bills. In effect the only liquid assets a business has are cash, debtors and any short-term investment such as bank deposits or government securities. For High Note this ratio is £12,000/£4,908 = 2.44:1. The ratio should be greater than 1:1 for a business to be sufficiently liquid.

Average collection period

We can see that High Note's current ratio is high, which is an indication that some elements of working capital are being used inefficiently. The business has £12,000 owed by customers on sales of £60,000 over a six-month period. The average period it takes High Note to collect money owed is calculated by dividing the sales made on credit by the money owed (debtors) and multiplying it by the time period, in days; in this case the sum is as follows: £12,000/£60,000 × 182.5 = 36.5 days.

If the credit terms are cash with order or seven days, then something is going seriously wrong. If it is net 30 days then it is probably about right. In this example it has been assumed that all the sales were made on credit.

Average payment period

This ratio shows how long a company is taking on average to pay its suppliers. The calculation is as for average collection period, but substituting creditors for debtors and purchase for sales.

Days stock held

High Note is carrying £9,108 stock of sheet music, CDs, etc and over the period it sold £30,000 of stock at cost. (The cost of sales is £30,000 to support £60,000 of invoiced sales as the mark up in this case is 100 per cent.) Using a similar sum as with average collection period we can calculate that the stock being held is sufficient to support 55.41 days sales (£9,108/£10,000 × 182.5). If High Note's suppliers can make weekly deliveries then this is almost certainly too high a stock figure to hold. Cutting stock back from nearly eight weeks (55.41 days) to one week (7 days) would trim 48.41 days or £7,957.38 worth of stock out of working capital. This in turn would bring the current ratio down to 2.68:1.

Circulation of working capital

This is a measure used to evaluate the overall efficiency with which working capital is being used. That is the sales divided by the working capital (current assets – current liabilities). In this example that sum is: £60,000/ £16,420 = 3.65 times. In other words we are turning over the working capital over three and a half times each year. There are no hard and fast rules as to what is an acceptable ratio. Clearly the more times working capital is turned over, stock sold for example, the more chance a business has to make a profit on that activity.

Tests of solvency

These measures see how a company is managing its long-term liabilities. There are two principal ratios used here: gearing and interest cover.

Gearing

This measures as a percentage the proportion of all borrowing, including long-term loans and bank overdrafts, to either the total of shareholders funds – share capital and all reserves. The gearing ratio is sometimes also known as the *debt/equity ratio*. For High Note this is: (£4,908 + £10,000)/ £18,800 = £14,908/£18,800 = 0.79: 1. In other words, for every £ the shareholders have invested in High Note they have borrowed a further 79 p. This ratio is usually not expected to exceed 1:1 for long periods.

Interest cover

This is a measure of the proportion of profit taken up by interest payments and can be found by dividing the annual interest payment into the annual profit before interest, tax and dividend payments. The greater the number, the less vulnerable the company will be to any setback in profits, or rise in interest rates on variable loans. The smaller the number, the more risk that level of borrowing represents to the company. A figure of between two and five times would be considered acceptable.

Tests of growth

These are arrived at by comparing one year with another, usually for elements of the profit and loss account such as sales and profit. So, for example if next year High Note achieved sales of £100,000 and operating profits of £16,000 the growth ratios would be 67 per cent, that is £40,000 of extra sales as a proportion of the first year's sales of £60,000; and 84 per cent, that is £7,300 of extra operating profit as a percentage of the first year's operating profit of £8,700.

Some additional information can be gleaned from these two ratios. In this example we can see that profits are growing faster than sales, which indicates a healthier trend than if the situation were reversed.

Market tests

This is the name given to stock market measures of performance. The key ratios here are:

1 Earnings per share = net profit/shares outstanding.
2 The after-tax profit made by a company divided by the number of ordinary shares it has issued.
3 Price earnings ratio = market price per share/earnings per share.
4 The market price of an ordinary share divided by the earnings per share.

The PE Ratio expresses the market value placed on the expectation of future earnings, ie the number of years required to earn the price paid for the shares out of profits at the current rate.

$$\text{Yield} = \frac{\text{Dividends per Share}}{\text{Price per Share}}$$

The percentage return a shareholder gets on the 'opportunity' or current value of their investment:

$$\text{Dividend Cover} = \frac{\text{Net Income}}{\text{Dividend}}$$

The number of times the profit exceeds the dividend, the higher the ratio, the more retained profit to finance future growth.

Other ratios

There are a very large number of other ratios that businesses use for measuring aspects of their performance such as:

- Sales per $/£/€ invested in fixed assets – a measure of the use of those fixed assets.
- Sales per employee – showing if your headcount is exceeding your sales growth.
- Sales per manager, per support staff, etc – showing the effectiveness of overhead spending.

Table 3.4 shows some of the measures that Tesco, the leading UK retail chain, sees as important. It operates a balanced scorecard approach to managing the business that is known internally within the group as its 'Steering Wheel'. This is intended to unite resources and focuses the efforts of its staff on operations, financial performance and the delivery of customer metrics. Its philosophy is that if it looks after customers well and operates efficiently and effectively then the shareholders' interests will always be best served by the inevitable outputs of those – growth in sales, profits and returns. Table 3.4 shows some of the ratio's that Tesco views as key.

TABLE 3.4 Tesco's 'Steering Wheel' ratios

	2009	2008
Sales growth		
Change in Group sales over the year (including Value Added Tax)	15.1%	11.1%
UK sales growth	9.5%	6.7%
International sales growth	30.6%	25.3%
International sales growth (at constant exchange rates)	13.6%	22.5%
Retailing services sales growth	11%	–
Profit before tax	£2,954m	£2,803m
Underlying profit before tax	£3,128m	£2,846m
Trading margin		
UK trading margin	6.2%	5.9%
International trading margin (excluding the United States)	5.3%	5.6%
UK Market Share		
Grocery market share	22.2%	21.8%
Non-food market share	8.8%	8.5%
Employee retention	87%	84%
Reduction in CO_2 emissions		
UK	13.3%	3.8%
The Group	12.6%	3.8%
Reduction in CO_2 emissions, new stores	20.9%	11.7%

SOURCE: www.thesmehub.com. Register for free then go to Member Services, Company Accounts Lookup and enter name.

Combined ratios

No one would use a single ratio to decide whether one vehicle was a better or worse buy than another. MPG, MPH, annual depreciation percentage and residual value proportion are just a handful of the ratios that would need to be reviewed. So it is with a business. A combination of ratios can be used to form an opinion on the financial state of affairs at any one time.

The best know of these combination ratios is the Altman Z-Score (**www. creditguru.com/CalcAltZ.shtml**) that uses a combined set of five financial ratios derived from eight variables from a company's financial statements linked to some statistical techniques to predict a company's probability of failure. Entering the figures into the onscreen template at this website produces a score and an explanatory narrative giving a view on the business's financial strengths and weaknesses.

Some problems in using ratios

Finding the information to calculate business ratios is often not the major problem. Being sure of what the ratios are really telling you almost always is. The most common problems lie in the four following areas.

Which way is right?

There is natural feeling with financial ratios to think that high figures are good ones, and an upward trend represents the right direction. This theory is, to some extent, encouraged by the personal feeling of wealth that having a lot of cash engenders.

Unfortunately, there is no general rule on which way is right for financial ratios. In some cases a high figure is good; in others a low figure is best. Indeed, there are even circumstances in which ratios of the same value are not as good as each other. Look at the two working capital statements in Table 3.5.

TABLE 3.5 Difficult comparisons

Current assets	1		2	
	£	£	£	£
Stock	10,000		22,990	
Debtors	13,000		100	
Cash	100	23,100	10	23,100
Less current liabilities				
Overdraft	5,000		90	
Creditors	1,690	6,690	6,600	6,690
Working capital		16,410		16,410
Current ratio		3.4:1		3.4:1

The amount of working capital in each example is the same (£16,410) as are the current assets and current liabilities, at £23,100 and £6,690 respectively. It follows that any ratio using these factors would also be the same. For example, the current ratios in these two examples are both identical, 3.4:1, but in the first case there is a reasonable chance that some cash will come in from debtors, certainly enough to meet the modest creditor position. In the second example there is no possibility of useful amounts of cash coming in from trading, with debtors at only £100, while creditors at the relatively substantial figure of £6,600 will pose a real threat to financial stability.

So, in this case the current ratios are identical but the situations being compared are not. In fact, as a general rule, a higher working capital ratio is regarded as a move in the wrong direction. The more money a business has tied up in working capital the more difficult it is to make a satisfactory return on capital employed, simply because the larger the denominator the lower the return on capital employed.

In some cases the right direction is more obvious. A high return on capital employed is usually better than a low one, but even this can be a danger signal, warning that higher risks are being taken. And not all high profit ratios are good: sometimes a higher profit margin can lead to reduced sales volume and so lead to a lower ROCE (return on capital employed).

In general, business performance as measured by ratios is best thought of as lying within a range, liquidity (current ratio), for example, staying between 1.2:1 and 1.8:1. A change in either direction represents a cause for concern.

Accounting for inflation

In the UK, financial ratios all use pounds sterling as the basis for comparison: historical pounds at that. That would not be so bad if all these pounds were from the same date in the past, but that is not so. Comparing one year with another from three or four years ago may not be very meaningful unless we account for the change in the value of the pound.

One way of overcoming this problem is to adjust for inflation, perhaps using an index, such as that for consumer prices. Such indices usually take 100 as their base at some time in the past, for example, 2000. Then an index value for each subsequent year is produced showing the relative movement in the item being indexed.

Apples and pears

There are particular problems in trying to compare one business's ratios with another. A small new business can achieve quite startling sales growth ratios in the early months and years. Expanding from £10,000 sales in the first six months to £50,000 in the second would not be unusual. To expect a mature business to achieve the same growth would be unrealistic. For Tesco to grow from sales of £10 billion to £50 billion would imply wiping out every other supermarket chain. So some care must be taken to make sure that like is being compared with like, and allowances made for differing circumstances in the businesses being compared (or if the same business, the trading/economic environment of the years being compared).

It is also important to check that one business's idea of an account category, say current assets, is the same as the one you want to compare it with. The concepts and principles used to prepare accounts leave some scope for differences.

Seasonal factors

Many of the ratios that we have looked at make use of information in the balance sheet. Balance sheets are prepared at one moment in time, and reflect the position at that moment; they may not represent the average situation. For example, seasonal factors can cause a business's sales to be particularly high once or twice a year, as with fashion retailers for example. A balance sheet prepared just before one of these seasonal upturns might show very high stocks, bought in specially to meet this demand. Conversely, a look at the balance just after the upturn might show very high cash and low stocks. If either of those stock figures were to be treated as an average it would give a false picture.

Getting company accounts

It will be very useful to look at other comparable businesses to see their ratios as a yardstick against which to compare your own business's performance. For publicly quoted and larger business whose accounts are audited this should not be too difficult; for smaller private companies the position is not quite so simple. In the first place small companies in the UK, that is those with annual turnover below £6 million, need only file an abbreviated balance sheet. Only public companies listed on a stock market and larger companies have to provide full financial statements. Despite this it is still possible to glean some valuable information on financial performance using the following sources.

Companies House (**www.companieshouse.gov.uk**) is the official repository of all company information in the UK. Its WebCHeck service offers a free of charge searchable Company Names and Address Index covering 2 million companies either by name or unique company registration number. You can use WebCHeck to purchase a company's latest accounts giving details of sales, profits, margins, directors, shareholders and bank borrowings at a cost of £1 ($1.6/€1.18) per company.

Credit reports such as those provided by **www.ukdata.com, www.checksure. biz** and **www.business-inc.co.uk** cost around £8 ($12.8/€9.4), are available online and provide basic business performance ratios.

FAME (Financial Analysis Made Easy) is a powerful database that contains information on 3.4 million companies in the UK and Ireland. Typically the following information is included: contact information including phone, e-mail and web addresses plus main and other trading addresses, activity details, 29 profit and loss account and 63 balance sheet items, cash flow and ratios, credit score and rating, security and price information (listed companies only), names of bankers, auditors, previous auditors and advisers, details of holdings and subsidiaries (including foreign holdings and subsidiaries), names of current and previous directors with home addresses and shareholder indicator, heads of department, and shareholders. You can compare each company with detailed financials with its peer group based on its activity codes, and the software lets you search for companies that comply with your own criteria, combining as many conditions as you like. FAME is available in business libraries and on CD from the publishers, which also offer free a trial (**www.bvdep.com/en/companyInformationHome.html**>Company data – national>FAME).

Keynote (**www.keynote.co.uk**) operates in 18 countries providing business ratios and trends for 140 industry sectors to assess accurately the financial health of each industry sector. Using this service you can find out how profitable a business sector is and how successful the main companies operating in each sector are. Executive summaries are free, but expect to pay between £250 ($400/€295) and £500 ($800/€590) for most reports. See also the London Stock Exchange's website (**www.londonstockexchange.com**).

Proshare (**www.proshareclubs.co.uk**>Research Centre>Performance Tables) is an investment club website, where you can register for free, which has a number of tools that crunch public company ratios for you. Select the companies you want to look at, then the ratios you are most interested in – EPS, P/E, ROI, Dividend Yield and so forth. Press the button and in couple of seconds all is revealed. You can then rank the companies by performance in more or less any way you want.

Yahoo (**http://uk.finance.yahoo.com**>Free annual reports) has direct links to several thousand public companies' reports and accounts online, so you can save yourself the time and trouble of hunting down company websites.

Examples of the accounting information readily available on most limited companies and all public companies are shown in Tables 3.6 and 3.7.

Free tools that calculate financial ratios from your financial data are available from abiz/ed (**www.bized.co.uk**>Company Information>Financial Ratio Analysis) and Harvard Business School (**http://harvardbusinessonline. hbsp.harvard.edu/b02/en/academic/edu_tk_acct_fin_ratio.jhtml**). They also provide useful introductions to ratio analysis as well as defining each ratio and the formula used to calculate it. You need to register on the Harvard website to be able to download the spreadsheet.

TABLE 3.6 Google Inc company accounts

Consolidated Statements of Income Data:

| | Year Ended 31 December, | | | | |
	2003	2004	2005	2006	2007
	(in thousands, except per share amounts)				
Revenues	$1,465,934	$3,189,223	$6,138,560	$10,604,917	$16,593,986
Costs and expenses:					
Cost of revenues	634,411	1,468,967	2,577,088	4,225,027	6,649,085
Research and development	229,605	395,164	599,510	1,228,589	2,119,985
Sales and marketing	164,935	295,749	468,152	849,518	1,461,266
General and administrative	94,519	188,151	386,532	751,787	1,279,250
Contribution to Google Foundation	–	–	90,000	–	–
Non-recurring portion of settlement of disputes with Yahoo!	–	201,000	–	–	–
Total costs and expenses	1,123,470	2,549,031	4,121,282	7,054,921	11,509,586

TABLE 3.6 *Continued*

	Year Ended 31 December,				
	2003	2004	2005	2006	2007
	(in thousands, except per share amounts)				
Income from operations	342,464	640,192	2,017,278	3,549,996	5,084,400
Interest income and other, net	4,190	10,042	124,399	461,044	589,580
Income before income taxes	346,654	650,234	2,141,677	4,011,040	5,673,980
Provision for income taxes	241,006	251,115	676,280	933,594	1,470,260
Net income	$105,648	$399,119	$1,465,397	$3,077,446	$4,203,720
Net income per share of Class A and Class B common stock					
Basic	$0.77	$2.07	$5.31	$10.21	$13.53
Diluted	$0.41	$1.46	$5.02	$9.94	$13.29

TABLE 3.6 *Continued*

Consolidated Balance Sheet Data:

	As of 31 December, (in thousands)				
	2003	**2004**	**2005**	**2006**	**2007**
Cash, cash equivalents and marketable securities	$334,718	$2,132,297	$8,034,247	$11,243,914	$14,218,613
Total assets	871,458	3,313,351	10,271,813	18,473,351	25,335,806
Total long-term liabilities	33,365	43,927	107,472	128,924	610,525
Redeemable convertible preferred stock warrant	13,871	–	–	–	–
Deferred stock-based compensation	(369,668)	(249,470)	(119,015)	–	–
Total stockholders' equity	588,770	2,929,056	9,418,957	17,039,840	22,689,679

SOURCE: http://investor.google.com/earnings.html

TABLE 3.7 Tesco company accounts – group income statement

53 weeks ended 28 February 2009	2009 £m	2008 £m
Continuing operations		
Revenue (sales excluding VAT)	54,327	47,298
Cost of sales	(50,109)	(43,668)
Gross profit	4,218	3,630
Administrative expenses	(1,248)	(1,027)
Profit arising on property-related items	236	188
Operating profit	3,206	2,791
Share of post-tax profits of joint ventures and associates	110	75
Finance income	116	187
Finance costs	(478)	(250)
Profit before tax	2,954	2,803
Taxation	(788)	(673)
Profit for the year	2,166	2,130

SOURCE: **www.investorcentre.tescoplc.com**

Using financial data to improve performance

A priority task for any MBA will be to assist managers in improving business performance. This is an area in which the MBA will be best able to demonstrate the value of his or her skills and so build allies in the organization. The most successful businesses, when it comes to becoming more profitable (the acid test of business improvement), concentrate their efforts in three areas: optimizing resources, maintaining or improving profit margins and of course building up sales revenue. It is this last strategy that draws the most attention, but not pursuing the other two may lead only to unprofitable growth, so leaving a business more vulnerable as it gets bigger. All three of these generic growth strategies are to a greater or lesser extent intertwined, so you should look on this categorization process more as an aide-memoire rather than a rigid structure.

Put simply you can see that any action that tends to increase profits while either not increasing or actually reducing the resources employed to generate those profits produces healthy growth. Using the summarized financial statements for High Note shown in Table 3.8 we can see the effect of various

TABLE 3.8   High Note's profit and loss account and balance sheet

Profit and loss account		Balance sheet		
	£		£	£
Sales	60,000	Fixed assets		
Less the cost of goods to be sold (materials, labour, etc)	30,000	Garage conversion, etc		11,500
		Computer		1,000
Gross profit	30,000	Total fixed assets		12,500
Less operating expenses (rent, utilities, admin, etc)	21,300			
Operating profit	8,700	Working capital		
Less interest due to bank	600	Current assets		
Profit before tax	8,100	Stock	9,108	
Less tax	1,377	Debtors	12,000	
Profit after tax	6,723	Cash	0	
(11.21%)			21,108	
		Less Current liabilities		
		Overdraft	4,908	
		Creditors	0	
			4,908	
		Working capital (CA–CL)		16,200
		Total assets		28,700

growth strategies. If we can increase sales, say, by £10,000 while maintaining the profit margin at 11.21 per cent we will have grown profits by £1,121. So both sales and profits will have grown by 17 per cent. If that can also be done without needing any more working space or money tied up in stocks, so much the better. Our return on capital will also improve. Contrast that with a strategy that grows sales while costs rise disproportionately and more assets are employed to achieve that growth, and an unhealthy growth pattern will emerge.

Optimizing resources

The first and in some ways the simplest way to grow profits is to get more of what you sell ready for market using fewer resources. This strategy improves profit margins while either reducing the actual amount of money needed to run the business, or allows you to grow without recourse to additional financing. Both are desirable outcomes as it leaves you with a more secure venture as well as a bigger one.

Reviewing working methods

The richest source of opportunities to optimize comes from finding ways to work smarter rather than harder. Finding out about better ways to work can be difficult for a small firm where the founder has few senior employees to learn from – one of the benefits big businesses get by virtue of continuously recruiting new people. Owner-managers can compensate by getting out themselves and seeing what is going on in their industry. Below are some ways you can keep abreast of the latest developments in your filed.

Read widely both the magazines that relate to your industry and those of neighbouring topics. In particular read magazines and articles published in the area that is at the leading edge of your business world; Silicon Valley for the internet, Germany for the motor industry, Japan for cameras and photography. You don't have to rush out and buy hundreds of magazines and learned journals. Use Find Articles (**www.findarticles.com**), which has a database of over 10 million articles on a range of topics, many of which are free and online.

See if your competitors are doing much better than you and then try to find out why. Get their catalogues, leaflets and price lists and examine their websites. Get their accounts from Companies House (**www.companies-house.gov.uk**) and calculate some key ratio to compare performance such as show in biz/ed (**www.bized.co.uk**>Company Information>Financial Ratio Analysis>Inter-firm Comparisons) and use Google News (**www.google.co.uk**>News) to read stories about them in the press (announcing new products, recruiting more staff, etc).

Attend exhibitions, conferences and seminars where you are likely to meet and hear movers and shakers in your industry. Esources (**www. esources.co.uk**) lists trade shows, fairs and exhibitions in the UK, and All Conferences.com (**www.allconferences.com**) is a directory focusing on conferences, conventions, trade shows, exhibitions and workshops that can be searched by category, key word, date and venue as well as by title.

Control working capital

The main levers for getting quick wins when it comes to improving performance lie in the working capital area. If sales and profit growth can be achieved using the same proportion of working capital or less a then healthy growth is being achieved.

Debtor control

If you are selling on credit and take 90 days to collect your money from customers, which is by no means uncommon, then you are tying up an extra £150,000 cash for every £1 million of sales, compared to a firm getting its money in 35 days. Even quite small firms, say with a turnover of around £3 million a year, could eliminate the whole value of their overdraft by taking simple measures to improve in this respect. Looking at it another way, getting paid a week earlier would free up nearly £60,000 of lifesaving cash in such a venture.

A very small amount of extra effort put in here can pay great dividends and it's important to remember the less cash needed to finance the business the more profitable that business will be. Here are some things you can do to get paid faster.

If you sell on credit set out your terms of trade clearly on your invoices. Unless customers know when you expect to be paid, they will pay when it suits them. Find out when your biggest customers have their monthly cheque run and make sure your bills reach them in time. Send out statements promptly to chase up late payers, and always follow up with a phone call. Always take trade references when giving credit and look at their accounts to see how sound they are.

Normally the rule is to take credit from your suppliers up to the maximum time allowed. But sometimes it may make good business sense to pay up promptly. While this may sound insane, sometimes suppliers with cash flow difficulties of their own offer what amounts to excessively high rates of interest for settling up promptly.

If a supplier offers 2 per cent to pay up in seven days rather than the 40 days they would usually take, what is on offer is in effect a 22.65 per cent equivalent interest. (Follow the steps below to work out if prompt payment is a good investment.) So if that figure is higher than the return you are making in the business, and your cash flow can stand the pain, paying promptly may be a better way to grow profits than many other options, particularly during a recession. You can use the same arithmetic to work out what you can afford to pay out to get your money in earlier; see Table 3.9.

TABLE 3.9   Evaluating a discount offer

Step 1	Agree discount	2%
Step 2	100 – discount on offer	98%
Step 3	Divide step 1 by step 2	0.02048
Step 4	Normal payment period in days	40
Step 5	Payment period to get discount	7
Step 6	Step 4 minus step 5	33
Step 7	365 divided by step 6	11.06061
Step 8	Step 7 times × step 3 × 100	22.65%

Inventory management

High inventory levels are popular with marketing departments as having them makes satisfying customers an easier task; they are less popular with production departments, which have to carry inventory costs in their budgets. Finance departments insist on having the lowest possible stock levels, as high stock pushes working capital levels up and return on investment down. This tussle between departments is a strategic issue that has to be resolved by top management. The birth of Waterstone's, the bookshop business founded by Tim Waterstone, fortuitously a marketing visionary, qualified accountant and the company's managing director, provides an interesting illustration of the dimension of the stock control issue. Up until the advent of Waterstone's the convention had been to store books spine out on shelves, in alphabetical order, under major subject headings – computing, sport, travel, etc. This had the added advantage of making it easy to see what books needed reordering and stock counts were a simple process. Waterstone, however, knew that 'browsers', the majority (60 per cent, according to his research) of people who go into bookshops to look around, had no idea what book they wanted, so didn't know where to start looking. His differentiating strategy was, as well as following the conventional model of having books on shelves, scattering the books in piles around the store using a variety of methods: new books in one pile, special offers in another. Sales and profits soared sufficiently to more than compensate for the near doubling of book stock.

Inventory categories

There are three different categories of inventory that a business needs to have and keep track of:

1 *Finished goods:* these are products ready to ship out to customers. For Apple these would be computers, iPods and so forth, for General Motors vehicles and for a baker loaves of bread.

2 *Work in progress (WIP):* these are products in the process of being completed. They have used up some raw materials and had workers paid to start the manufacturing process, so the cost will reflect those inputs. For General Motors WIP would include vehicles awaiting paint or a pre-delivery inspection.

3 *Raw materials:* These are the basic materials from which the end product is made. For General Motors this would include metal and paint, but it could also include a complete bought-in engine for the vehicles in which it uses third-party power units.

Economic order quantity (EOQ)

Businesses have to carry a certain minimum amount of stock to ensure the production pipeline works efficiently and likely demand is met. So the costs associated with ordering large quantities infrequently and so reducing the order cost but increasing the cost of holding stock has to be balanced with placing frequent orders, so pushing up the costs of placing orders but reducing stock-holding costs. EOQ is basically an accounting formula that calculates the point at which the combination of order costs and inventory carrying costs are the least, so arriving at the most cost effective quantity to order. The formula for EOQ is:

$$\text{Economic Order Quantity} = \frac{\sqrt{(2 \times R \times O)}}{C}$$

where: R = Annual demand in units; O = Cost of placing an order; C = Cost of carrying a unit of inventory for the year.

InventoryOps.com, a website created and run by Dave Piasecki to support his book *Inventory Accuracy: People, processes, & technology* (2003, Ops Publishing), provides a useful starting point in your quest for information on all aspects of inventory management and warehouse operations. You will find a full explanation of how to use EOQ at (**www.inventoryops. com/economic_order_quantity.htm**).

Improving profit margins

Over time costs tend to creep ahead of the value you are getting for the money spent. The rises happen steadily, often nearly invisibly and in increments some-times apparently insignificant in themselves. For example, employees expect an annual pay review, which usually means a pay rise not necessarily related to any improvement in performance; suppliers regularly increase prises; the cost of utilities and government taxes consistently rise faster than inflation. Unless you are getting more sales as a result of these cost rises, profits will shrink. There are four courses of action we can take to improve margins.

1. Charge more

It is never easy raising prices but it can, if done selectively, be a path to healthy growth. First, let's examine the potential rewards and risks. Using High Note as our working model, assume its £60,000 of sales come from 60 customers all buying £1,000 worth of goods and services from us, at 50 per cent gross profit margin. If by raising our prices by 10 per cent we lost no customers then our profit would rise by £6,000, all of which would drop to the bottom line, before tax, as there are no additional costs involved; almost doubling our profit before tax.

What would happen if we lost six customers (10 per cent) as a result of the price rise? Now we would only have 54 customers paying £1,100 each, or £59,400. That's only £600 less than before and there are other benefits that have not been shown. Putting the pressure on price rather than volume means carrying less stock, having fewer bills to chase, using less capital and wear-ing out equipment less quickly. That is not to imply that putting up prices is an easy task, but it may not be much harder than finding new customers, and it is nearly always more profitable. When raising prices try to offer some extra value in return in terms of improved service or extra features.

These sums depend on your level of gross profit. The lower your gross profit the less business you can afford to lose for any given price rise. Download this spreadsheet from Innovator.com; it does all the arithmetic of changing prices for you (**www.innovator.com**>Free Business Plan Templates and Financial Plan Models>Free Break Even Model and Pricing Tools – Full Version).

2. Change product/service mix

If you sell more than one product or service, or are planning to introduce new ones as part of your growth strategy, analyse costs so that energies are focused on those with the highest profit margin. Very few owner-managers have any true idea as to which products or services generate the most profit, so collecting that data has to be the first step. (If you are a little rusty on costing, read Chapter 4 first.)

Look at the example in Table 3.10. This business makes three products. Product C is bulky, complicated and a comparatively slow seller. It uses all the same sort of equipment, storage space and sales efforts as products A and B, only more so. When fixed costs are allocated across the range it draws the greatest share.

TABLE 3.10 Product profitability (1)

	A	B	C	Total
	£	£	£	£
Sales	30,000	50,000	20,000	100,000
Variable costs	20,000	30,000	10,000	60,000
Allocated fixed costs	4,500	9,000	11,500	25,000
Total costs	24,500	39,000	21,500	85,000
Operating profit	5,500	11,000	(1,500)	15,000

These figures seem to show that product C is losing money and should be eliminated. Doing so will produce the situation shown in Table 3.11.

TABLE 3.11 Product profitability (2)

	A	B	Total
	£	£	£
Sales	30,000	50,000	80,000
Variable costs	20,000	30,000	50,000
New allocated fixed costs	8,333	16,667	25,000
Total costs	28,333	46,667	75,000
Operating profit	1,667	3,333	5,000

Fixed costs will not change just because we have dropped a product; our property and any other element of fixed costs will still need to be covered. So dropping the 'unprofitable' C product has actually resulted in less profit than before. This full costing system has given the wrong signal as it ignores any contribution (the difference between selling price and variable costs) that product C makes.

If we allocate fixed costs by reference to the amount of contribution a product makes we will end up with a very different calculation; see Table 3.12.

TABLE 3.12 Fixed costs allocated by contribution level

		Contribution		Fixed cost allocated
		£	%	£
Product	A	10,000	25	6,250
	B	20,000	50	12,500
	C	10,000	25	6,250
Total		40,000	100	25,000

Recasting the profit and loss account using the contribution each product makes rather than full costing reveals a quite different profit picture; see Table 3.13.

TABLE 3.13 Product profitability using contribution

	A		B		C		Total
	£	%	£	%	£	%	£
Sales	30,000		50,000		20,000		100,000
Marginal costs	20,000		30,000		10,000		60,000
Contribution	10,000	33	20,000	40	10,000	50	40,000
Fixed costs	6,250		12,500		6,250		25,000
Product profit	3,750	13	7,500	15	3,750	19	15,000

Given that we can't eliminate many fixed costs in a home-based business, contribution as a basis for allocating fixed costs give a more useful signal as to where to concentrate efforts. Far from eliminating product C, all things being equal we should try to sell more.

3. Buy less

The challenge here is to strip out waste or find ways to step up yield. When you are working on your own this will probably not be a fertile field; once you have employees, however dedicated, the problems start. The classic question when people want to buy something is to ask, 'If it were your money would you spend it this way?' One entrepreneur who has built his company to a £3 million business from a standing start five years earlier formed his 20 employees into what he called 'Smart Circles'. He challenged them to find ways the firm could do things faster, better and at a lower cost. In year one he doubled profits and within a five years his business was valued at £10 million.

4. Reducing the tax take

Tax on profits is often a small business's biggest single expense, slicing anything from 20 to 40 per cent off the bottom line. All money that goes in taxes can be consider a waste as far as a business is concerned, as unlike individuals who may see something of value for their tax a business gets nothing back. So the rule here is to minimize tax within the law. The big companies have got this down to a fine art; the top 800 UK companies paid no tax at all in 2008/9. These are some strategies for reducing taxes and so increasing retained profits, though some of that may not then be available as cash to the business. This is a job for your treasury department, if you have one. If not get specialist tax advice, but as an MBA you should be able to act as the catalyst to ensure this area is reviewed frequently.

04 Finance as a value creator

- Breaking even, where value begins
- Realizing profit goals
- Profit maximization vs shareholder value
- Putting a cost on capital
- Assessing future profitability.

Financial management is not just about historical data and esoteric arguments about the valuation of assets and liabilities. The most useful application of financial tools, from an MBA's perspective, are some powerful but simple techniques to help managers make better decisions now and have a more accurate picture of the likely outcomes, from a financial perspective at least, of future performance. These tools are simple and certainly not new – for example articles assessing the use of break-even analysis had started to appear by 1962 (*Break-Even Analysis: Its uses and misuses,* Howard F Stettler, 1962, American Accounting Association). But most managers have never heard of these tools and those very few that have don't know how to use them. This gives MBAs a powerful edge and allows them to muscle into decisions that are normally the prerogative of those several pay grades higher.

Three further factors work to the MBA's advantage when it comes to appreciating the interplay between financial performance and value. In the first instance profit alone is far less important than accountants would like to have you believe: a glance a Figure 4.1 showing the steady rise in Amazon's share price, while racking up accelerating losses, is sufficient to prove that point. So the MBA can bring his or her wider skills to bear, while fully understanding the part finance plays, to get a more rounded picture of what drives value.

The second factor that an MBA needs to keep in mind is that management below the very top matters very little in the eyes of those who assess

FIGURE 4.1   Amazon: The more it lost the more it was worth!

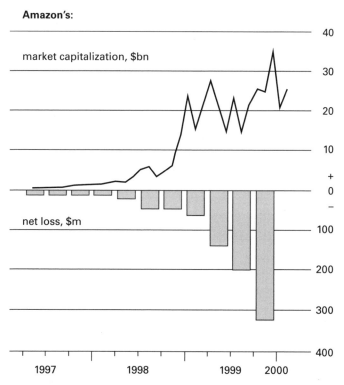

Amazon's:

market capitalization, $bn

net loss, $m

1997   1998   1999   2000

SOURCE: http://phx.corporate-ir.net/phoenix.zhtml?c=97664&p=irol-irhome

value, but financial results do. In a study by DDI, a talent management company, in February 2010, of 50 financial analysts only eight said that leadership accounted for over 25 per cent of the criteria they used in assigning value to a company's shares. Financial elements accounted for the remaining 75 per cent. Some 84 per cent rated consistent growth in turnover a most important factor, while 94 per cent ranked the experience of the person at the very top as key. The Ocado case study, later in this chapter, seems to support these findings.

Third, it is quite possible for a business that is very profitable in one period to be completely worthless in a matter of months or even days. If you think this an unlikely scenario, look back to Lehman Brothers, the 158-year-old bank that failed in September 2008. It was listed as 37th in the Fortune 500 in 2008, up from 47th the preceding year. Its last accounts showed $4,192 million profits, up 4.6 per cent on the year before. Its 'stock in trade' was investment advice, which became worthless as its business model imploded. The MBA should be aware that the wheel is always in spin and yesterday's accounts are just that: yesterday's story.

Cost, volume, pricing and profit decisions

Working out the cost of making a product or delivering a service and consequently how much to charge doesn't seem too complicated. At first glance the problem is simple. You just add up all the costs and charge a bit more. The more you charge above your costs, provided the customers will keep on buying, the more profit you make. Unfortunately, as soon as you start to do the sums the problem gets a little more complex. For a start, not all costs have the same characteristics. Some costs, for example, do not change however much you sell. If you are running a shop, the rent and rates are relatively constant figures, completely independent of the volume of your sales. On the other hand, the cost of the products sold from the shop is completely dependent on volume. The more you sell, the more it costs you to buy in stock.

	€
Rent and rates for shop	2,500
Cost of 1,000 units of volume of product	1,000
Total costs	3,500

You can't really add up those two types of costs until you have made an assumption about volume – how much you plan to sell. Look at the simple example above. Until we decide to buy, and we hope sell, 1,000 units of our product, we cannot total the costs. With the volume hypothesized we can arrive at a cost per unit of product of:

$$\text{Total costs} \div \text{Number of units} = €3,500 \div 1,000 = €3.50$$

Now, provided we sell out all the above at €3.50, we shall always be profitable. But will we? Suppose we do not sell all the 1,000 units, what then? With a selling price of €4.50 we could, in theory, make a profit of €1,000 if we sell all 1,000 units. That is a total sales revenue of €4,500, minus total costs of €3,500. But if we only sell 500 units, our total revenue drops to €2,250 and we actually lose €1,250 (total revenue €2,250 – total costs €3,500). So at one level of sales a selling price of €4.50 is satisfactory, and at another it is a disaster. This very simple example shows that all those decisions are intertwined. Costs, sales volume, selling prices and profits are all linked together. A decision taken in any one of these areas has an impact on the others. To understand the relationship between these factors, we need a picture or model of how they link up. Before we can build this model, we need some more information on each of the component parts of cost.

The components of cost

Understanding the behaviour of costs as the trading patterns in a business change is of vital importance to decision makers. It is this 'dynamic' nature in every business that makes good costing decisions the key to survival and provides the MBA with a wealth of opportunities to demonstrate his or her skill and knowledge.

The last example showed that if the situation was static and predictable, a profit was certain, but if any one component in the equation was not a certainty (in that example it was volume), then the situation was quite different. To see how costs behave under changing conditions we first have to identify the different types of cost.

Fixed costs

Fixed costs are costs that happen, by and large, whatever the level of activity. For example, the cost of buying a car is the same whether it is driven 100 miles a year or 20,000 miles. The same is also true of the road tax, insurance and any extras, such as a stereo system or navigator.

In a business, as well as the cost of buying cars, there are other fixed costs such as plant, equipment, computers, desks and answering machines. But certain less tangible items can also be fixed costs, for example rent, rates, insurance and so on, which are usually set quite independent of how successful or otherwise a business is.

Costs such as most of those mentioned above are fixed irrespective of the timescale under consideration. Other costs, such as those of employing people, while theoretically variable in the short term, in practice are fixed. In other words, if sales demand goes down and a business needs fewer people, the costs cannot be shed for several weeks (notice, holiday pay, redundancy, etc). Also, if the people involved are highly skilled or expensive to recruit and train (or in some other way particularly valuable) and the downturn looks a short one, it may not be cost-effective to reduce those short-run costs in line with falling demand. So viewed over a period of weeks and months, labour is a fixed cost. Over a longer period it may not be fixed. We could draw a simple chart showing how fixed costs behave as the 'dynamic' volume changes. The first phase of our cost model is shown in Figure 4.2. This shows a static level of fixed costs over a particular range of output. To return to the previous example, this could show the fixed cost, rent and rates for a shop to be constant over a wide range of sales levels. Once the shop owner has reached a satisfactory sales and profit level in one shop, he or she may decide to rent another one, in which case the fixed costs will 'step up'. This can be shown in the variation on the fixed cost model in Figure 4.3.

FIGURE 4.2   Cost model 1: showing fixed costs

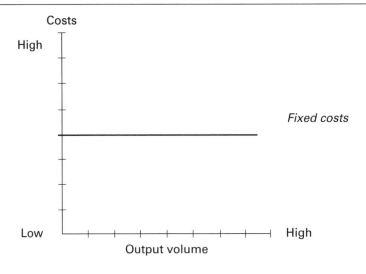

FIGURE 4.3   Variation on cost model 1: showing a 'step up' in fixed costs

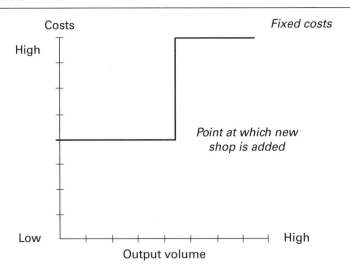

Variable costs

These are costs that change in line with output. Raw materials for production, packaging materials, bonuses, piece rates, sales commission and postage are some examples. The important characteristic of a variable cost is that it rises or falls in direct proportion to any growth or decline in output volumes. We can now draw a chart showing how variable costs

FIGURE 4.4 Cost model 2: showing behaviour of variable costs as volume changes

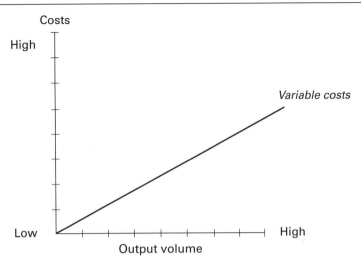

behave as volume changes. The second phase of our cost model will look like Figure 4.4.

There is a popular misconception that defines fixed costs as those costs that are predictable, and variable costs as those that are subject to change at any moment. The definitions already given are the only valid ones for costing purposes.

Semi-variable costs

Unfortunately not all costs fit easily into either the fixed or variable category. Some costs have both a fixed and a variable element. For example, a mobile phone has a monthly rental cost that is fixed, and a cost per unit consumed over and above a set usage rate, which is variable. In this particular example low-usage consumers can be seriously penalized. If only a few calls are made each month, their total cost per call (fixed rental + cost per unit ÷ number of calls) can be relatively high. Other examples of this dual-component cost are photocopier rentals, electricity and gas.

These semi-variable costs must be split into their fixed and variable elements. For most small businesses this will be a fairly simple process; nevertheless it is essential to do it accurately or else much of the purpose and benefits of this method of cost analysis will be wasted.

Break-even analysis

Bring both fixed and variable costs together we can build a costing model that shows how total costs behave for different levels of output; see Figure 4.5.

FIGURE 4.5   Cost model showing total costs and fixed costs

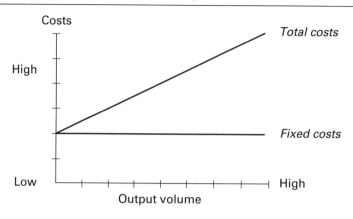

Any company capturing a sizeable market share will have an implied cost advantage over any competitor with a smaller market share. That cost advantage can be used to make more profit, lower prices and compete for an even greater share of the market or invest in making the product better and so stealing a march on competitors. By starting the variable costs from the plateau of the fixed costs, we can produce a line showing the total costs. Taking vertical and horizontal lines from any point in the total cost line will give the total costs for any chosen output volume. This is an essential feature of the costing model that lets us see how costs change with different output volumes: in other words, accommodating the dynamic nature of a business. It is to be hoped that we are not simply producing things and creating costs: we are also selling things and creating income. So a further line can be added to the model to show sales revenue as it comes in. To help bring the model to life, let's add some figures, for illustration purposes only.

Figure 4.6 shows the break-even point (BEP). Perhaps the most important single calculation in the whole costing exercise is to find the point at which real profits start to be made. The point where the sales revenue line crosses the total costs line is the break-even point. It is only after that point has been reached that a business can start to make a profit. We can work this out by drawing a graph or by using a simple formula. The advantage of using the formula as well as a graph is that you can experiment by quickly changing the values of some of the elements in the model.

The equation for the BEP is:

$$\frac{\text{Fixed costs}}{\text{Unit selling price} - \text{Variable costs per unit}}$$

This is quite logical. Before you can reach profits you must pay for the variable costs. This is done by deducting those costs from the unit selling price.

FIGURE 4.6   Cost model showing a break-even point

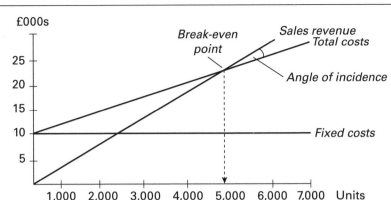

What is left (usually called the 'unit contribution') is available to meet the fixed costs. Once enough units have been sold to meet these fixed costs, the BEP has been reached. Let's try the sum out, given the following information shown on the break-even chart:

Fixed costs = £10,000

Selling price = £5 per unit

Variable cost = £3 per unit

So BEP = 5,000 units (£5 − £3 = £2)

Now we can see that 5,000 units must be sold at £5 each before we can start to make a profit. We can also see that if 7,000 is our maximum output we have only 2,000 units available to make our required profit target. Obviously, the more units we have available for sale (ie the maximum output that can realistically be sold) after our break-even point, the better. The relationship between total sales and the break-even point is called the margin of safety.

Margin of safety

This is usually expressed as a percentage and can be calculated as shown in Table 4.1. Clearly, the lower this percentage, the lower the business's capacity for generating profits. A low margin of safety might signal the need to rethink fixed costs, selling price or the maximum output of the business. The angle formed at the BEP between the sales revenue line and the total costs line is called the 'angle of incidence'. The size of the angle shows the rate at which profit is made after the break-even point. A large angle means a high rate of profit per unit sold after the BEP.

TABLE 4.1   Calculating a margin of safety

	£	
Total sales	35,000	(7,000 units × £5 selling price)
Minus break-even point	25,000	(5,000 units × £5 selling price)
Margin of safety	10,000	
Margin of safety as a percentage of sales	29%	(10,000 ÷ 35,000)

Meeting profit objectives

By adding in the final element, desired profits, we can have a comprehensive model to help us with costing and pricing decisions. Supposing in the previous example we knew that we had to make £10,000 profit to achieve a satisfactory return on the capital invested in the business, we could amend our BEP formula to take account of this objective:

$$\text{BEPP (break-even profit point)} = \frac{\text{Fixed costs + Profit objective}}{\text{Unit selling price} - \text{Variable costs per unit}}$$

Putting some figures from our last example into this equation, and choosing £10,000 as our profit objective, we can see how it works. Unfortunately, without further investment in fixed costs, the maximum output in our example is only 7,000 units, so unless we change something the profit objective will not be met.

$$\frac{£10,000 + £10,000}{\text{BEPP}} = \frac{£20,000}{10,000 \text{ units}}$$
$$£5 - £3 = 2$$

The great strength of this model is that each element can be changed in turn, on an experimental basis, to arrive at a satisfactory and achievable result. Let us return to this example. We could start our experimenting by seeing what the selling price would have to be to meet our profit objective. In this case we leave the selling price as the unknown, but we have to decide the BEP in advance (you cannot solve a single equation with more than one unknown). It would not be unreasonable to say that we would be prepared to sell our total output to meet the profit objective. So the equation now works out as follows:

$$\frac{20,000}{7,000} = £ \text{ Unit selling price} - £3$$

Moving the unknown over to the left-hand side of the equation we get:

$$£ \text{ Unit selling price} = £3 + 2.86 = £5.86$$

We now know that with a maximum capacity of 7,000 units and a profit objective of £10,000, we have to sell at £5.86 per unit. Now if the market will stand that price, then this is a satisfactory result. If it will not, then we are back to experimenting with the other variables. We must find ways of decreasing the fixed or variable costs, or increasing the output of the plant, by an amount sufficient to meet our profit objective.

Negotiating special deals

Managers are frequently laid open to the temptation of taking a particularly big order at a 'cut-throat' price and it is the MBA's role to make sure that however attractive the proposition may look at first glance, certain conditions are met before the order can be safely accepted. Let us look at an example – a slight variation on the last one. Your company has a maximum output of 10,000 units, without any major investment in fixed costs. At present you are just not prepared to invest more money until the business has proved itself. The background information is:

Maximum output	10,000 units
Output to meet profit objective	7,000 units
Selling price	£5.86
Fixed costs	£10,000
Unit variable cost	£3.00
Profitability objective	£10,000

The break-even chart will look like Figure 4.7.

FIGURE 4.7   Break-even chart for special deals

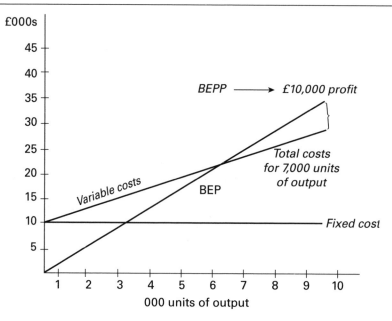

The managers you are advising are fairly confident that they can sell 7,000 units at £5.86 each, but that still leaves 3,000 units unsold – should they decide to produce them. Out of the blue an enquiry comes in for about 3,000 units, but a strong hint is given that nothing less than a 33 per cent discount will clinch the deal. What should you recommend? Using the costing information assembled so far, you can show the present breakdown of costs and arrive at your selling price:

Unit cost breakdown	£3.00
Variable costs	£1.43 (£10,000 fixed costs ÷ 7,000 units)
Contribution to fixed costs	
Contribution to meet profit objective	£1.43 (£10,000 profit objective ÷ 7,000 units)
Selling price	£5.86

As all fixed costs are met on the 7,000 units sold (or to be sold), the remaining units can be sold at a price that covers both variable costs and the profitability contribution, so you can negotiate at the same level of profitability, down to £4.43, just under 25 per cent off the current selling price. However, any selling price above the £3.00 variable cost will generate extra profits, but these sales will be at the expense of your profit margin. A lower profit margin in itself is not necessarily a bad thing if it results in a higher return on capital employed, but first you must do the sums. There is a great danger with negotiating orders at marginal costs, as these costs are called, in that you do not achieve your break-even point and so perpetuate losses.

Dealing with multiple products and services

The examples used to illustrate the break-even profit point model were of necessity simple. Few if any businesses sell only one product or service, so a more general equation may be more useful to deal with real world situations.

In such a business, to calculate your break-even point you must first establish your gross profit. This is calculated by deducting the money paid out to suppliers from the money received from customers. (Look back to Chapter 3 for more on this subject.) For example, if you are aiming for a 40 per cent gross profit, expressed in decimals as 0.4, your fixed costs are £10,000 and your overall profit objective is £4,000, then the sum will be as follows:

$$\text{BEPP} = \frac{£10,000 + £4,000}{0.4} = \frac{£14,000}{0.4} = £35,000$$

So, to reach the target you must achieve a £35,000 turnover. (You can check this out for yourself: look back to the previous example where the BEPP was 7,000 units, and the selling price was £5 each. Multiplying those figures gives a turnover of £35,000. The gross profit in that example was 2/5, or 40 per cent, also.)

Getting help with break-even

You have quite a few options to get help with making breakeven calculations. If your algebra is a bit rusty you can take a quick refresher at the BBC's Bite Size site (**www.bbc.co.uk/schools/gcsebitesize/maths**).

Alternatively there are a number of online spreadsheets and tutorials that will take you through the process. biz/ed (**www.bized.co.uk**>Virtual Worlds>Virtual Learning Arcade>Break-even Analysis) is a simulation that lets you see the effect of changing variables on a fairly complex break-even calculation. Score (**www.score.org**>Business Tools>Template Gallery>Break Even Analysis) and BizPep (**www.bizpeponline.com/PricingBreakeven.html**) sell a software program that calculates your break-even for prices plus or minus 50 per cent of your proposed selling price. You can tweak costs to see how to optimize your selling price and so hit your profit goal.

Harvard Business School (**http://hbswk.hbs.edu/archive/1262.html**) has a whole teaching module online, where you can see what you would have learnt about the subject had you gone there!

Knowledge Dynamics (**http://www.knowledgedynamics.com/demos/ BreakevenFlash)** has a neat e-learning simulation that also explains the impact of various manufacturing and marketing decisions on the break-even volume and date as you try out alternative decisions on prices and costs.

Profit maximization vs shareholder value

Operating managers are focused firmly on the bottom line and usually their rewards and promotion prospects are directly influenced by their ability to maximize profits. Shareholders, on the other hand, and this usually includes the board of directors and a handful of other senior staff whom an MBA could be wise to cultivate, have a different but related goal. They as the owners of the business want to maximize the value of the business, a sum derived by multiplying the number of shares issued by the market price of those shares.

While a business clearly needs money to operate and grow it doesn't all have to come from shareholders who expect to enjoy all the future increase in value, but could be provided by banks, for example, which have much lower expectations for their share in any additional value. They are usually satisfied with a set level of interest and their capital returned intact. (This subject, known as gearing or leverage, is covered more fully in Chapter 10.)

The factors that influence share price go way beyond a simple measure of the amount of profit. First, the efficiency with which that profit was made will weigh heavily on shareholders' minds, so the return on capital and profit margins will count too. Think about which business you would rather have a stake in: one that employed £100 million to make £20 million profit, or one that employed £50 million to make £19 million profit. Cash generation is also a vital factor in value. Profit is an accounting estimate of value, which can be adversely affected by all manner of factors. It's not until profit is turned into cash that shareholders have any real certainty as to the value of their stake. So for otherwise identical ventures, the one that generates the most cash the fastest is likely to be the more valuable in the eyes of the stock market. Factors such as the ability to innovate – Apple for example, or that have global reach and appeal – McDonald's or Coca Cola, will also keep relative value high.

CASE STUDY   Ocado

On 7 February 2010 the rumour in the City was that Ocado, which sells food sourced from supermarket operator Waitrose (part of John Lewis), was to launch an initial public offering (IPO) putting a value of between £1 ($1.6/€1.18) billion and £1.1 ($1.76/€1.29) billion on the business. Three investment banks, Goldman Sachs, UBS and JP Morgan Cazenove, it was further rumoured, where seen as front-runners to lead the float. There was nothing surprising in the story: it was long known that the company's strategy called for a voracious consumption of cash. In various rounds of fundraising the company had raised just short of £300 ($480/€354) million, more than any other European internet start-up. The company hoped to raise a further £160 ($256/€189) million from the flotation, to help it sustain its 30 per cent rise in sales, that by December 2009 had reached £40.8 ($65.3/€48) million.

Nor was it especially surprising that it hadn't turned in a profit in any year since start-up. Losses in the last two years ran to around £100 ($160/€118) million. PeaPod Inc, a company based in Illinois, United States, had tried to make a similar business profitable and failed over the 12 years from its start-up to August 2001, when Royal Ahold, operator of American chains Stop & Shop and Giant Food, bought out the entire company.

Ocado was launched in partnership with Waitrose in January 2002 and its service is now available to over 13.5 million households across the South East, the Midlands, the North West and the South Coast. Charging £5.99 ($9.58/€7.07) a go or £9.99 ($15.60/€11.75) a month for unlimited deliveries for customers spending £40 ($64/€47) a time, Ocado was established with a clear vision: to offer busy people an alternative to going to the supermarket every week. By fulfilling orders from a dedicated warehouse, Ocado aims to show a virtually live inventory on its web shop, enabling customers to choose from a range of groceries that are actually in stock. The company has developed its own unique logistics software intended to ensure the right goods are delivered to the right place at the right time. Its warehouse in Hatfield, Hertfordshire, stores some 20,000 products, more than the largest Waitrose branch, pumping them round some 10 miles of conveyor belts to make over 80,000 deliveries a week. Ocado claims to have 20 per cent of Britain's online grocery sales, putting it third behind Tesco and Sainsbury's. Putting it in perspective, this represents only 2 per cent of the UK's £130 ($208/€153) billion online grocery sales.

Ocado's founders all have impressive track records in the investment banking field, a definite asset when it comes to pumping up value and raising cash; Tim Steiner, the CEO, spent eight years as a banker at Goldman Sachs, as did Jason Gissing, now in charge of marketing and external communications and formerly Chief Financial Officer. Neill Abrams, the third member of the start-up trio, is Director of Legal & Business Affairs and only differs from his colleagues in that he spent nine years at Goldman Sachs. Michael Grade, formerly chairman of ITV, was appointed chairman in 2009. Losses in the past three years at £22.5 ($36/€26.5) million, £43.5 ($69.6/€51.3) million and £45.5 ($72.8/€53.7) million are on an improving trend, albeit a fairly shallow one. If the company manages a successful IPO at anything resembling the mooted figure of around £1 ($1.6/€1.18) billion it will demonstrate clearly that investors see value in market share and turnover, while being prepared to wait patiently for profits to come through.

The cost of capital

A business needs to keep track of how much it is paying for the capital it uses, as that is the threshold that has to be passed before value is being added to the business. It is also the minimum hurdle rate for any investment it may make. It also needs to be aware that if new money being raised is more costly than that already in the business, it will only be profitable if it raises the hurdle rate for new projects accordingly.

Cost of debt

This can be very straightforward. If a company takes out a bank loan at a fixed rate of interest of say, 8 per cent, then this is the cost before any tax relief. Taking tax relief at 40 per cent into account then the net cost of debt comes down to 4.8 per cent. In the case of a public offer for bonds or debentures, the rate of interest that has to be paid on new loans to get them taken up by investors at par can be regarded as the cost of borrowed capital.

Cost of equity

Put simply, the cost of equity is the return shareholders expect the company to earn on their money. It is their estimation, often not scientifically calculated, of the rate of return that will be obtained both from future dividends and an increased share value.

Dividend valuation model

One approach to finding the cost of equity is to take the current gross dividend yield for a company and add the expected annual growth.

For example, XYZ plc has forecast payment of a gross equivalent dividend of 10 cents on each ordinary share in the coming year. The company's shares are quoted on the stock exchange and currently trade at $2.00. Growth of profits and dividends has averaged 15 per cent over the last few years. The cost of equity for XYZ plc can be calculated as:

$$\text{Cost of equity capital} = \frac{\text{Current dividend (gross) \%}}{\text{Current market price}} + \text{Growth rate \%}$$

$$= \frac{(\$0.10 \times 100)\%}{\$2} + 15\% = 20\%$$

With this method, dividends are assumed to grow in the future at the constant rate achieved by averaging the last few years' performance.

Capital asset pricing model (CAPM)

Before turning to the next method, we need to clarify some aspects of risk. There are two broad types of risk: specific and systematic.

Specific risk applies to one particular business. It includes, for example, the risk of losing the chief executive; the risk of someone else bringing out a similar or better product; or the risk of labour problems. Shareholders are expected not to want compensation for this type of risk as it can be diversified away by holding a sufficient number of investments in their portfolios.

Systematic risk derives from global or macro-economic events that can damage all investments to some extent and therefore holders require compensation for this risk to their wealth. This compensation takes the form of a higher required rate of return.

A slightly more complicated approach to the cost of equity tries to take the systematic risk element into account. It is known as the 'capital asset pricing model' or CAPM. Put simply, CAPM states that investors' required rate of return on a share is composed of two parts: a risk-free rate similar to that obtainable on a risk-free investment in short-term government securities; and an additional premium to compensate for the systematic risk involved in investing in shares. This systematic risk for a company's shares is measured by the size of its beta factor. A beta of 1.0 for a company means that its shares have the same systematic risk as the average for the whole market. If the beta is 1.4 then systematic risk for the share is 40 per cent higher than the market average. A company's share beta is applied to the market premium that is obtained from the excess of the return on a market portfolio of shares over the risk-free rate of return. The formula to calculate cost of equity capital using CAPM is:

$$Ke = Rf + B(Rm - Rf)$$

where: Ke = cost of equity, Rf = risk-free return, Rm = return on market portfolio of shares and B = beta factor.

For example, if the risk-free rate of return is 5.5 per cent and the return on a market portfolio is 12 per cent, then for a company with a beta of 0.7 for its ordinary shares the cost of equity is:

$$\begin{aligned} Ke &= Rf + B(Rm - Rf) \\ &= 5.5\% + 0.7(12\% - 5.5\%) \\ &= 10.05\% \end{aligned}$$

Of the two methods described for finding the cost of equity for a company, the CAPM method is the more scientific. Ideally, the risk-free and market rates of return should reflect the future but current rates of return are used as substitutes. Beta factors measure how sensitive each company's share price movements are relative to market movements over a period of a few years.

The weakness of CAPM lies in it assuming all investors are rational and well-informed and that markets are perfect and there is an unlimited supply of risk-free money. There are even more complex models for calculating the cost of equity capital, but none are without their critics.

Weighted average cost of capital

Having identified the cost of equity and the cost of borrowed capital (and that of any other long-term source of finance such as hire purchase or mortgages), we need to combine them into one overall cost of capital. This is primarily for use in project appraisals as justification of those that yield a return in excess of their cost of capital.

An average cost is required because we do not usually identify each individual project with one particular source of finance. Because equity and debt capital have very different costs, we would make illogical decisions and accept a project financed by debt capital only to reject a similar project next time round when it was financed by equity capital. Generally businesses take the view that all projects have been financed from a common pool of money except for the relatively rare case when project-specific finance is raised. The weightings used in the calculations should be based on the market value of the securities and not on their book or balance sheet values.

As an example, assume your company intends to keep the gearing ratio of borrowed capital to equity in the proportion of 20:80. The nominal cost of new capital from these sources has been assessed, say, at 10 per cent and 15 per cent respectively and corporation tax is 30 per cent. The calculation of the overall weighted average cost is as follows:

Type of capital	Proportion (a)	After-tax cost (b)	Weighted cost (a × b)
10% loan capital	0.20	7.0%	1.4%
Equity	0.80	15.0%	12.0%
			13.4%

The resulting weighted average cost of 13.4 per cent is the minimum rate that this company should accept on proposed investments. Any investment that is not expected to achieve this return is not a viable proposition. Risk has been allowed for in the calculation of the beta factor used in the CAPM method of identifying the cost of equity. This relates to the risk of the whole existing business. If a company embarks on a project of significantly different risk, or has a divisional structure of activities of varying risk levels, then a single cost of equity for the whole company is inappropriate. In this situation, the average beta of proxy companies operating in the same field as a division can be used.

Future investment decisions

The cost of capital is an important figure as it is in essence the threshold for future investments. Using the figures shown above, if our weighted average cost of capital is 13.4 per cent, taking on any new activity that makes a lower profit ratio will be lowering the performance, hardly an MBA type of activity.

Investment decisions, where the decisions have cost and revenue implications for years, perhaps even decades, fall into a number of categories:

- *Bolt-on investments:* these are where an investment will be supporting and enhancing an existing operation, for example if part of a production process is being slowed down for want of some new equipment to eliminate a bottleneck.

- *Standalone single project:* this involves a simple accept or reject decision.

- *Competing projects:* this requires a choice of which produces the best results either because only one can be pursued or because of limited finance. In the latter case this is describes a *capital rationing.*

What follows is an examination of the financial aspects of investment decisions. There may well be other strategic reasons for taking investment decisions including those that might be more important than finance alone. For example, it could be imperative to deny a competitor a particular opportunity, or if part of achieving a national or global strategy calls for disproportionate expenses in one or more areas. However, there are *no* circumstances when any investment decision should not be subjected to proper financial appraisal and so at least seeing the cost of accepting a lower return than required by the cost of capital being used.

It is also important to note that any methodology for appraising investments requires that cash is used rather than profits, for reasons that will become apparent as the techniques are explained. Profit is not ignored; it is simply allowed to work its way through in the timing of events.

Payback period

The most popular method for evaluating investment decisions is the *payback* method. To arrive at the payback period you have to work out how many years it takes to recover your *cash* investment. Table 4.2 shows two investment projects that require respectively £20,000 and £40,000 cash now to get a series of cash returns spread over the next five years.

TABLE 4.2   The payback method

	Investment A £	Investment B £
Initial cash cost *now* (Year 0)	20,000	40,000
Net cash flows		
Year 1	1,000	10,000
Year 2	4,000	10,000
Year 3	8,000	16,000
Year 4	7,000	4,000
Year 5	5,000	28,000
Total cash in over period	25,000	68,000
Cash surplus	5,000	28,000

Although both propositions call for different amounts of cash to be invested we can see that both recover all their cash outlays by year four. So we can say these investments have a four-year payback. But as a matter of fact investment B produces a much bigger surplus than the other project and it returns half our initial cash outlay in two years. Investment A has only returned a quarter of our cash over that time period.

Payback may be simple, but it is not much use when it comes to dealing with either the timing or with comparing different investment amounts.

Discounted cash flow

We know intuitively that getting cash in sooner is better than getting it in later. In other words, a dollar received now is worth more than a dollar that will arrive in one, two or more years in the future because of what we could do with that money ourselves, or because of what we have to pay out to have use of that money (see the cost of capital, above). To make sound investment decisions we need to ascribe a value to a future stream of earnings to arrive at what is known as *the present value*. If we know we could earn 20 per cent on any money we have than the maximum we would be prepared to pay for a dollar coming in one year hence would be around 80 cents. If we were to pay one dollar now to get a dollar back in a year's time we would in effect be losing money.

The technique used to handle this is known as 'discounting' and the process is termed 'discounted cash flow' (DCF) and the residual discounted cash is called the 'net present value'. The first column in Table 4.3 shows the simple cash flow implications of an investment proposition; a surplus of 5,000 comes after five years from putting 20,000 into a project. But if we accept the proposition that future cash is worth less than current cash the only question we need to answer is how much less. If we assume take our weighted average cost of capital as a sensible starting point we would select 13.4 per cent as an appropriate rate at which to discount future cash flows. To keep the numbers simple and to add a small margin of safety let's assume 15 per cent is the rate we have selected (this doesn't matter too much as you will see in the section on internal rate of return).

TABLE 4.3   Using discounted cash flow (DCF)

	£ Cash Flow A	Discount Factor at 15% B	Discounted Cash Flow A × B
Initial cash cost *now* (Year 0)	20,000	1.00	20,000
Net cash flows			
Year 1	1,000	0.8695	870
Year 2	4,000	0.7561	3,024
Year 3	8,000	0.6575	5,260
Year 4	7,000	0.5717	4,002
Year 5	5,000	0.4972	2,486
Total	25,000		15,642
Cash surplus	5,000	Net Present Value	(4,358)

The formulae for calculating what a £ received at some future date is:

$$\text{Present Value (PV)} = \pounds P \times 1/(1 + r)^n$$

where £P is the initial cash cost, r is the interest rate expressed in decimals and n is the year in which the cash will arrive. So if we decide on a discount rate of 15 per cent, the present value of a £ received in one year's time is:

$$\text{Present Value} = \pounds 1 \times 1/(1 + 0.15)^1$$
$$= \pounds 0.87 \text{ (rounded to two decimal places)}$$

So we can see that our £1,000 arriving at the end of year one has a present value of £870; the £4,000 in year two has a present value of £3,024 and by year five the present value reduces cash flows to barely half their original figure. In fact far from having a real payback in year four and generating a cash surplus of £5,000, this project will make us £4,358 worse off than we had hoped to be if we wanted to make a return of 15 per cent. The project, in other words, fails to meet our criteria using DCF but may well have been pursued using payback.

Internal rate of return (IRR)

DCF is a useful starting point but does not give us any definitive information. For example, all we know about the above project is that it doesn't make a return of 15 per cent. In order to know the actual rate of return we need to choose a discount rate that produces a net present value of the entire cash flow of zero, known as the 'internal rate of return'. The maths is time-consuming but the Solutions Matrix website (**www.solutionmatrix.com**) has a tool for working out payback, discounted cash flow, internal rate of return, and a lot more calculations relating to capital budgeting. You have to register on the site first before downloading the free capital budgeting spreadsheet suite and tutorial. From the home page you should click on 'Download Center' and 'Download Financial Metrics Lite for Microsoft Excel'. Using this spreadsheet you will see that the IRR for the project in question is slightly under 7 per cent, not much better than might be obtained through bank interest and certainly insufficient to warrant taking any risks for.

Outsourcing

Outsourcing is the activity of contracting out the elements that are not considered core or central to the business. It is an important financial strategy open to a business that will help it limit the amount of cash it has to raise and utilize to function and so help it make a superior return on the funds invested. There are obvious advantages to outsourcing: the best people can do what they are best at. But the approach can get out of hand, if left unmanaged. In 2008 IBM completed a major overhaul of its value chain and for the first time in its century-long history created an Integrated Supply Chain (ISC) – a centralized worldwide approach to deciding what to do itself, what to buy in and where to buy in from. Suppliers were halved from 66,000 to 33,000; support locations from 300 to three global centres in Bangalore, Budapest and Shanghai. Manufacturing sites reduced from 15 to nine, all 'globally enabled' in that they can make almost any of the company's products at each plant and deliver them anywhere in the world. In the process IBM has lowered operating costs by more than $4 (£2.56/€4.72) billion a year.

CASE STUDY

No manufacturing. No salesmen. No research and development. Jill Brown grew her business from a standing start to a turnover of £2 ($3.2/€2.36) million a year in just five years, as much by deciding what not to do as by what to actually do. The business she founded, Brown Electronics, supplies switches for computer equipment, the kind of gadget that, for example, allows half a dozen personal computers to use one printer between them.

She says: 'I didn't want to get into manufacturing myself, but I save myself the headaches. Why should I start manufacturing as long as I've got my bottom line right? Turnover is vanity, profit is sanity. I have worked for other people who wanted to grow big just for the kudos.'

Instead, Jill contracts out to other manufacturers' factories. She feels she still has control over quality, since any item that is not up to standard can be sent back. She also has the ultimate threat of taking away trade, which would leave the manufacturers she uses with a large void to fill. 'We would do so if quality was not good enough. Many manufacturers have under-utilized capacity.'

Jill uses freelance salesmen on a commission basis. She explains: 'I didn't want a huge sales force. Most sales managers sit in their cars at the side of the road filling in swindle sheets. Research and development is another area where expenses would be terrific. We have freelance design teams working on specific products. We give them a brief and they quote a price. The cost still works out at twice what you expected, but at least you have a measure of control. I could not afford to employ R & D staff full-time and I would not need them full-time. My system minimizes the risks and gives us a quality we could not afford as a small business.'

Indirectly, Jill provides work for about 380 elsewhere, while still being able to operate out of a space not much larger than a two-bedroom flat.

Pros and cons of outsourcing

Outsourcing has many benefits for a new business and for an established one for that matter. But there are also some inherent dangers.

The pros are:

- *Access to expertise:* it can be almost impossible for a small firm, especially in the start-up phase, to have a team onboard with the latest expertise. It is easier for larger established firms to attract the best staff and to have the latest equipment. That in turn means you as a new entrant can have access to state-of-the-art products and services from the outset.

- *Greater scalability:* it just isn't cost-effective to have production resources on hand from the outset to meet possible future demand. By outsourcing to one or more suppliers you can have, in effect, any level of output you want, all at a variable cost rather than a fixed cost.

- *More predictable costs:* while outside suppliers and manufacturers can sometimes provide products and services at a lower cost than doing it yourself, the main financial reason for choosing outsourcing is to make costs more predictable and establish a smoother cash flow.

- *Free-up your time:* turning over non-core functions leaves you and your team free to concentrate on strategic development and core business functions.

- *Economies of scale:* an outsource supplier has a higher volume of throughput than you or any of its other customers is likely to have. That means better negotiating leverage, lower material prices and better equipment utilization. So its fixed costs are spread over more than one client and part of that benefit can come to you in lower prices.

The cons are:

- *Confidentiality of data:* this is a fundamental concern for any business, and if the activity concerned involves giving another business access to such information it may not be a good one to outsource. If you do outsource anything involving company secrets ensure that basic contractual provisions, including intellectual property rights and non-disclosure agreements, are established to protect confidential information.

- *Quality control:* this is a strategic issue when it comes to outsourcing and an emerging danger with the arrival of the 'socially minded customer' in that people are looking more closely at companies and their products before buying from them. Getting garments made cheaply by child labour is very much an issue on consumers' radar. So while outsourcing plays a vital role in operations it still has to be managed and to conform to corporate ethical standards. There are a number of well-regarded quality standards that may help you monitor and control your quality. The BS EN ISO 9000 series is perhaps the best-known group of standards. They can ensure that your operating procedure delivers a consistent and acceptable standard of products or services. If you are supplying to large firms they may insist on your meeting these quality standards, or on auditing your premises to satisfy themselves. The British Standards Institution (**www.bsi-global.com**) can provide details of the standards.

- *Loss of control:* although you can change outsource suppliers, as long as an activity is bought in you will never have full control over it. You will also find it difficult to develop the skills needed to keep abreast of changes in the field.

Setting the boundaries

The starting point in outsourcing is to decide what you are good at then consider outsourcing everything else. Focus your company on your core competency, and stick to the knitting. There are some things that are central to your business that you should probably not outsource at the outset. You need to keep an eye on them until you have them fully under control. These include cash flow management and most aspects of customer relations. Later on you may consider, for example, outsourcing collecting cash from customers to an invoice discounter or factoring service that may have better processes in place to handle larger volumes of invoices than you could afford.

Some tasks make sense to outsource initially and bring in-house later. If you plan to offer a product or service that you're not expert at, it makes sense to contract out the core function, at least until you gain confidence and expertise.

Shares and markets

The magic of multiples

By the time the business you are working in has successfully grown to the point where profits are above £1 ($1.6/€1.18) million it will be possible to give some serious thought to floating on a stock market. (See Chapter 7 for more on the practical steps to achieve this.) That means selling shares in your business to the public at large and perhaps, in time, getting your company bought out by a bigger fish still. The logic of the maths is as follows. Your business with a profit of £1 ($1.6/€1.18) million would in all probability be valued at £4 ($6.4/€4.720) million, give or take half a million, based on a P/E ratio of 4. However, the same business on a stock market could be valued on a much higher P/E ratio, perhaps as much as double. The logic is that the shares are liquid; that is, investors know their value from day to day and can sell up and move on any time they like. Also, companies on a stock market are subject to a greater degree of scrutiny and so investors can be more confident in their accounts – although the market crash of October 2008 left that argument in some doubt.

You also have a powerful way to accelerate value, once your company has been floated off. If you now buy a private business that is making profits of £250,000 in your business sector it would in all probability be sold on a P/E of around 4, so costing you about £1 million. But now that profit is in a public company and as you are on a P/E of 8 it would add £2 million to your value (8 × £250,000). So, in effect, for £1 million of investment you have instantly added £2 million to your value, and of course the profit stream of £250,000 should continue and there may well be synergies from cost savings and economies of scale. Thus the alchemy of market multiples.

Share buyback and other market manipulation techniques

Companies can buy back their shares and that reduces the number of shares outstanding, giving each remaining shareholder a larger percentage ownership of the company. This is usually considered a sign that the company's management believes its share price is undervalued. Other reasons for buybacks include putting unused cash to use, raising earnings per share and obtaining stock for employee stock option plans or pension plans.

Buying back shares doesn't actually change anything in the business. Customers, products, employees, operations and strategies are all unchanged: just a piece of financial sleight of hand has been used in an effort to manipulate the share price. But do analysts, the people who tell the market what a share is likely to be worth in the future, really fall for such transparent tricks? Apparently they do. A study, 'A matter of appearances: How corporate leaders manage the impressions of financial analysts', by two academics, James Westphal and Melissa Graebner published in the *Academy of Management Journal* in February 2010, provides compelling evidence to support that view.

The study of 1,300 analysts and corporate bosses found that the CEO was more likely to resort to managing appearances when his or her company received a negative appraisal from Wall Street, rather than make any substantive changes. Aside from share buybacks, designed to send a signal of confidence in value to the market, other techniques include appointing more independent directors. In theory that should improve corporate governance and hold the working board to account more effectively. In practice, although such external appointments may have no formal ties to the company, they very often have 'friendship' ties to the boss. This is the case in some 45 per cent of the cases in this study. More blatant still are the incidents where CEOs secure jobs and club memberships for analysts in an attempt to prevent stock prices being downgraded.

Apparently these tactics pay off handsomely. Firms that take these measures see the chances of having their stock upgraded, and hence the nominal value of the business increased, by 36 per cent. The chance of a downgrade, the study concluded, falls by 45 per cent. Amazingly, public companies enjoy lasting share price gains from plans that please analysts even when the plans aren't actually implemented. The announcement alone seems sufficient to please the market.

PART TWO
Corporate capital structures

In this part the role of business structures in financing business is examined. Those structures include: sole traders, partnerships, limited partnerships, companies – private and public. In practice sole traders are limited to borrowing as a source of finance, while the others can use equity.

The forms of debt finance examined include those provided by banks such as overdrafts and term loans, and the Enterprise Finance Guarantee Scheme. Other debt instruments reviewed include bonds and convertibles, syndicated loans, commercial paper, leasing finance, hire purchase, sale and leaseback, factoring, invoice discounting and bills of exchange.

For equity finance the different shares structures – ordinary, preference and convertible – are examined. The alternative sources of equity finance are also discussed in this part, including business angels and seed corn funding, business incubators, venture capital – private and publicly funded, corporate venture funding, stock markets, and hybrid structures such as mezzanine finance.

The role of business structures in financing business

- A brief history of corporate structures
- Working alone
- Forming partnerships
- Limiting liabilities
- Cooperatives

In this chapter we will examine how businesses are legally constituted, how those structures came about and the bearing they have on the financial options open to a firm. In the following chapters we will look at the different financing options in detail.

There are at least two reasons why an MBA student should acquire a basic appreciation of the milestone events that have led up to the current theories of how businesses organizations are constituted and financed. The first is much the same reason as why most people learn something of the history of their country, its neighbours, its friends and enemies. Such a study lends interest, context and an appreciation of how we got to where we are today. It is much easier to understand, for example, the enmity between the French and the British with a smattering of information on the smouldering commercial and territorial disputes that ranged around the world from the Americas to India as well as across the African continent.

The second reason is perhaps even more important. Harvard Professor Geoffrey Jones, who edited *The Oxford Handbook of Business History* (2008, Oxford Handbooks in Business & Management) with University of

Wisconsin-Madison Professor Jonathan Zeitlin, claims in his core history text used at Harvard that: 'Over the last few decades, business historians have generated rich empirical data that in some cases confirms and in other cases contradicts many of today's fashionable theories and assumptions by other disciplines.' This loss of history has resulted in the spread of influential theories based on ill-informed understandings of the past. 'For example,' Jones claims, 'current accepted advice is that wealth and growth will come to countries that open their borders to foreign direct investment. The historical evidence shows clearly that this is an article of faith rather than proven by the historical evidence of the past.'

Businesses are themselves legal entities and the complexity of commercial life means that, sooner or later, you will find yourself taking, or defending yourself against, legal action. Ignorance does not form the basis of a satisfactory defence so every MBA needs to know enough law to know when he or she might need legal advice. Some business schools take law very seriously; for example at Northwestern University's Kellogg School and George Washington University MBA students can take a joint MBA and JD (*juris doctor*), the basic professional degree for lawyers. Babson in Wellesley, Massachusetts, has law as one of its core subjects. Penn State, on the other hand, offers only an optional module in the second year on 'Business Law for Innovation and Competition'.

Nevertheless, lawyers dominate big businesses in the United States and both Congress and the Senate. In the UK around 12 per cent of MPs are either barristers or solicitors, the largest professional grouping in the House of Commons. Other than very large businesses it is not usual to have either a qualified lawyer or a legal department in businesses in the UK. Such services are usually bought in either on a contractual or ad hoc basis. Law is an imprecise field.

Corporate structures

As an MBA it's highly likely that you will be working for a conventional company, private or public. There are, however, a number of distinct forms that a business can take, the choice depending on a number of factors: commercial needs, financial risk and the need for outside capital.

Each of these forms is explained briefly below, primarily as they apply in the UK, together with the procedure to follow on setting them up. You can change your ownership status later as your circumstances change, so while this is an important decision it is not a final one.

Sole trader

Over 80 per cent of businesses start up as sole traders and indeed around 55 per cent of all businesses in the UK employing fewer than 50 people still use this legal structure. It has the merit of being relatively formality free and, unless you intend to register for VAT, there are few rules about the records you have to keep. There is no requirement for your accounts to be audited, or for financial information on your business to be filed at Companies House.

As a sole trader there is no legal distinction between you and your business – your business is one of your assets, just as your house or car is. It follows from this that if your business should fail, your creditors have a right not only to the assets of the business but also to your personal assets, subject only to the provisions of the Bankruptcy Acts. The capital to get the business going must come from you – or from loans. There is no access to equity capital.

Partnerships

Partnerships are effectively collections of sole traders and, as such, share the legal problems attached to personal liability. There are very few restrictions to setting up in business with another person (or persons) in partnership, and several definite advantages. By pooling resources you may have more capital; you will be bringing, hopefully, several sets of skills to the business; and if you are ill the business can still carry on.

There are two serious drawbacks that you should certainly consider. First, if one of the partners makes a business mistake, perhaps by signing a disastrous contract, without the knowledge or consent of the others, every member of the partnership must shoulder the consequences. Under these circumstances your personal assets could be taken to pay the creditors even though the mistake was no fault of your own.

Second, if a partner goes bankrupt in his or her personal capacity, for whatever reason, his or her share of the partnership can be seized by creditors. As a private individual you are not liable for your partner's private debts, but having to buy him or her out of the partnership at short notice could put you and the business in financial jeopardy. Even death may not release you from partnership obligations and in some circumstances your estate can remain liable. Unless you take 'public' leave of your partnership by notifying your business contacts and legally bringing your partnership to an end, you could remain liable.

The legal regulations governing this field are set out in the Partnership Act 1890, which in essence assumes that competent businesspeople should know what they are doing. The Act merely provides a framework of agreement that applies 'in the absence of agreement to the contrary'. It follows from this that many partnerships are entered into without legal formalities – and sometimes without the parties themselves being aware that they have entered a partnership!

The main provisions of the Partnership Act state:

- All partners contribute capital equally.
- All partners share profits and losses equally.

- No partner shall have interest paid on his capital.
- No partner shall be paid a salary.
- All partners have an equal say in the management of the business.
- Unless you are a member of certain professions (law, accountancy, etc) you are restricted to a maximum of 20 partners in any partnership.

It is unlikely that all these provisions will suit you, so you would be well advised to get a written 'partnership agreement' drawn up by a solicitor at the outset of your venture.

Limited partnerships

One possibility that can reduce the more painful consequences of entering a partnership is to form a limited partnership, combining the best attributes of a partnership and a company.

A limited partnership works like this. There must be one or more general partners with the same basic rights and responsibilities (including unlimited liability) as in any general partnership, and one or more limited partners who are usually passive investors. The big difference between a general partner and a limited partner is that the limited partner isn't personally liable for the debts of the partnership. The most a limited partner can lose is the amount that he or she paid or agreed to pay into the partnership as a capital contribution or received from the partnership after it became insolvent.

To keep this limited liability, a limited partner may not participate in the management of the business, with very few exceptions. A limited partner who does get actively involved in the management of the business risks losing immunity from personal liability and having the same legal exposure as a general partner.

The advantage of a limited partnership as a business structure is that it provides a way for business owners to raise money (from the limited partners) without having to either take in new partners who will be active in the business, or having to form a limited company. A general partnership that's been operating for years can also create a limited partnership to finance expansion.

Limited companies

How they came about

From the earliest trading times to the present day the most popular legal structure under which to operate has been as a sole trader, which in effect means everyone for themselves. In the beginning merchants always risked their own money, if they had any to invest; if they travelled, as most did, they risked their lives on the journey. The caravan trade of Asia, Asia Minor, and North and Central Africa ploughed its way through the sands that separated distant cities and seaports. The largest caravans comprised thousands of camels and required careful administration. They also stimulated people to band together in partnerships, pooling protection costs and profits to spread the risks. The partnerships would usually last only for the particular journey. Later on, older merchants who had made money from earlier ventures could join such expeditions by putting up money, without the hardship of making the trip themselves. This could be seen as an early form of limited partnership.

As the ventures became more costly and of longer duration, partnership structures of fixed duration of one, three or five years became common, with an ever increasing range of partners with differing shares in the venture. To add to the complications these partners could join and leave, perhaps for no more sinister reason than death, at different times.

The concept of limited liability, where the shareholders are not liable, in the last resort, for the debts of their business, changed the whole nature of business and risk taking. It opened the floodgates, encouraging a new generation of entrepreneurs to undertake much larger scale ventures without taking on all the consequences of failure. As the name suggests, in this form of business liability is limited to the amount you contribute by way of share capital and, in the event of failure, creditors' claims are restricted to the assets of the company. The shareholders of the business are not normally liable as individuals for the business debts beyond the paid-up value of their shares.

The concept itself can be traced back to Roman times, when it was granted, albeit infrequently, as a special favour to friends for large undertakings by those in power. The idea was resurrected in 1811 when New York State brought in a general limited liability law for manufacturing companies. Most US states followed suit and eventually Britain caught up in 1854. Today most countries have a legal structure incorporating the concept of limited liability.

Limited companies today

Of the 4.5 million businesses trading in the UK, over 1.4 million are limited companies. As the name suggests, in this form of business your liability is limited to the amount you state that you will contribute by way of share capital, though you may not actually have to put that money in.

A limited company has a legal identity of its own, separate from the people who own or run it. This means that, in the event of failure, creditors' claims are restricted to the assets of the company. The shareholders of the business are not liable as individuals for the business debts beyond the paid-up value of their shares. This applies even if the shareholders are working directors, unless of course the company has been trading fraudulently. Other advantages include the freedom to raise capital by selling shares.

Disadvantages include the cost involved in setting up the company and the legal requirement in some cases for the company's accounts to be audited by a chartered or certified accountant.

Public Limited Company (plc)

A plc is a company that can sell shares to the public at large either through a recognized stock market or by advertising in the press or through intermediaries. It needs to fulfil some minimum, not too onerous, conditions. These conditions vary from country to country but generally:

- It must state that it is a plc in its articles of association.
- It must have a five-figure authorized share capital.
- Before it can trade a quarter of that must be actually paid up.
- Each allotted share must be paid up to at least a quarter of its nominal value.
- There must be at least two shareholders, two directors and a company secretary who meets certain standards in terms of qualifications or experience.

City code on takeovers and mergers

Buying up a plc is a more complicated process than taking over a private company or business. The Take Over Panel (**www.thetakeoverpanel.org.uk**) rules on taking over another company quoted on a stock market run to 266 pages!

In the first instance shareholders in the business being acquired have to be offered the same deal. Family, directors and those with major blocks of shares can't be offered preferential treatment. The buying company must be able to fulfil the cash consideration involved before making any announcement. There are conditions under which a potential bidder must either make a formal offer or walk away from the target for at least six months. Once 90 per cent of a target company's shares have been acquired the remaining shareholders have to accept the deal.

Company limited by guarantee

This type of incorporation is used for non-profit organizations that require corporate status as a means of protecting participants. There are no shareholders but members give an undertaking to contribute a nominal amount towards the winding up of the company in the event of a shortfall when it closes down. It cannot distribute its profits to its members, and is therefore eligible to apply for charitable status if necessary. You may find this type of structure being used by a business as a means of isolating part of its activities such as clubs or sports associations that are not part of its profit-generating business.

Cooperative

A cooperative is an enterprise owned and controlled by the people working in it. Once in danger of becoming extinct, the workers' cooperative is enjoying something of a comeback, and there are over 4,370 operating in the UK, employing 195,000 people. They are growing at the rate of 20 per cent per annum.

Help and advice on business corporate structure

A guidance note entitled 'Business ownership' is available from Companies House (**www.companieshouse.gov.uk**>Guidance Booklets>).

Business Link (**www.businesslink.gov.uk**>Taxes, returns and payroll> choosing and setting up a legal structure>Legal structure: the basics) has a guide to putting your business on a proper legal footing, explaining the tax and other implications of different ownership structures.

Cooperatives UK (**www.cooperatives-uk.coop**>Services>Co-operative Development) is the central membership organization for cooperative enterprises throughout the UK. This link is to the regional network.

Desktop Lawyer (**www.desktoplawyer.co.uk**>BUSINESS>BUSINESS START-UP>Choosing a business structure>The Partnership) has a summary of the pros and cons of partnerships as well as inexpensive partnership deeds.

06 Debt finance

- Borrowing options
- Bank finance
- Government-supported lending
- General bonds
- Specialist bonds
- Asset-based lending

Debt finance and its regulation are hardly new: its practice stretches far before arrival such firms as Banca Monte dei Paschi di Siena SpA (MPS) in 1472, though that is now the oldest operating bank. As far back as 1795 BC Hammurabi, a Babylonian lawmaker, had already established a code of behaviour for money lenders and merchants to adhere to. 'If the agent accept money from the merchant, but have a quarrel with the merchant (denying the receipt), then shall the merchant swear before God and witnesses that he has given this money to the agent, and the agent shall pay him three times the sum', is one example of the fine detail of these dozens of interlocking laws. Hammurabi's code was certainly not the earliest. Preceding sets of laws have disappeared, but several traces of them have been found, and Hammurabi's own code clearly implies their existence. He only claimed to be reorganizing a legal system long established. The introduction of coined money in about 600 BC by the Greeks allowed bankers to keep account books, change and lend money, and even arrange for cash transfers for citizens through affiliate banks in cities thousands of miles away.

Despite being remembered mostly for their military prowess during the crusades the Knights Templar became, in part by accident, the first major international banking institution. Their specific forte was in keeping the highways open to allow pilgrims to come to the Holy Land unmolested. This goal inevitably meant the Templars owned some of the mightiest castles, and because of their awesome reputation as fighting men, their castles served as ideal places to deposit money and other valuables. A French knight, for example, could deposit money or mortgage his chateau through the Templars in Paris and pick up gold coins along the route to Jerusalem and on the way back, if he survived! The Templars charged a fee for both the transaction and for converting the money into various currencies along the route. Over the years the business grew and eventually the Templars ran a network of full service banks providing lending and ancillary services across Europe, from England to Jerusalem. At their maximum strength the Templars employed about 7,000 people, owned 870 castles and fortified houses and were the principal bankers to popes and kings.

Bank lending

Towards the lower risk end of the financing spectrum are the various organizations that lend money to businesses. They all try hard to take little or no risk, but expect some reward irrespective of performance. They want interest payments on money lent, usually from day one, though sometimes they are content to roll interest payments up until some future date. While they hope the management is competent, they are more interested in securing a charge against any assets the business or its managers may own. At the end of the day they want all their money back. It would be more prudent to think of these organizations as people who will help you turn a proportion of an illiquid asset such as property, stock in trade or customers who have not yet paid up, into a more liquid asset such as cash, but of course at some discount.

CASE STUDY Hippychick

When new mother Julie Minchin discovered the Hipseat she knew she had found a helpful product. Anything that makes carrying a baby around all day without ending up with excruciating backache has got to be a benefit. It was only later that she realized that selling the product for the German company that made the Hipseat could be the right way to launch her into business. At first Julie acted as its UK distributor but later she wanted to make some major improvements to the product. That meant finding a manufacturer to make the product especially for her business. China was the logical place to find a company flexible enough to make small quantities as well as being able to help her keep the cost of the end product competitive.

She funded the business with a small family loan, an overdraft facility and a variety of grants secured with the help of Business Link. Now in its tenth year the company has a turnover of £3 ($4.8/€3.5) million a year and sells 14 unique products aimed at the baby market. It supplies national chains such as Boots and Mothercare as well as independents. It also sells via its catalogue and website and is in the process of building a network of distributors for its branded products.

Banks are the principal, and frequently the only, source of finance for nine out of every 10 unquoted businesses. Firms around the world rely on banks for their funding. In the UK, for example, they have borrowed nearly £55 ($88/€65) billion from the banks. Despite newspaper headlines to the contrary, according to the Bank of England (**www.bankofengland.co.uk/ publications/other/monetary/creditconditions.htm**) 'the overall availability of credit to corporates was broadly unchanged in 2010 Q4, following a period of rising availability for most of the previous two years, and was expected to remain broadly unchanged in 2011 Q1'.

Bankers, and indeed any other sources of debt capital, are looking for asset security to back their loan and provide a near-certainty of getting their money back. They will also charge an interest rate that reflects current market conditions and their view of the risk level of the proposal; usually anything from 0.25 per cent to upwards of 3 or 4 per cent for more risky or smaller firms.

Bankers like to speak of the 'five Cs' of credit analysis, factors they look at when they evaluate a loan request. When applying to a bank for a loan, be prepared to address the following points:

1 *Character:* bankers lend money to borrowers who appear honest and have a good credit history. Before you apply for a loan, it makes sense to obtain a copy of your credit report and clean up any problems.

2 *Capacity:* this is a prediction of the borrower's ability to repay the loan. For a new business, bankers look at the business plan. For an existing business, bankers consider financial statements and industry trends.

3 *Collateral:* bankers generally want a borrower to pledge an asset that can be sold to pay off the loan if the borrower lacks funds.

4 *Capital:* bankers scrutinize a borrower's net worth, the amount by which assets exceed debts.

5 *Conditions:* whether bankers give a loan can be influenced by the current economic climate as well as by the amount.

Types of bank funding

Banks usually offer three types of loan:

1 *Overdrafts:* though technically short-term money as they can be called in at a moment's notice, these tend to form a part of the permanent capital of a business, albeit a fluctuating one.

2 *Term loans:* offered for set periods.

3 *Government-backed loans:* these are available to some types of business, usually small or new ventures, where the banker's normal criteria might not be met, but the government would like to encourage the sector.

1. Overdrafts

The principal form of short-term bank funding is an overdraft, secured by a charge over the assets of the business. A little over a quarter of all bank finance for small firms is in the form of an overdraft. If you are starting out in a contract cleaning business, say, with a major contract, you need sufficient funds initially to buy the mop and bucket. Three months into the contract they will have been paid for, so there is no point in getting a five-year bank loan to cover this as within a year you will have cash in the bank and a loan with an early redemption penalty! However, if your bank account does not get out of the red at any stage during the year, you will need to re-examine your financing. All too often companies utilize an overdraft to acquire long-term assets, and that overdraft never seems to disappear, eventually constraining the business.

The attraction of overdrafts is that they are very easy to arrange and take little time to set up. That is also their inherent weakness. The key words in the arrangement document are 'repayable on demand', which leaves the bank free to make and change the rules as it sees fit. (This term is under constant review, and some banks may remove it from the arrangement.) With other forms of borrowing, as long as you stick to the terms and conditions, the loan is yours for the duration. It is not so with overdrafts.

2. Term loans

Term loans, as long-term bank borrowings are generally known, are funds provided by a bank for a number of years. Just over a third of all term loans are for periods greater than 10 years, and a quarter are for three years or less.

The interest can either be variable, changing with general interest rates, or fixed for a number of years ahead. The proportion of fixed-rate loans has increased from a third of all term loans to around one in two. In some cases it may be possible to move between having a fixed interest rate and a variable one at certain intervals. It may even be possible to have a moratorium on interest payments for a short period, to give the business some breathing space. Provided the conditions of the loan are met in such matters as repayment, interest and security cover, the money is available for the period of the loan. Unlike in the case of an overdraft, the bank cannot pull the rug from under you if circumstances (or the local manager) change.

3. Government-backed loans

The Enterprise Finance Guarantee Scheme (formerly the Small Firms Loan Guarantee) is operated by banks at the instigation of governments in the UK; there are similar schemes in Australia, the United States and elsewhere. The UK scheme guarantees loans from banks and other financial institutions for small businesses with viable business proposals that have tried and failed to obtain a conventional loan because of a lack of security. Loans are available for periods of between two and 10 years on sums up to £1 ($1.6/€1.8) million.

The government guarantees 70–90 per cent of the loan. In return for the guarantee, the borrower pays a premium of 1–2 per cent per year on the outstanding amount of the loan. The commercial aspects of the loan are matters between the borrower and the lender. You can find out more about the details of the scheme on the Business Link website (**www.businesslink.gov.uk**>Finance and grants>Borrowing>Loans and overdrafts> Enterprise Finance Guarantee). Banks operating the scheme are listed on the Business Enterprise website (**www.berr.gov.uk**>What we do>Enterprise & Business Support>Enterprise and Small Business>Information for Small Business Owners and Entrepreneurs>Access to Finance>Small Firms Loan Guarantee).

CASE STUDY   Tim Waterstone and his eponymous bookstore

Waterstone's funding is an example of a new venture, funded initially by debt capital that has netted its founder both a fortune and a place in business history as someone who has changed the way an entire sector works, very much for the better. When Waterstone was trying to raise money, books were not exactly sexy and no one could see anything that could be done with the sector that hadn't been done before. Books and their distribution systems had endured in principle while changing in method over the centuries. From 1403 when the earliest known book was printed from movable type in Korea, through to Gutenberg's 42-line Bible printed in 1450, which in turn laid the foundation for the mass book market, the product, at least from a reader's perspective, has had many similarities. Even the latest developments of in-store print-on-demand and e-book delivery such as Amazon's Kindle look like leaving the reader holding much the same product.

When Tim Waterstone was fired from WH Smith's US operation he was already halfway to rethinking the way in which books were to be sold. In the UK the business model comprised rows of books stacked on shelves, spine out in alphabetical order sectioned off by subject. Bookshops were drab, operated a leisurely 9 to 5 existence, Monday to Friday and mornings only on Saturdays, staffed by assistants with no real understanding of books. Manhattan bookshops around where Waterstone lived were, by contrast, brilliant places: lively and consumer-led with huge stock, accessible and knowledgeable staff and long opening hours. The US model addressed several major problems for their customers. In the first place book buyers are usually in a job; were they not they would use a library. So not being open evenings or weekends effectively constrained customers to a quick visit sacrificing part of, if not their entire lunch break. The second problem concerned the way that people browse for books. Research shows that nearly two-thirds of book purchases are unplanned in the sense that customers either had no firm idea of what they were looking for, or they simply stumbled across an appealing title while in the shop. With this in mind books had to be distributed around the shop to maximize the opportunities for customers to stumble across an interesting title. While the spine-out bookshelf layout was highly economic in terms of floor space and stockholding it was unappealing and a further factor limiting sales prospects. The third problem that Waterstone set out to address was to staff his bookshops with people who could offer advice and information on authors and their books. He set out to create an environment that would appeal to literate young graduates rather than to barely articulate shop assistants. Had Waterstone simply wanted to open a bookshop he could have started straight away. The equity in his house would have been more than enough to finance the venture. But his bookshop concept called for a fundamental change in the way books were to be sold in the UK that in turn meant, in his opinion, opening a chain of 100 shops.

Despite having a comprehensive business plan he found it impossible to get backing. High street banks turned him down in droves. But Waterstone had never run a bookshop and didn't want to. His talent and experience were in running a business and as such would have been underutilized at best and wasted at worst in trying to set up a single outlet. In any event the success or otherwise of a single outlet would not prove conclusively one way or another his business concept. Waterstone knew that without investment he could never hope to get his business off the ground. The trick was to find a way of raising enough money to prove the concept, while leaving the door open to raising more once success was in sight. He wrote a detailed business plan and took it round numerous financial institutions. There was little enthusiasm for backing his plans for 100 shops but with a mixture of money from a finance house, pledging his house, personal savings, borrowings from his father-in-law, and making use of the government's loan guarantee scheme, he raised enough funds to test his strategy.

Within three months the first Waterstone's opened, based on a simple store plan an art student sketched out for £25 ($40/€29). Waterstone achieved scale quickly as opening new branches was a well-planned and simple procedure. A handful of head office staff found new locations, bought stock and hired shop managers. Soon the company employed 500 people in 40 branches, with a turnover of £35 ($56/€41) million a year. The ultimate achievement was to sell back the company to WH Smith for £50 ($80/€59) million barely a decade after starting up.

Local financing initiatives

Many communities, particularly those operating in rundown areas in need of regeneration, have a facility to lend or even invest in businesses that could bring employment to the area. The case below is one such example. Funding from these sources could be for anything from start-up, right through to expansion or in some cases even rescue finance to help prevent a business from folding, shedding a large number of jobs or relocating to a more benign business environment.

CASE STUDY

Rachel Lowe, a 29-year-old single mother with two children came up with her winning business idea while working part-time as a taxi driver in Portsmouth. She invented a game involving players throwing a dice to move taxi pieces around a board collecting fares to travel to famous destinations while aiming to get back to the taxi rank before they run out of fuel. Being able to run the business from home meant Rachel could spend more time with her children and still be a breadwinner. But despite having a business plan written up when she entered a local business competition, she had serious hurdles to cross before she could get started. With a deal from Hamley's, the London toyshop, in the bag and a manufacturer and distributor lined up, all that was missing was a modest amount of additional funding to help with marketing and stock.

She pitched her proposal to the BBC's 'Dragons Den' and was given a thorough roasting. To say the Dragons were not enthusiastic would be a serious understatement. They reckoned Monopoly would wipe the floor with her. Bowed but far from beaten Rachel then turned to South Coast Money Line, a Community Development Finance Institution and part of the Portsmouth Area Regeneration Trust Group (**www.part.org.uk**). With a loan from them she propelled her game – Destination London – into the top 10 best selling games, even beating Monopoly! A deal with Debenhams to stock regional versions of the game and signing up to produce Harry Potter and Disney versions left her with a business worth £2 ($3.2/€2.36) million, at a conservative estimate.

Bonds, debentures and mortgages

Bonds, debentures and mortgages are all kinds of borrowing with different rights and obligations for the parties concerned. For a business, a mortgage is much the same as for an individual. The loan is for a specific event, buying a particular property asset such as a factory, office or warehouse. Interest is payable and the loan itself is secured against the property, so should the business fail the mortgage can substantially be redeemed.

Companies that want to raise funds for general business purposes, rather than as with a mortgage where a particular property is being bought, issue debentures or bonds. These run for a number of years, typically three years and upwards, with the bond or debenture holder receiving interest over the life of the loan, and the capital is returned at the end of the period.

The key difference between debentures and bonds lies in their security and ranking. Debentures are unsecured and so in the event of the company being unable to pay interest or repay loans holders may well get little or nothing back. Bonds are secured against specific assets and so rank ahead of debentures for any pay-out.

Unlike bank loans that are usually held by the issuing bank, though even that assumption is being challenged by the escalation of securitization of debt being packaged up and sold on, bonds and debentures are sold to the public in much the same way as shares. The interest demanded will be a factor of the prevailing market conditions and the financial strength of the borrower.

Categories of bond

There are several general categories of bond that companies can tap into. *Standard bonds* pay interest, a coupon, half-yearly on the principal amount, known as the face or par value. At the maturity date the principal is repaid. The value of bonds fluctuates depending on market condition, the length of time to maturity and the likelihood of the borrower defaulting. None of these matters are of immediate concern to the recipient of the funds, as long as they can service the interest. The risk is for the bondholder who can see the value of the investment alter over time.

Zero coupon bonds pay no interest over their life but pay a lump sum at maturity equivalent to the value of the interest such an investment would normally bear. The buyer of the bond receives a return by the gradual appreciation of the bonds' price in the marketplace. This could be an attractive financing strategy for a business making an investment that itself will not bear fruit for a number of years.

Junk bonds are bonds usually subordinated to, that is put below in the pecking order of who gets paid in tough times, other regular bonds. Such bonds carry a higher interest burden.

Callable bonds are used when an issuer wants to retain the option to buy back the bonds from the public if general interest rates fall sharply after the issue date. The issuer notifies bondholders that after a certain date no further interest will be paid, leaving the holders with no reason to keep the bond. The company issuing the bond can then go out to the market and launch a new bond at a lower rate of interest and so lower its cost of capital. This process is also known as refinancing.

Commercial paper

Banks and big companies such as General Electric and AT&T regularly raise cash for operations by issuing paper to investors that often matures in six months or less. Private investors, especially money-market funds, buy this debt because as well as being very safe it pays an interest rate slightly higher than comparable US Treasury notes or UK Government Gilts. Although commercial paper is technically repayable in under six months in practice the corporate borrower repays investors by issuing more paper, effectively paying back investors with more borrowed cash. The attraction to the borrower over other forms of lending is that as long as it matures before nine months (270 days) it doesn't have to be registered with any regulatory body, making it in effect 'off-balance sheet', which in turn reduces gearing (see Chapter 8 for more on gearing and financial risk). The exception to this rule is if the proceeds from this type of financing are to be used for anything other than current assets (inventories, debtors, etc), for example fixed assets, such as a new plant. In such cases the relevant regulatory body has to be informed. However, in practice business funds tend to go into a pot and tracing where a particular sum of money came from and what was done with it is virtually impossible.

Syndicated loan

This is a loan offered by a group of lenders (a syndicate) who work together to provide funds usually though by no means always for a single borrower. The borrower could be a business, a large project, or a government. The loans are usually so large as to be potentially fatal to any single lender in the event of a default – hence the syndication. Borrowers who need a sophisticated facility or multiple types of facility find that using a syndicated loan agreement simplifies the borrowing process by using a single agreement covering the whole group of banks and different types of facility rather than entering into a series of separate bilateral loans. A syndicated loan agreement could contain a fixed term or revolving facility that is in effect permanent; or it can contain a combination of both or several of each type (multiple term loans in different currencies and with different maturity dates are fairly typical of the more complex syndicated loan). The syndicated loan can be for one borrower, a group of borrowers or allow for new borrowers to join in under certain circumstances from time to time. Four important pieces of documentation accompany syndicated loans:

1 *Term sheet:* this sets out the terms of the proposed financing, the parties involved, their expected roles and the key features of the loan including the type of facilities, the amounts, the pricing, the term of the loan and the covenant (any conditions and restrictions).

2 *Information memorandum:* this contains a commercial description of the borrower's business, management and accounts as well as details of the proposed loan facilities required. This document contains more information than is usually in the public domain so potential lenders will be expect to sign a confidentiality undertaking.

3 *Syndicated loan agreement:* the loan agreement sets out the detailed terms and conditions on which the facility is made available to the borrower.

4 *Fee letters:* borrower pay fees to those banks in the syndicate that have performed additional work or taken on greater responsibility in the loan process, including the arranger, the agent and the security trustee. Details of these fees are usually put in separate side letters to

ensure confidentiality. These fees are in addition to paying interest on the loan and any related bank expenses.

CASE STUDY Cobra Beer

In 1990 Cambridge-educated and recently qualified accountant Karan Bilimoria started importing and distributing Cobra beer, a name he chose because it appeared to work well in lots of different languages. He initially supplied his beer to complement Indian restaurant food in the UK. Lord Bilimoria, as he now is, started out with debts of £20,000 ($32,000/€23,600), but from a small flat in Fulham and with just a Citroen CV by way of assets he has grown his business to sales of over £100 ($160/€118) million a year.

Three factors have been key to its success. Cobra was originally sold in large 660 ml bottles and so was more likely to be shared by diners. Also, as Cobra is less fizzy than European lagers, drinkers are less likely to feel bloated and can eat and drink more. The third factor was Bilimoria's extensive knowledge through his training as an accountant of sources of finance for a growing business. He was fortunate in having an old-style bank manager who had such belief in Cobra that he agreed a loan of £30,000 ($48,000/€35,400) but since then has tapped into every possible type of funding (see Figure 6.1; Source: **www.thesmehub.com** – register for free then go to Member Services, Company Accounts Lookup and enter name), including selling a 28 per cent stake in his firm in 1995.

Payment in kind (PIK)

A PIK Loan usually doesn't require any cash payment of either capital or interest until it matures. Such loans are typically unsecured with maturity dates usually exceeding five years. These loans usually carry a detachable warrant, which is the right to purchase a certain number of shares at a given price for a certain period of time, or some such mechanism. This allows the lender to share in the future success of the business by way of compensation for its risk.

PIKs are something of a controversial debt structure and can ratchet substantial amounts of interest every year, which can ultimately destroy a company. Paramount Restaurants, the owner of Chez Gerard and Cafe Uno, is an example of the distress this form of finance can cause. In March 2010 the company saw its PIK notes stand at over £78 ($125/€92) million, up from £51.5 ($82.4/€60.7) million three years earlier. The debt was provided by Silverfleet, which backed a £107 ($171/€126) million buy-out. The PIK element was rolling up a crippling 15.5 per cent interest annually.

Paramount's bankers, including Royal Bank of Scotland, HSBC and Barclays had to take the company over from Silverfleet, taking a 60 per cent equity stake in the business themselves, in an effort to save the business from failure.

FIGURE 6.1 Cobra Beer's financing strategy

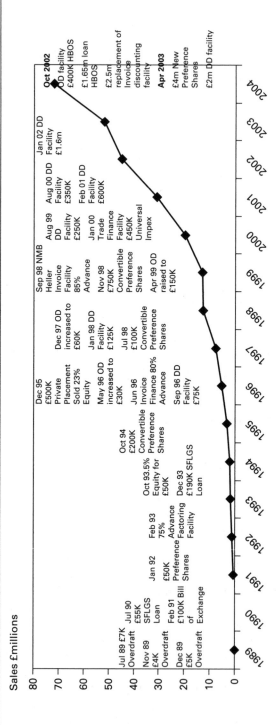

Sales £millions

Asset usage financing

The banks are more covert when it comes to looking for security for money lent. Some other major sources of funds are less circumspect; indeed their whole prospectus is predicated on a precise relationship between what a business has or will shortly have by way of assets, and what they are prepared to advance. Such products play an important role in financing businesses.

Leasing companies

Physical assets such as cars, vans, computers, office equipment and the like can usually be financed by leasing them, rather as a house or flat may be rented. Alternatively, they can be bought on hire purchase. This leaves other funds free to cover the less tangible elements in your cash flow.

Leasing is a way of getting the use of vehicles, plant and equipment without paying the full cost all at once. Operating leases are taken out where you will use the equipment (for example a car, photocopier, vending machine or kitchen equipment) for less than its full economic life. The lessor takes the risk of the equipment becoming obsolete, and assumes responsibility for repairs, maintenance and insurance. As you, the lessee, are paying for this service, it is more expensive than a finance lease, where you lease the equipment for most of its economic life and maintain and insure it yourself. Leases can normally be extended, often for fairly nominal sums, in the latter years.

Hire purchase differs from leasing in that you have the option to eventually become the owner of the asset, after a series of payments. You can find a leasing company via The Finance and Leasing Association (**www.fla.org**> For Businesses>Business Finance Directory), which gives details of all UK-based businesses offering this type of finance. The website also has general information on terms of trade and code of conduct.

Discounting and factoring

Customers often take time to pay up. In the meantime you have to pay those who work for you and your less patient suppliers. So, the more you grow, the more funds you need. It is often possible to 'factor' your creditworthy customers' bills to a financial institution, receiving some of the funds as your goods leave the door, hence speeding up cash flow.

Factoring is generally only available to a business that invoices other business customers, either in its home market or internationally, for its products or services. Factoring can be made available to new businesses, although its services are usually of most value during the early stages of growth. It is an arrangement that allows you to receive up to 80 per cent of the cash due from your customers more quickly than they would normally pay. The factoring company in effect buys your trade debts, and can also provide a debtor accounting and administration service. You will, of course, have to pay for factoring services. Having the cash before your customers pay will cost you a little more than normal overdraft rates. The factoring service will cost between 0.5 and 3.5 per cent of the turnover, depending on volume of work, the number of debtors, average invoice amount and other related factors. You can get up to 80 per cent of the value of your invoice in advance, with the remainder paid when your customer settles up, less the various charges just mentioned.

If you sell direct to the public, sell complex and expensive capital equipment, or expect progress payments on long-term projects, then factoring is not for you. If you are expanding more rapidly than other sources of finance will allow, this may be a useful service that is worth exploring.

Invoice discounting is a variation on the same theme where you are responsible for collecting the money from debtors; this is not a service available to new or very small businesses. You can find an Invoice Discounter or Factor through The Asset Based Finance Association (**www.thefda.org.uk/public/membersList.asp**), the association representing the UK's 41 factoring and invoice discounting businesses.

Letters of credit and bills of exchange

Until the 19th century the branch banking system was fairly limited and postal services relatively slow. A system of transferring money, in particularly between countries, but also within countries was established. Initially under the general heading of 'bills of exchange' these financial instruments were in effect promissory notes, much like the modern day cheque, drawn up by one party who promises to pay another a certain sum on a certain day. Variations on this theme also became established, letters of credit being one of the most common. These were and to some extent still are used for buyers and sellers of international goods to transfer money to facilitate transactions. These letters can be irrevocable, that is payment must be made if all conditions are met; revocable – these can be cancelled or amended without prior notice; transferrable where the letter concerned and the money attached can be passed to another party, usually a 'middleman' or agent. An MBA needs only a nodding acquaintance with these types of financial instruments and when you need to know more you can read up on them at SITPRO (Simplifying International Trade) (**http://www.sitpro.org.uk/trade/lettcredintro.html**), where you will find a series of checklists to guide you through the maze.

Sell and leaseback assets

August 2009 saw broadcaster ITV reporting full-year losses of £2.59 ($4.14/ €3.1) billion, a consequence of the collapse in advertising revenue brought about by the prevailing economic crisis. By the time it reported these figures the company had already cut 1,000 jobs, secured £155 ($248/€183) million in cost savings and had its sights set on cutting a further £215 ($344/€254) million out of overheads in 2010. In fact the company's advertising revenue decline of 15 per cent was a little better than that of the market as a whole, which had slipped back 17 per cent. Nevertheless Michael Grade, the outgoing chairman, felt the situation drastic enough to call for further action. He sold the Friends Reunited website to Scottish publisher D C Thompson, of *Beano* fame, for £25 ($40/€29.5) million, some £150 ($240/€177) million less than ITV had paid for it four years earlier. The assets that Grade sold off were considered non-core and so could safely be sacrificed. But what if you want to keep assets but still need cash, perhaps for less pressing needs than survival?

Sale and leaseback can be seen as a less desperate measure than selling off assets. At least using this strategy you live and get to fight another day. The process involves selling some or all of your fixed assets including property and vehicles to another company, becoming a tenant in what were your premises or leasing your former cars and delivery fleet. The benefits are a large slug of cash to help ride out a storm, but also it's a way to reduce operating costs going forward, as amongst other things there is a tax benefit to be realized by offsetting lease costs as an operating expense. IBM, for example, sold and leased back four of its five remaining owned sites in the UK in 2006, leaving only its Hursley software laboratory in company ownership. As well as reducing costs, IBM is increasingly trying to have only sufficient property on the books to meet business demands, and leasing on relatively short terms helps in this respect. Other big users of sale and leaseback include Tesco, which recently made a £366 ($585/€432) million property sale and leaseback of 12 stores and two distribution centres.

CASE STUDY
British International Helicopters (BIH) – Penzance

By December 2008 BIH's managing director, Tony Jones, was facing a dilemma. His company, based on the edge of Penzance and close to the main rail station and harbour, provided one of a number of vital links between the mainland and the Isles of Scilly. Annual passenger numbers had declined from 133,000 in 2002 to 100,000 in 2008 and the prospects for tourism in the credit crunch environment of 2009/10 did not augur well. Along with the rising costs of spare parts and fuel, the service has steadily become less viable over the past four years. The company's operating profit has reduced by £1.2 ($1.9/€1.4) million a year and something drastic had to be done to keep the business going and preserve the firm's 86 jobs.

Raising fares was not an option. Flying by helicopter was an already costly, if convenient, option. BIH's standard fare of £170 ($272/€200) for the 20-minute flight compared unfavourably with Skybus's fixed wing service at £140 ($224/€165) delivered from Land's End aerodrome, some 30 minutes drive away, and the 2½ hour ferry crossing on the Scillonian for £95 ($152/€112).

One of BIH's proposed recovery strategies involves selling off the Penzance Heliport, which is on prime land on the edge of town, sandwiched between branches of Morrison's and Tesco, and transferring flights to the Land's End airport. As well as freeing up a substantial capital sum, BIH's operating costs would drop sharply as it would be sharing the costs of running Land's End airport with Skybus, and its flying time (and hence fuel and operating costs) would be shortened significantly. Fire-fighters, baggage handlers and administrative staff would be transferred to Land's End but many staff would stay in or near the existing heliport. In the event this decision was postponed to allow time to explore other options including sale and leaseback.

Equity

07

- Understanding equity
- The role of venture capital
- Using business angels
- Corporate venturing
- Floating on a stock market

There are many sources of funds available to businesses but not all of them are equally appropriate to all businesses at all times. These different sources of finance carry very different obligations, responsibilities and opportunities for profitable business, and having some appreciation of these differences will enable the MBA to help managers and directors make informed choices.

Most businesses initially and often until they go public, floating their shares on a stock market, confine their financial strategy to bank loans, either long- or short-term, or other financing methods that require the loan to be repaid with interest – this field of finance was the subject of Chapter 6. Often this strategy is adopted as managers view the other financing methods as either too complex or too risky. In many respects the reverse is true. Almost every finance source other than banks will to a greater or lesser extent share some of the risks of doing business with the recipient of the funds. (The appropriate balance of risk to be selected between differing sources of finance is covered in Chapter 10.)

Businesses operating as a limited company or limited partnership have a potentially valuable opportunity to raise relatively risk-free money. It is risk-free to the business but risky, sometimes extremely so, to anyone investing. Essentially this type of capital, known collectively as 'equity', consists of the issued share capital and reserves of various kinds. It represents the amount of money that shareholders have invested directly into the company by buying shares, together with retained profits that belong to shareholders but which the company uses as additional capital. As with debt, equity comes in a number of forms with differing rights and privileges.

Ordinary shares form the bulk of the shares issued by most companies and are the shares, which carry the ordinary risks, associated with being in business. All the profits of the business, including past retained profits, belong to the ordinary shareholders once any preference share dividends have been deducted. Ordinary shares have no fixed rate of dividend; indeed over half the companies listed on US stock markets pay no or virtually no dividend. These include high growth companies such as Google and Microsoft, which argue that by retaining and reinvesting all their profits they can create better value for shareholders than by distributing dividends.

A company does not have to issue all its share capital at once. The total amount it is authorized to issue must be shown somewhere in the accounts, but only the issued share capital is counted in the balance sheet. Although shares can be partly paid, this is a rare occurrence.

Preference shares get their name for two reasons. First, they receive their fixed rate of dividend before ordinary shareholders. Second, in the event of winding up a company, any funds remaining go to repay preference share capital before any ordinary share capital. In a forced liquidation this may be of little comfort as shareholders of any type come last in the queue after all other claims from creditors have been met.

Class A and class B shares are cases where categories of shareholder are singled out for more or less favourable treatment. For example, class A shares are often given up to five votes per share, while class B shares get one. In extreme cases class B shareholders can get no votes at all. Companies will often try to disguise the disadvantages associated with owning shares with less voting rights. One of the most famous examples of this was their use by the Savoy Hotel Group to ward off an unwanted takeover by Trusthouse Forte. While Trusthouse was able to buy 70 per cent of Savoy shares on the open market, it could only secure 42 per cent of the voting rights as it was only able to buy class B shares, the A shares being in the hands of Savoy family and allies.

'Reserves', a typically misleading term in all accounting, means profits of various kinds that have been retained in the company as extra capital. Also important is what the term 'reserves' does not mean. It does not mean actual money held back in reserve in bank accounts or elsewhere. Reserves come from retained profits over many years but are reinvested in buildings, equipment, stocks or company debts, just like any other source of capital and rarely held in cash. The main categories of reserves are as follows:

- Profit and loss account: the cumulative retained profits from ordinary trading activities.

- Revaluation reserve: the paper-profit that can arise if certain assets are re-valued to current price levels without the assets concerned being sold.

- Share premium account: the excess over the original par value of a share when new shares are offered for sale at an enhanced price. Only the original par value is ever shown as issued share capital.

There are two broad sources of equity: *private equity* usually put in by individuals or small groups of individuals who, for the potential of greater returns, will take on greater risks; or *public capital* through a share issue on a stock market.

Private equity

There are three main sources of private equity: business angels, venture capital firms and corporate venture funding.

Business angels

One likely first source of equity or risk capital will be a private individual with his or her own funds, and perhaps some knowledge of your type of business. In return for a share in the business, such investors will put in money at their own risk. They have been christened 'business angels', a term first coined to describe private wealthy individuals who back a play on Broadway or in London's West End.

Most angels are determined upon some involvement beyond merely signing a cheque and may hope to play a part in your business is some way. They are hoping for big rewards – one angel who backed Sage with £10,000 ($16,000/€12,000) in its first round of £250,000 ($5000,000/€295,000) financing saw his stake rise to £40 ($64/€47) million.

These angels frequently operate through managed networks, usually on the internet. In the UK and the United States there are hundreds of networks, with tens of thousands of business angels prepared to put up several billion each year into new or small business.

Here are 10 things worth knowing about business angels:

1 40 per cent suffer partial or complete loss of their investment;
2 50 per cent don't conduct research into prospective investments;
3 55 per cent don't take up personal references, compared with only 6 per cent of venture capital providers in general;
4 90 per cent have worked in a small firm or owned their own business;
5 business angels meet owners five times on average before investing, compared with venture capital providers in general who require 10 meetings;
6 10 per cent of business angel investment is for less than $10,000 (£6,250/€8,475) and 45 per cent is for over $50,000 (£31,250/€42,370);
7 most business angels invest close to home. Up to 50 miles is usual, with 200 miles as the limit. Angels rarely invest abroad;
8 only 2 per cent have made overseas investments;

9   angels often flock together. Syndicated deals make up more than a quarter of all deals, where two or more angels band together to invest;

10   angels are up to five times more likely to invest in start-ups and early stage investments than venture capital providers in general.

Finding a business angel

The British Business Angels Association (**www.bbaa.org.uk**) has an online directory of UK business angels. The European Business Angels Network (eban) has directories of national business angel associations both inside and outside of Europe; see (**www.eban.org**>Members) where you can find individual business angels.

CASE STUDY

Calum Brannan was just 15 and taking his GCSEs when he stared up PPLParty.com from his bedroom in Coventry. Brannon felt there was an unexploited niche providing a website to share pictures and information on clubbing. He invested £200 ($320/€236) earned from his part-time job at Pizza Hut and through little more than word of mouth now has over 400,000 members. Next came a small amount of money from a business angel to help pay for his eight staff and now he is looking for around £400,000 ($640,000/€472,000) from a venture capital firm to enable him to move his business to the next stage.

Venture capital

Venture capitalists (VCs), sometimes unflatteringly referred to as 'vulture capitalists', are investing other people's money, often from pension funds. They have a different agenda from that of business angels, and are more likely to be interested in investing more money for a larger stake. In general, VCs expect their investment to have paid off within seven years, but they are hardened realists. Two in every 10 investments they make are total write-offs, and six perform averagely well at best. So, the one star in every 10 investments they make has to cover a lot of duds. VCs have a target rate of return of 30 per cent plus, to cover this poor hit rate.

Raising venture capital is not a cheap option and deals are not quick to arrange either. Six months is not unusual, and over a year has been known. Every VC has a deal done in six weeks in its portfolio, but that truly is the exception. Fees will run to hundreds of thousands of pounds, the sweetener being that these can be taken from the money raised.

Risk capital, or equity as it is also know, has a very limited appetite for serious risk taking, in the UK at least. Over the five years to December 2009 venture capital firms invested an average of just over 1 per cent of their capital into around a score of start-up companies. The rest of the funds went into either established businesses (29 per cent) or management buy-outs (MBOs) (70 per cent). That latter figure really says it all about the average VC's appetite for risk: an MBO involves backing an established business with a track record and part, hopefully the best part, of an incumbent management team.

Still, you can hardly blame the UK venture capital industry for its caution when it comes to start-ups. Over the past 20 years the UK venture capital industry has made an IRR (internal rate of return, about which more later), of around 2 per cent. That's a whole lot better than the European VC performance who achieved −1.1 per cent over the same period. The US experience is rather different: the average return over 20 years on start-up investments is 21.8 per cent (source: Thomson Reuters). US venture capital investment is around six times that of the UK. European VC as a whole is roughly the same size as for the UK, and the rest of the world about the same again.

The good news, however, is that the UK has the largest VC industry outside of the US, accounting for some 12 per cent of the world's total capital provision. The 214 VC firms and several thousand business angels that make up the sector are actively looking for growing businesses to invest in. As the case study below shows, new players are coming into the market all the time. The catch is that they are only interested in businesses capable of generating superior profits, calculated using their preferred yardstick of IRR.

CASE STUDY European Founders Capital (EFC)

In April 2009 two of Britain's most successful internet entrepreneurs pumped £20 ($32/€236) million of their own money into a new early stage venture capital fund. Michael Birch, who set up Bebo, the social networking website and Bent Hoberman, co-founder with Martha Lane Fox of lastminute.com the travel booking service, teamed up to exploit what they saw as the great opportunities that will be thrown up as the world comes out of the worst economic downturn in over half a century. Rogan Angelini-Hurl, a close friend of Hoberman who missed out on an opportunity to co-found lastminute.com back in 2000, has joined in this venture, bringing to it his experience as a City analyst. EFC plans to exploit the gap between business angels, who typically invest in the tens of thousands, and venture capitalists that look to invest several million pounds, usually in more established firms.

Finding venture capital

The British Venture Capital Association (**www.bvca.co.uk**) and the European Venture Capital Association (**www.evca.com**) both have online directories giving details of hundreds of venture capital providers. The Australian Government (**www.austradeict.gov.au/Globl-VC-directory/default.aspx**) has a global venture capital directory on this website, and the National Venture Capital Association in the US has directories of international of venture capital associations both inside and outside the United States (**www.nvca.org>** Resources).

You can see how those negotiating with or receiving venture capital rate the firm in question at The Funded website (**www.thefunded.com**) in terms of the deal offered, the firm's apparent competence and how good it is at managing the relationship. There is also a link to the VCs website. The Funded has 2,500 members.

CASE STUDY
The Internet Bookshop and why it was eclipsed by Amazon

UK entrepreneur Darryl Mattocks, a software engineer and computer enthusiast, entered the market in 1994 a year ahead of Amazon, but his approach was profoundly different. Mattock went into a bookshop in Oxford and picked up a book he had ordered a few days before. He paid for it, walked a few doors down to the Post Office and despatched it to the customer who had e-mailed his order the previous week. He was constrained initially to financing the business using credit cards, though later a friend introduced him to James Blackwell, a member of the family behind the Oxford booksellers, who put up £50,000 ($80,000/€59,000) for a 50 per cent stake in the venture.

Jeff Bezos, a former investment banker, raised $11 (£6.9/€9.3) million from Silicon Valley venture capitalists before starting up, and invested $8 (£5/€6.8) million of that in marketing. Mattock's Internet Bookshop had a database of 16,000 books, while Amazon was selling nearly $16 (£10/€13.5) million worth of books. In 1988, around the time it was buying Waterstone's, WH Smith bought out bookshop.co.uk, parent company of The Internet Bookshop, for £9.4 ($15/€11) million. Amazon was then valued at $10.1 (£6.3/€8.6) billion.

Corporate venturing

Venture capital firms often take a hand in the management of the businesses they invest in. Another type of venturer is also in the risk capital business, without it necessarily being their main line of business. These firms, known as corporate venturers, usually want an inside track to new developments in and around the edges of their own fields of interest.

Sinclair Beecham and Julian Metcalfe, who started with a £17,000 ($27,000/€20,000) loan and a name borrowed from a boarded-up shop, founded Prêt a Manger. They were not entrepreneurs content with doing their own thing. They had global ambitions and it was only by cutting in McDonald's the burger giant, that they could see any realistic way to dominate the world. They sold a 33 per cent stake for £25 ($40/€29.5) million in 2001 to McDonald's Ventures LLC, a wholly-owned subsidiary of McDonald's Corporation, the arm of McDonalds' that looks after its corporate venturing activities. They joined forces with the corporate venturing arm of a big firm.

They could also have considered Cisco, Apple Computers, IBM and Microsoft, which also all have corporate venturing arms. Other corporate venturers include Deutsche Bank, which set up DB eVentures to get a window on the 'digital revolution'. Reuters Greenhouse has stakes in 85 companies and even the late and unlamented Enron had venture investments (totalling $110/£176/€130 million). For an entrepreneur this approach can provide a 'friendly customer' and help open doors. For the 'parent' it provides a privileged ringside seat as a business grows and the opportunity to decide if the area is worth plunging into more deeply, or at least provides valuable insights into new technologies or business processes.

Recent research into corporate venturing by Ashridge (**www.ashridge. org.uk**>Research and Faculty) business school concluded that less than 5 per cent of corporate venturing units created new businesses that were taken up by the parent company. Moreover, many failed to make any positive contribution whatsoever. There are some success stories, however. In 2008 McDonald's offloaded its Prêt stake to Bridgepoint, a private equity firm that bought a majority stake including McDonald's 33 per cent shareholding, for £345 ($552/€407) million. That would suggest that McDonald's at least quadrupled the value of its initial stake. Nokia Venture Partners (NVP), which makes significant minority investments in start-ups in the wireless internet space, had as its biggest success to date the initial public offering of PayPal, in 2002. At a conference in July 1999, NVP and Deutsche Bank used Paypal's (then called Confinnity) encryption technology to send founders Peter Thiel and Max Levchin $3 (£4.8/€3.5) million in venture capital via a Palm Pilot as their initial stake. Corporate venturing entrepreneurs think big and are happy to cut others with cash in on the deal, if it will help make them rich. Independence for independence's sake is not a high priority.

HM Revenue & Customs (**www.hmrc.gov.uk/guidance/cvs.htm**) has a useful guide entitled 'The Corporate Venturing Scheme', explaining the scheme, tax implications and sources of further information.

CASE STUDY Innocent

In the summer of 1998 when Richard Reed, Adam Balon and Jon Wright had developed their first smoothie recipes but were still nervous about giving up their jobs, they bought £500 ($800/€590) worth of fruit, turned it into smoothies and sold them from a stall at a London music festival. They put up a sign saying, 'Do you think we should give up our jobs to make these smoothies?' next to bins labelled 'YES' and 'NO', inviting people to put the empty bottle in the appropriate bin. At the end of the weekend the 'YES' bin was full, so they went in the next day and resigned. The rest, as they say, is history. Virtually a household name, the business has experienced a decade of rapid growth. But the business stalled in 2008, with sales slipping back and their European expansion soaking up cash at a rapid rate.

The founders, average age 28, decided that they needed some heavyweight advice and talked to Charles Dunstone, Carphone Warehouse founder, and Mervyn Davies, chairman of Standard Chartered. The strong advice was to get an investor with deep pockets and ideally something else to bring to the party to augment the youthful enthusiasm of the founders. They launched their search for an investor the day that Lehman Brothers filed for bankruptcy. In April 2009 the Innocent team accepted Coca-Cola as a minority investor in their business, paying £30 ($48/€35) million for a stake of between 10 and 20 per cent. They chose Coca-Cola because as well as providing the funds, it can help get their products out to more people in more places. Also, with Coca-Cola having been in business for over 120 years, there will be things they can learn from it.

Family, friends and business associates of the board

Those close to your company, family and friends of the board of directors, key suppliers or customers can often be persuaded to either lend or invest in your business. This helps you avoid the problem of pleading your case to outsiders and enduring extra paperwork and bureaucratic delays. Help from friends, relatives and business associates can be especially valuable if your business has credit problems that would make raising money from a commercial funding source difficult or impossible.

Such sources of finance bring a range of extra potential benefits, costs and risks that are not a feature of most other types of finance. You need to decide if these are acceptable and incorporate this into your assessment of whether or not to recommend going down this route.

Some advantages of raising money from people you know well are that you may be get easier terms, may be able to delay paying back money until you are in better financial shape and may be given more flexibility if your firm gets into difficulties. But once the loan or investment terms are agreed, the same legal obligations apply as with any other source of finance.

In addition, raising money from such sources can have a major disadvantage. If your business does poorly and those close to you end up losing money, you may well damage a good personal relationship. So, in dealing with friends, relatives and business associates, be extra careful not only to establish clearly the terms of the deal and put them in writing but also to make an extra effort to explain the risks. In short, it's your job to make sure your helpful friend, relative, supplier or customer won't suffer a true hardship if you're unable to meet your financial commitments. Don't accept money from those who can't afford to risk it.

Here are 10 things to remember about raising money from family, friends and business associates:

1 Do agree proper terms for the loan or investment.

2 Do put the agreement in writing and if involves a share transaction or guarantee, have a legal agreement drawn up.

3 Do make an extra effort to explain the risks of the business and the possible downside implications to their money.

4 Do make sure when raising money from parents to advise those concerned that other siblings are compensated in some way, perhaps via a will.

5 Do make sure you or your fellow directors want to run a family business before raising money in this way as family investors always want to get involved.

6 Don't borrow from people on fixed incomes.

7 Don't borrow from people who can't afford to lose money.

8 Don't make the possible rewards sound more attractive than you would to any other investor.

9 Don't offer jobs in your business to anyone providing money unless they are the best person for the job.

10 Don't change the normal pattern of social contact with family, friends or business associates after they have put up the money.

CASE STUDY Poncho Ocho

In the autumn of 2009 when Nick Troen and Frank Yeung set up their 'gourmet' burritos venture in London's Spitalfields Market, they had Innocent (see the case study earlier in this chapter) as their business model. The duo, friends since university days, had tried out every Mexican eatery in London, New York and Los Angeles to sharpen up their proposition. Troen had even based his MA thesis, done at the London School of Economics, on the casual food market in the Spitalfields area. The business exudes an air of hippy healthiness intended to excite bored office workers looking for something different for lunch.

Before starting their business Yeung worked for Goldman Sachs, the investment bank and Troen was at KPMG, the accountancy firm, before putting in a spell at Innocent, the smoothie maker. It was this depth of theoretical knowledge and practical hands-on experience, brought together into a comprehensive business plan, that made them comfortable about tapping into family and friends to invest the £140,000 ($224,000/€165,000) start-up funds required.

Private capital preliminaries

Two important stages will be gone through before a private investor will put cash into a business. The emphasis put on these stages will vary according to the complexity of the deal, the amount of money and the legal ownership of the funds concerned. For example, business angels investing on their own account can accept greater uncertainty than, say, a venture capital fund using a pension fund's money.

1. Due diligence

Usually, after a private equity firm signs a letter of intent to provide capital and you accept, it will conduct a due diligence investigation of both the management and the company. During this period the private equity firm will have access to all financial and other records, facilities, employees, etc, to investigate before finalizing the deal. The material to be examined will include copies of all leases, contracts and loan agreements in addition to copious financial records and statements. The equity firm will want to see any management reports such as sales reports, inventory records, detailed lists of assets, facility maintenance records, aged receivables and payables reports, employee organization charts, payroll and benefits records, customer records and marketing materials. It will want to know about any pending litigation, tax audits or insurance disputes. Depending on the nature of the business, it might also consider getting an environmental audit and an insurance check-up. The sting in the due diligence tail is that the current owners of the business will be required to personally warrant that everything they have said or revealed is both true and complete. In the event that proves not to be so, they will be personally liable to the extent of any loss incurred by those buying the shares.

2. Term sheet

A term sheet is a funding offer from a capital provider. It lays out the amount of an investment and the conditions under which the new investors expect the business owners to work using their money.

The first page of the term sheet states the amount offered and the form of the funds (a bond, common stock, preferred stock, a promissory note or a combination of these). A price, either per 1,000 units of debt or per share of stock, is quoted to set the cost basis for investors 'getting in' on your company. Later that starting price will be very important in deciding capital gains and any taxes due at acquisition, IPO (initial public offering) or shares/units transferred.

Another key component of the term sheet is the 'post-closing capitalization'. This is the proposed cash value of the venture on the day the terms are accepted. For example, investors may offer £500,000 in series A preferred stock at 50 pence per share (1 million shares) with a post-closing cap of £2 million. This translates into a 25 per cent ownership stake in the firm (£500,000 divided by £2 million).

The next section of the term sheet is typically a table that summarizes the capital structure of your company. Investors generally start with preferred stock to gain a priority of distribution, should the enterprise fail and the liquidation of assets occur. The typical way to handle this is to have the preferred stock convertible into common stock on a 1:1 ratio at the investors' option, such that the preferred position is essentially a common stock position, but with priority of repayment over the founders' own common stock position.

Other terms included on the sheet could cover rents, equipment, levels of debt vs equity, minimum and maximum time periods associated with the transfer of shares, vesting in additional shares, option periods for making subsequent investments and having 'right of first refusal' when other rounds of funding are sought in the future.

Public capital

Stock markets are the place where serious businesses raise serious money. It's possible to raise anything from a few million to tens of billions; expect the costs and efforts in getting listed to match those stellar figures. The basic idea is that owners sell shares in their businesses, which in effect brings in a whole raft of new 'owners' who in turn have a stake in a business's future profits. When they want out they sell their shares to other investors. The share price moves up and down to ensure that there are as many buyers as sellers at any one time.

Going public also puts a stamp of respectability on you and your company. It will enhance the status and credibility of your business, and it will enable you to borrow more against the 'security' provided by your new shareholders, should you so wish. Your shares will also provide an attractive way to retain and motivate key staff. If they are given, or rather are allowed to earn, share options at discounted prices, they too can participate in the capital gains you are making. With a public share listing you can join in the takeover and asset-stripping game. When your share price is high and things are going well you can look out for weaker firms to gobble up – all you have to do is to offer them more of your shares in return for theirs; you do not even have to find real money. But of course this is a two-sided game and you also may now become the target of a hostile bid.

You may find that being in the public eye not only cramps your style but also fills up your engagement diary. Most CEOs of public companies find that they have to spend up to a quarter of their time 'in the City' explaining their strategies, in the months preceding and the first years after going public. It is not unusual for so much management time to have been devoted to answering accountants' and stockbrokers' questions that there is not enough time to run the day-to-day business, and profits drop as a direct consequence.

The City also creates its own 'pressure' both to seduce companies onto the market and then by expecting them to perform beyond any reasonable expectation. There have been a number of high profile examples of companies that have floated their shares on a stock market then changed their minds and withdrawn, buying out all outside shareholders. The rationale for taking a company back into private hands is that owners feel that they can run the company better without the need to justify their decisions to other shareholders, or the complex and burdensome regulations that public companies must comply with.

CASE STUDY   The Saga saga

The name that is synonymous with providing holidays exclusively for the over-50s is undoubtedly Saga. The business, started out in 1951 with the daunting name of 'Old People's Travel Bureau', was an experiment by Folkestone hotelier Sidney De Haan. He believed that older holidaymakers would appreciate a quieter off-season break by the sea, charging just £6.10 ($9.75/€7.20), including travel, full board and three excursions. Over the next decade the company chartered trains and planes and finally bought its own charter boat, the Saga Rose. Along the way it launched a magazine, insurance business and a clutch of FM radio stations. Over a third of the UK's over-50s are on Saga's database, which holds records of 7 million individuals of whom over 2 million actively buy from Saga each year. By January 2007 the company was making £158.2 ($253/€186.7 million in profits and employing 3,800 people worldwide.

The company's financing history has been something of a roller coaster. Initially financed using family money and bank debt, the firm was floated on the stock market in 1978. Saga was not a hit with investors though, partly because of the weakening UK holiday's market. The De Haan family took the group private in 1990, buying out all the other investors. By 2004 the company was preparing to go back onto the stock market when the private equity firm, Charterhouse Capital Partners, paid £1.35 ($2.2/€1.6) billion to take control of the group, and it pulled its IPO at the last minute. The acquisition was by way of a buyout, with Charterhouse taking an 80 per cent stake and the management the remainder. Charterhouse funded the acquisition of Saga with £500 ($800/€590) million of equity. The remainder was funded with debt, which it has since refinanced.

In January 2007, just three years later, the company, then thought to be worth around £3 ($4.8/€3.5) billion, was again exploring its financing strategy. A sale or flotation could value the 20 per cent stake held by staff and senior management at £500 ($800/€590) million, with the 8 per cent stake of Andrew Goodsell, Saga's chief executive, worth a couple of hundred million. Mr Goodsell stated, 'We've smashed through all of our plans, repaid large amounts of debt and [Charterhouse] has achieved what it wanted to achieve.' Once again stock-market flotation was on the cards, but a very different opportunity emerged. In June 2007 Permira and CVC, the two private equity firms that owned the bulk of the AA, approached Saga's majority owner Charterhouse to ask it to consider a merger. The result was a £6.15 ($9.8/€7.3) billion surprise move that created one of the country's largest private equity-backed companies.

Initial public offer – criteria for getting a stock market listing

The rules vary from market to market but these are the conditions that are likely to apply to get a company listed on an exchange.

Getting listed on a major stock exchange calls for a track record of making substantial profits with decent seven-figure sums being made in the year you plan to 'float', as this process is known. A listing also calls for a large proportion, usually at least 25 per cent, of the company's shares being put up for sale at the outset. In addition, you would be expected to have 100 shareholders now and be able to demonstrate that 100 more will come on board as a result of the listing.

As you draw up your flotation plan and timetable you should have the following matters in mind:

- *Advisers:* you will need to be supported by a team that will include a sponsor, stockbroker, reporting accountant and solicitor. These should be respected firms, active in flotation work and familiar with the company's type of business. You and your company may be judged by the company you keep, so choose advisers of good repute and make sure that the people work effectively together. It is very unlikely that a small local firm of accountants, however satisfactory, will be up to this task.

- *Sponsor:* you will need to appoint a financial institution, usually a merchant banker, to fill this important role. If you do not already have a merchant bank in mind, your accountant will offer guidance. The job of the sponsor is to coordinate and drive the project forward.

- *Timetable:* it is essential to have a timetable for the final months in the run-up to a float – and to adhere to it. The company's directors and senior staff will be fully occupied in providing information and attending meetings. They will have to delegate and there must be sufficient back-up support to ensure that the business does not suffer (see below for an example of a timetable).

- *Management team:* a potential investor will want to be satisfied that your company is well managed, at board level and below. It is important to ensure succession, perhaps by offering key directors and managers service agreements and share options. It is wise to draw on the experience of well-qualified non-executive directors.

- *Accounts:* the objective is to have a profit record that is rising but, in achieving this, you will need to take into account directors' remuneration, pension contributions and the elimination of any expenditure that might be acceptable in a privately owned company but would not be acceptable in a public one, namely excessive perks such as yachts, luxury cars, lavish expense accounts and holiday homes.

Accounts must be consolidated and audited to appropriate accounting standards and the audit reports must not contain any major qualifications. The auditors will need to be satisfied that there are proper stock records and a consistent basis of valuing stock during the years prior to flotation. Accounts for the last three years will need to be disclosed and the date of the last accounts must be within six months of the issue.

AIM

London's Alternative Investment Market (AIM) was formed in the 1990s specifically to provide risk capital for new rather than established ventures. AIM raised around £12.5 ($20/€14.7) billion last year – a 76 per cent leap from the previous year and a record number of companies floated on the exchange, bringing the total to 1,634.

AIM is particularly attractive to any dynamic company of any size, age or business sector that has rapid growth in mind. The smallest firm on AIM entered at under £640,000 ($1 million/€755,000) capitalization and the largest at over £500 ($800/€590) million. The formalities are minimal, but the costs of entry are high and you must have a nominated adviser, such as a major accountancy firm, stockbroker or banker. A survey showed that costs of floating on the junior market are around 6.5 per cent of all funds raised, and companies valued at less than £2 ($3.2/€2.36) million can expect to shell out a quarter of funds raised in costs alone. The market is regulated by the London Stock Exchange (**www.londonstockexchange.com**>AIM).

PLUS

One rung down from AIM is PLUS-Quoted Market, whose roots lie in the market formerly known as Ofex. It began life in November 2004 and was granted Recognised Investment Exchange (RIE) status by the Financial

Services Authority (FSA) in 2007. Aimed at smaller companies wanting to raise up to £10 ($1.6/€1.18) million it draws on a pool of capital primarily from private investors. The market is regulated, but requirements are not as stringent as those of AIM or the main market, and the costs of flotation and ongoing costs are lower. Keycom used this market to raise £4.4 ($7.04/ €5.19) million in September 2008 to buy out a competitor to give it a combined contract to provide broadband access to 40,000 student rooms in UK universities. There are 174 companies quoted on PLUS; even in 2009, a particularly bad year for stock market activity, 30 companies applied for entry to PLUS and 18 were admitted. You can find out more about PLUS at **www.plusmarketsgroup.com**.

CASE STUDY NCC Group

Not everyone was enthralled by either the economic downturn or the publicity highlighting the UK government's data protection failures. But to the NCC Group, which provides escrow software that ensures business-critical material or source code is protected and accessible should anything happen to a key supplier, these factors helped grow turnover and 2008 profit to £35.7 ($57.1/€42) million and £8.7 ($13.9/€10.3) million respectively. The rise in turnover was helped by two acquisitions, but around a fifth of revenue growth was organic. The CEO Rob Cotton, a chartered accountant who was with what is now PricewaterhouseCoopers, was headhunted by the National Computer Centre in 2000 to help the company develop its strategy for rapid growth. It didn't take Cotton long to see that the jewel in NCC's crown was the escrow business: this division, one of three, accounted for £8 ($12.8/€9.4) million out of total sales of £12 ($19/€14) million. By 2002 the company was due for another round of financing. The original venture capitalist (ECI), which had put in £3 ($4.8/€3.5) million in 1999, had always envisaged a trade sale, but in 2002 the aftershock of the dotcom bust was still reverberating round the high tech market.

So, led by Cotton, it was decided on a management buyout and five VCs contacted and invited to fund the plan. By October 2002 Cotton had a shortlist of two, which came back at the end of January 2003 with their final bids. These included banking details, investment levels, legal aspects and service agreements for directors. At the next round, after weighing up all the factors, the warranties, banking relationships and the people in the VC firm NCC would have to live with, it was decided to go with Barclays Private Equity. While the exact shape of the £31 ($49.6/€36.6) million deal had still to be thrashed out, BPE was given a one-month exclusive period and NCC's number two string was kept warm.

The management, who was going to take the money and leave, fell out with aspects of the deal and refused to talk to Cotton for three months. Intensive negotiations with managers, VCs and everyone else concerned had to take place and the business, in a highly competitive market, had still to be run. Cotton says the key for him was having a great corporate financier. The NCC Group had for some time been using Stuart Moss, a partner in Rickitt Mitchell, a local Manchester firm. Moss knew Cotton, NCC's technology, business and management team. The parties were pulled back together and a rigid timetable got the deal concluded and the management paid off by April. Good professional advice saved 20 per cent in fees and was critical in resolving conflicts. The company was admitted to the AIM in July 2004 and the main London Stock Market three years later.

The world's stock markets

How many stock exchanges are there? You may have heard of the LSE (London Stock Exchange and NYSE (New York Stock Exchange), with the more informed adding Frankfurt, Tokyo and perhaps Paris. Those guessing five, or even 10 or 20, are way off. The answer is around 200. The big markets compete with alternative platforms, brokerage networks for market share and about a third of equities trading occurs off-exchange. Alternative trading outfits, such as Direct Edge, won share with innovative pricing and are seeking the legitimacy of exchange status. PLUS, AIM and Peer BATS, already exchanges, are themselves launching new platforms, such as CBOE's C2, a new European exchange.

Dozens of unfamiliar names are crowding onto the stage. Chi-X, only launched in 2008, became the second largest European bourse by turnover in less than three years, overtaking old hands such as Deutsche Bourse in the process. Chi-X, BATS Europe and Turquoise were launched on the back of new European Commission rules that broke the national monopoly of the exchanges. These and others were all backed by banks, the exchanges' largest customers, irritated by the old guard's high fees and slow technology.

The goal of these exchanges is to tailor charges and rebates to attract different order flows – from retail money to the high-frequency traders – and in the process create what every listed company requires, liquidity, so generating a ready market in their shares. This competition has reduced execution costs for all traders and spurred companies into listing on several exchanges at the same time.

You can check out all the world stock markets, from Australia to Zagreb on Stock Exchanges World Wide Links (**www.tdd.lt/slnews/Stock_Exchanges/ Stock.Exchanges.htm**) maintained by Aldas Kirvaitis of Lithuania and at World Wide-Tax.com (**www.worldwide-tax.com**>World Stock Exchanges). Once in the stock exchanges' websites, almost all of which have pages in English, look for a term such as 'Listing Center', 'Listing' or 'Rules'. There you will find the latest criteria for floating a company on that particular exchange.

Timetable to a float

While you may never have done an IPO, as the first launch of shares to the public is known, an MBA Business Finance will have to be able to appear as though he or she knows the ropes thoroughly. Copenhagen Business

School's Professor Luiss Guido Carli lectures on the dangers of under-pricing IPOs and Harvard Business School has a whole library of articles on IPO strategies.

The process used to take about six months to execute; now it is routinely being done in half that time. Though it may vary from exchange to exchange the timetable looks broadly like the following.

Week 1. Pick underwriters to take your company to market. This involves listening to a dozen or more bankers telling you why they are number one in doing your type of IPO. At the rate of three a day this can be a wearying experience, listening to depressingly similar presentations. The bankers will all have done successful IPOs before, probably by the dozen, so you will be looking more for empathy than technical competence. At the end of the week you need to have chosen a lead and probably a couple of co-managers to help spread the good word about your great business to the share-buying community.

Week 2. The lead manager begins drafting the company's prospectus. This involves sucking dry the board, management team and your account-ants of background information. Your CFO will be involved full-time in this process, so better get some financial back-up in place to deal with routine matters.

Week 3. The company team and bankers collaborate on the prospectus. By now fairly junior staff will be handling the process. The stars your com-pany met on week one's presentations have moved on to sell the next deal. This process can involve several eight-hour days with people from your law, banking and accounting firms going through the documentation line by line.

This involves a delicate balance between outlining the risks while simul-taneously describing the business and the investment prospects in a way that will appeal. You can see how other companies have gone about this process by looking at their filings on the London Stock Exchange and Securities and Exchange Commission (SEC) websites. In the end this due diligence process should have flushed out any worries and concerns about you or your business.

Week 4. The lead manager files the registration document with the LSE/ SEC, or its equivalent in the country you plan to list.

Weeks 5–8. The lead bankers and you and your team prepare the road-show presentation and wait for the LSE/SEC to digest your documents.

Week 9. The LSE/SEC responds with 20 pages of nitpicking questions: 'What do you mean by "online response times"?' and, 'Can you provide evidence that your client x is one of the largest drinks manufacturers in Spain?' There may well be a second round of questions a few weeks later, but by now you will have got the measure of how to reply.

Probity is important in this whole process. What is required is trans-parency, the Nirvana of the share-dealing community. The World Online float on the Amsterdam Exchange (AEX) in the spring of 2000 is a salutary warning on disclosure. The company was at the time Europe's largest internet service provider. It generated an enormous amount of interest among Dutch private investors, the company's home base, with 150,000 subscribing in the March IPO at a price of €43 (£36.4/$58.2). Within six weeks the price was down to €14.80 (£12.5/$20). The reason given for the slump in price was that World Online's chairman, Nina Brink, had disposed of some of her shares to US private equity fund Baystar Capital, three months before the float. The price she sold at was €6.04 (£5.11/$8.19) and Baystar sold in the first few days of trading at over €30 (£25.4/$40.7). Brink was accused of making allegedly misleading statements during the offer period, and was forced to resign. Unhappy shareholders immediately reached for their lawyers.

Week 10. The lead manager plans the roadshow. Your team go to the bank and sell the company to its institutional sales force. They then get to work with their clients to persuade them to subscribe for your stock. Everyone is bound by what are known as 'the rules' that govern the 'quiet period', which extends from due diligence until a set time after the IPO. Over this period the company must be careful not to hype the stock or do anything that would lead to speculation about your firm's performance in the press.

There are also rules explaining exactly what you can and cannot say to the press. It's generally best to say nothing. If one of your competitors is doing an IPO their quiet period is a good time to hit at them in the press, or to go out and buy a business you know they might want. They are in effect in limbo and can't retaliate.

This is where the institutional sales team come into their own. Via an ancient ritual of winks, nudges, passive verbs, rhetorical questions and comparisons, they get their story across. The lead bank's sales team can be a mighty force indeed. Goldman Sachs, for example has several hundred front-line sales people in its IPO team, and that can result in a very big message reaching a lot of potential investors.

Weeks 11–12. A glorified travel agent in the bank fixes up a punishing schedule, known as the 'roadshow'. This is the reverse of week one, when people were selling to you. Now your team are selling the stock to institutional investors. This could involve as many as 80 meetings across three continents in 13 days. A lot can be said at roadshow meetings, but the only document that can be handed out is the approved prospectus. Anything else could be a violation of the rules.

Commitments start to come in from the institutions. 'I'll take 250,000, but only if it's priced below £20. At £25 I'll only take 100,000.' The bank's syndicate manager has to make sense of this anticipated demand to come up with an IPO price.

Week 13. The day of the IPO. Assuming stock markets have not gone into one of their all too frequent nose dives, the bank's market maker figures out the highest price someone will sell and someone will buy at and set a price, usually above the opening price and the price at which the institutions have bought. If the markets have plunged and you have to pull the IPO, it's like slipping down a long snake back to the bottom of the snakes and ladders board. You may get another crack at it in six months, or perhaps never. One entrepreneur likened doing his IPO to childbirth: painful, glorious, but not to be done again (see the Travelport case study below).

Your company is now public, the bank collects 7 per cent of the proceeds, your board and shareholders are rich, as are you if you negotiated stock options into your employment terms. Your company now has the funds and credibility to get back to growing the business.

If the market maker has got the price too high and the shares plunge quickly it will leave a sour taste in everyone's mouth. The pre-float shareholders can't realize their gain for months after the float, and having a paper profit slashed in half, as for example with lastminute.com's float, will not endear you to the staff. The institutions will be sitting on a loss, and while they are grown up enough to take it on the chin, they will be very wary when you come back for more money. It is usually best to set the price at a rate that will see the shares rising in the weeks and months following a float. That makes for better press coverage too, which inevitably impacts on customers, suppliers and potential employees.

CASE STUDY Travelport

On Thursday 11 February 2010 Jeff Clarke, chief executive of Travelport, the US travel group, had a tough decision to make. The group, which includes Worldspan and Galileo that provide reservation software systems to the travel industry, and Gullivers Travel Associates, a wholesaler of accommodation, ground travel and tours, was profitable and growing well.

For weeks he had been touring the boardrooms of institutional investors trying to drum up support for the IPO planned for later in the year. Blackstone, the private equity group that owned 70 per cent of Travelport, hoped the float would raise $1.9 billion and so allow it to reduce its stake to 30 per cent, half the group's debt, and bring in cash needed for other investment opportunities. But serious market volatility and growing uncertainty in the equity meant there was little appetite for the shares, and what appetite there was at a strike price of 190 cents, a long way below the 210–290 that was required to achieve its goals. The group's detractors claimed the gearing was too high and the P/E (price earnings) too expensive to be the sort of seriously compelling proposition that was essential to get IPOs off the ground in uncertain times. Reluctantly, Clarke decided to postpone the float, while Credit Suisse, Deutsche Bank, UBS, Barclays and Citigroup, all joint book runners to the group, remained tight-lipped.

Travelport's experience in getting its IPO off the ground was by no means unusual in 2009/10. Back in 1996 over 600 companies went public in the

US alone. In 2009 just 41 new companies got listed, and the rest of the world didn't fare much better. One exception to this gloomy situation is China. In 2009 Chinese companies accounted for almost a quarter of all listings on US stock markets as well as number of local listings too.

Stock markets – a brief history

One thing that truly separates MBAs from the rest is having some appreciation of the history of major business milestones. Having such a grasp, used judiciously, never fails to impress. Stock markets have an interesting and longer pedigree than most people in business would guess. Many would put them down as a fairly modern phenomenon, perhaps even giving the start of the last century as their starting point. They would, however, be seriously wrong, if that were their view.

The need for stock exchanges developed out of early trading activities in agricultural and other commodities. During the Middle Ages, traders found it easier to use credit that required supporting documentation of drafts, notes and bills of exchange. The history of the earliest stock exchange, the French stock exchange, goes back to the 12th century when transactions occurred in commercial bills of exchange. To control this budding market, Phillip the Fair, of France (1268–1314) created the profession of *couratier de change*, which was the predecessor of the French stockbroker. At about the same time, in Bruges, merchants began gathering in front of the house of the Van Der Buerse family to engage in trading. Soon the name of the family became identified with trading and in time a 'bourse' came to signify a stock exchange. At the same time, stock exchanges began to materialize in other trading centres like the Netherlands (Amsterdam Bourse) and Frankfurt (the Deutsche Stock Exchange, formerly the Börse).

In 1698, when one John Castaing in 'Jonathan's Coffee-house' in Exchange Alley in the City of London began publishing a list of stock and commodity prices called 'The Course of the Exchange and other things', the business of stock exchanges really got under way. By 1761 a group of 150 stockbrokers and jobbers had formed a club at Jonathan's to buy and sell shares. In 1773 the brokers erected their own building in Sweeting's Alley, with a dealing room on the ground floor and a coffee room above. Briefly known as 'New Jonathan's', members soon altered the name to 'The Stock Exchange'.

It was not until 1791 that the United States had its first bourse when the Philadelphia traders organized a stock exchange. The following year, 21 New York traders agreed to deal with each other under a buttonwood tree on Wall Street. By 1794 the market had moved indoors. India's premier stock exchange, the Bombay Stock Exchange (BSE), can trace its origins as far back as 125 years when it started as a voluntary non-profit-making association. In the 1870s, a securities system was introduced in Japan and public bond negotiation began. This resulted in the request for a public trading institution, and the 'Stock Exchange Ordinance' was enacted in

May 1878. Based on this ordinance, the Tokyo Stock Exchange Co. Ltd. was established on 15 May 1878 and trading began on 1 June.

These early stock exchanges were gentlemen's clubs governed only by a few house rules. Trading rarely started before 10.30 am and was over by 15.30 pm. No records were filed, no rules governed the case of a trader who could not deliver what he had sold and nothing prevented prices being manipulated.

What investors want

The legal structures – partnerships and limited companies in their various forms (see Chapter 5) – have made it easier and safer for entrepreneurs to raise money. But what exactly do investors want in return? Well, unsurprisingly they too are using something like the factors outlined in Chapter 3, which I recommend you use to evaluate a business opportunity for yourself. Investors would like the problem your product or service addresses to be a big one; they would like to see that your solution is scalable and that there is some discernable barrier preventing others entering your market too quickly. They want a few other things as well.

Evidence of customer acceptance

Backers like to know that your new product or service will sell and is being used, even if only on a trial or demonstration basis. The founder of Solicitec, a company selling software to solicitors to enable them to process relatively standard documents such as wills, had little trouble getting support for his house conveyancing package once his product had been tried and approved by a leading building society for its panel of solicitors. If you are only at the prototype stage, then as well as having to assess your chances of succeeding with the technology, financiers have no immediate indication that, once made, your product will appeal to the market. Under these circumstances you have to show not only that the 'problem' your innovation seeks to solve is substantial but that your product is one that a large number of people will have a compelling need for, and be willing to pay for, in a foreseeable timescale.

There really is a market

One inventor from the Royal College of Art came up with a revolutionary toilet system design that, as well as being extremely thin, used 30 per cent less water per flush and had half the number of moving parts of a conventional product, all for no increase in price. Although he had only drawings to show, it was clear that with domestic metered water for all households a distinct possibility and a UK market for half a million new units per

FIGURE 7.1   Funding appetite

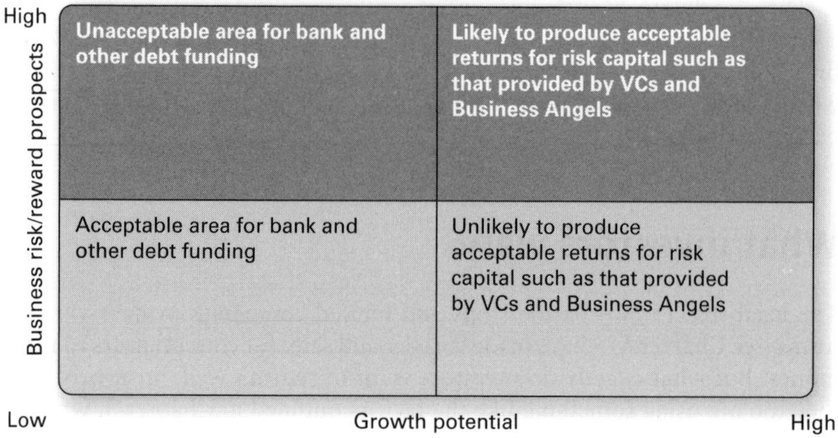

(vertical axis label: Business risk/reward prospects, from Low to High; horizontal axis label: Growth potential, from Low to High)

Unacceptable area for bank and other debt funding	**Likely to produce acceptable returns for risk capital such as that provided by VCs and Business Angels**
Acceptable area for bank and other debt funding	Unlikely to produce acceptable returns for risk capital such as that provided by VCs and Business Angels

annum, a sizeable acceptance was reasonably certain. As well as evidence of customer acceptance, entrepreneurs need to demonstrate that they know how and to whom their new product or service must be sold, and that they have a financially viable means of doing so.

Figure 7.1 shows the funding appetite of various sources of funds. VCs, business angels and indeed any source of share capital will only be attracted to propositions that combine high growth potential with a high risk/reward potential. Banks and other lenders will be attracted to almost the opposite profile, looking instead for a stable less risky proposition that at least offers some security for the capital sum they are putting up.

Personal qualities

At the end of the day every investment boils down to people. So you, your career progression, your knowledge, skills and experience will all be uppermost in an investor's mind when reviewing your proposition. Tim Waterstone, for example, the founder of the Waterstone's bookstore chain, had first-hand experience of running a chain of bookshops.

Team worker

Investors are rarely interested in supporting one-man bands. They want the security that having a team brings, even if it's only a team of two. They also know that few people have all the skills needed to get a substantial venture off the ground. Bebo and Money Supermarket (see the case studies below) are examples of the different skill sets that teams can bring beyond that of a single entrepreneur. Investors also know that teamwork is essential if the business is to become valuable and the sooner they see that attribute being exhibited the better.

CASE STUDY Bebo

Michael Birch had what might be seen as six dummy runs before co-founding Bebo. He was a pioneer in the world of social networking sites, starting up Ringo.com back in 2003 and selling it on quickly – with the benefit of hindsight, perhaps too quickly. Operating out of a 120 sq ft office in the suburbs of San Francisco, overwhelmed with the initial site traffic and lacking finance, he sold Ringo within six months.

Birch and his wife Xochi met up while studying physics at Imperial College London. After a six-year slog at Zurich Insurance in computer programming he left frustrated by the overly bureaucratic environment, a lesson in organizational behaviour that he was to apply to advantage in future ventures. The Birchs then started out on their path as serial entrepreneurs. Their first three dotcom start-ups were unsuccessful, then their luck changed. BirthdayAlarm.com, initially a simple alert service that evolved into an e-cards business, was followed by Ringo, whose sale gave them some cash to roll into a more substantial venture. Applying everything they had learnt from Ringo and what wasn't working on MySpace, the Birch's aimed Bebo squarely at the 30-somethings, but rapidly refocused on teenagers, the site's early adopters.

Within two years of starting, Bebo.com became the most visited social networking site from within the UK, attracting 10.6 million unique visitors, an increase of 63 per cent over the start, and ahead of Myspace.com, with just 10.1 million unique visitors. Selling up to AOL in March 2008 left the Birches some £295 ($472/€348) million for their 70 per cent stake and some pointers as to how their next venture will be run. Being able to attract and manage veterans of the internet from such as companies as Google, Yahoo! and MSN and fostering their loyalty, Birch claims, is the main 'non-marketing' key to their success.

Money Supermarket (www.moneysupermarket.com)

Founded in a bedroom by Simon Nixon and Duncan Cameron in 1999, Money Supermarket grew to have revenues in excess of £100 ($160/€118) million barely a decade later. Nixon was a drop-out from an accounting course at Nottingham University, leaving halfway through the second year. He initially worked as a self-employed financial consultant and persuaded Cameron, a computer geek and his girlfriend's brother, to give up a computer studies course at Liverpool University to write the software programs that were crucial to the launch of the venture.

By the summer of 2007, on the eve of its stock market float, it was valued at around £1 billion, more than 30 times its previous year's profits. As the name would suggest, the business is an internet-based price comparator that started out in the financial services sector and now covers a myriad of other sectors including utilities, travel and general shopping. The value proposition is that Money Supermarket saves you hours surfing the net yourself. But despite some fairly complicated technology the business model is little more than the tried and tested role of the intermediary or broker doing the sums for their client that Nixon started out with when he started his first business, Mortgage 2000.

Hybrids

A number of financing methods straddle the debt and equity boundary. These try to mitigate taking a bit more risk for the potential of a bit more return that would be usual with debt financing. But they also limit the upside that might be expected from pure equity, which would retain all of any increase in value from the outset.

Convertible preference shares operate as with preference shares, in that their holders rank before ordinary shareholders for dividend payments, or return of funds in the case of failure. They also have the option at some specified date in the future to convert to ordinary shares and so enjoy all of any increase in value.

Mezzanine finance has one or all of these characteristics: it ranks after other forms of debt but before equity for any payout in the event of a business failing; it pays higher, often significantly higher, interest than other debt; it can be held for up to 10 years; and it can be converted into ordinary shares. It is popular with VCs for management buy-outs.

Money for free

There is little an MBA can do that is viewed with greater favour than bringing cost-free money into a business. It's never easy to do, takes longer than you think and much more effort than the word 'free' might encourage you to think. But it can be done and the payback for both the business and the MBA who secures the funds can be disproportionately large.

Grants

Government agencies at both national and local government level as well as some extra-governmental bodies such as the EU offer grants, effectively free or nearly free money in return for certain behaviour. It may be to encourage research into a particular field, stimulate innovation or employment, or to persuade a company to locate in a particular area. Grants are constantly being introduced (and withdrawn), but there is no system that lets you know automatically. You have to keep yourself informed.

Business Link (**www.businesslink.gov.uk**>Finance and grants>Grants and government support), has advice on how to apply for a grant as well as a directory of grants on offer. Microsoft Small Business Centre (**www.micro-soft.com/uk/businesscentral/euga/home.aspx**) has a European Union Grant Adviser with a search facility to help you find which of the 6,000 grants on offer might suit your business needs. Grants.Gov (**www.grants.gov**) is a guide to how to apply for over 1,000 federal government grants in the United States.

CASE STUDY

Jason and Katherine Salisbury started up their business, Suffolk Farmhouse Cheeses, in a renovated rundown cowshed next to their home. They bought second-hand equipment and, despite having two young children, have put in 18-hour days since going it alone in 2004. Their annual turnover is now £275,000 ($440,000/€324,000) which they have financed in part with an £80,000 ($128,000/€94,000) bank loan from HSBC. Now they are entering business competitions to fund expansion. They narrowly missed out on £30,000 ($48,000/€35,000) government grant in their first year of operations, but since then have won through to the regional heats of the HSBC's Start-up Stars Awards from which they could win a similar sum.

Social enterprise

If the business you work for or a division of it is concerned primarily with achieving sustainable social change, then you are in a field that is fast becoming mainstream – social enterprise. There are plenty of government bodies and foundations around the world that could bankroll such activities. In the UK there is an annual Queen's Award for Industry for Sustainable Development, an ACCA Award for the Best Social Accounts and a School for Social Entrepreneurs (**www.sse.org.uk**) that helps would-be social entrepreneurs to get started. The Schwab Foundation (**www.schwabfound.org**) covers much the same ground in the United States.

According to government statistics, around 55,000 businesses trade with a social or environmental purpose across the UK. They contribute massively to the national economy and substantially benefit their local communities by creating employment opportunities, providing ethical products and services, and reinvesting surpluses into society. The primary motivation for this type of venture is to build an ethical business that is of benefit to the wider community. As one social entrepreneur put it, 'I am trying to build a little part of the world in which I would like to live.' Money is important, but getting rich is not.

CASE STUDY   Oneworld Health (**www.oneworldhealth.org**) – an agent of positive change

Established by Victoria Hale, a social entrepreneur and pharmacologist based in San Francisco, Oneworld Health is as different from mainstream drug companies as it is possible to be. It has as its vision to 'serve as a positive agent for change by saving lives, improving health, and fulfilling the promise of medicine for those most in need', and has 'Integrity,

Courage, Collaboration' as its values. Oneworld assembles experienced and dedicated teams of pharmaceutical scientists to identify the most promising drugs and vaccine candidates and develops them into safe, effective and affordable medicines. Then it partners with companies, not-for-profit hospitals and organizations in the developing world to conduct medical research on new cures. Oneworld manufactures and distributes newly approved therapies such as those that tackle malaria, the cause of 300–500 million acute illnesses and over 1 million deaths annually. The company scours the virtual shelves of big pharmaceutical companies looking for drugs that for some reason failed to get to market, perhaps because the market proved too small, the benefits too few or in some other way didn't meet the needs of an affluent western market. Hale even persuaded the University of California Santa Barbara to donate a patent for a discovery involving the novel use of calcium channel blockers to control the schistosomiasis parasite. Hale and her team believe that that there are huge inefficiencies in the way drugs are currently devised and produced in the western world and have secured $140 (£87.5/€103) million from the Bill and Melinda Gates Foundation to help in their work.

Using pension assets

Back in 2001 the UK's power supply industry won a landmark ruling in the House of Lords that allowed it to make use of the surplus in its employees' pension fund. This gave companies the green light to begin 'raiding' pension funds, which they duly did. Companies used surpluses for redundancy payments and to finance the pension holidays that allow companies to suspend contributions; all strategies that diverted some of the pension pot to other investments in the business. Although you may have thought pension holidays were ancient history, Shell surprised its employees and the world at large by announcing in October 2007 its 46,000 employees were taking one, giving the company a break too. Changes to pension regulations around the world have made it harder to take contribution holidays unless schemes are showing a healthy surplus of £5 ($8/€6) billion.

This financing strategy is one more likely to be available to private companies with a relatively limited number of participants, usually directors, partners, top managers and shareholders. In these cases the company can pay money out of company profits into either a Small Self-Administered Scheme (SSAS) or a Self-Invested Personal Pension plan (SIPP) and so avoid paying tax. That scheme can then invest in a narrow range of asset classes such as the company's own shares, purchase of commercial property and loans to the company, subject to certain conditions and with the approval of the pension trustees.

Both an SSAS and SIPP can, since April 2006, borrow a sum equivalent to 50 per cent of its net assets to purchase property. Information on SSAS and SIPP pension schemes is available from Westerby Trustee Service (**www.sipp-ssas-pensions.co.uk**) and Clear Financial Solutions (**www.clearfinancialsolutions.co.uk**>Business Solutions>SSAS/SIPP).

PART THREE
Financial strategies and special topics

MBAs are expected to have a grasp of financial management that goes substantially beyond the basics of accounting reports and sources of finance. Sitting near or in the boardroom will give an MBA a ringside seat on mergers, acquisitions, joint ventures and the like. In fact they should be in on every aspect of business planning and strategy formulation as this is where the next rungs up the career ladder will start to appear.

Though the MBA will rarely have much to do directly with tax or foreign exchange, for example – these are more likely to be under the wing of the treasury function – he or she must have a basic appreciation of the impact of these areas on business risk and performance. Tax affairs, if poorly managed, can consume a fifth of a business's hard-won profits and the vagaries of exchange rate fluctuations can erode that further still.

In addition to knowing where a business can raise funds, the MBA needs a sound appreciation of the risks associated with each source and in particular how funding sources can be best balanced to reduce those risks.

These areas are the subject of the third part of the book.

Risk management

08

- Setting an acceptable gearing level
- Dealing with defaulting customers
- Resorting to law
- Managing foreign exchange risks
- Protecting investors
- Finding financial facts

A useful fact for the MBA to know is that the rumour of calamities awaiting most ventures is just that – an unfounded and incorrect piece of oft-repeated misinformation. An exhaustive study of the eight-year destinations of all 814,000 US firms founded in a particular year by Bruce A Kirchoff, Professor of Management at New Jersey Institute of Technology, revealed that just 18 per cent actually failed, meaning that the entrepreneurs were put out of business by their financially backers, lack of demand or competitive pressures. True, some 28 per cent of businesses closed their doors voluntarily, their founders having decided for a variety of reasons that either working for themselves or this particular type of business was just not for them.

But the majority of the businesses studied in Kirchoff's mammoth and representative study survived and in many cases prospered. The European Observatory study carried out a few years later than Kirchoff's and using a smaller sample came to a similar conclusion on survival rates. However, this study added one important extra fact. The failure rate in the early years is much higher than in later years, and by year five of a firm's life the failure curve is flattening off (see Figure 8.1, produced from data in the quoted research studies). Nevertheless, businesses face real and constant dangers from areas of risk that managers can and should understand, and they should take action to limit the potential damage.

FIGURE 8.1 The truth about the risk of failure

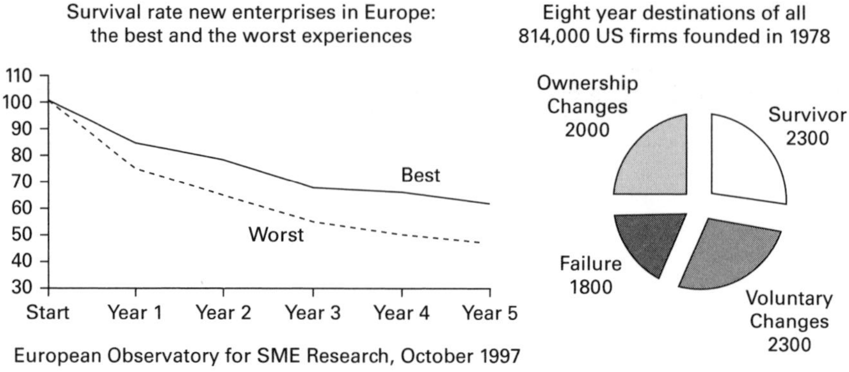
Survival rate new enterprises in Europe: the best and the worst experiences
110
100
90
80
70
60
50
40
30
Start
Year 1
Year 2
Year 3
Year 4
Year 5
Best
Worst
European Observatory for SME Research, October 1997
Eight year destinations of all 814,000 US firms founded in 1978
Ownership Changes 2000
Survivor 2300
Failure 1800
Voluntary Changes 2300

SOURCE: European xxx and Dynamic Capitalism. Kirchoff, 1994.

Gearing – leverage

Despite the esoteric names – debentures, convertible loan stock, preference shares – businesses have access to only two fundamentally different sorts of money. *Equity*, or owner's capital, including retained earnings, is money that is not a risk to the business. If no profits are made, then the owner and other shareholders simply do not get dividends. They may not be pleased, but they cannot usually sue, and even where they can the advisers who recommended the share purchase will be first in line.

Debt capital is money borrowed by the business from outside sources; it puts the business at financial risk and is also risky for the lenders. In return for taking that risk they expect an interest payment every year, irrespective of the performance of the business. 'High gearing' is the term used when a business has a high proportion of outside money to inside money. High gearing has considerable attractions to a business that wants to make high returns on shareholders' capital. But as with economies and consumers, the most common financial risk a business faces is borrowing more money than it can safely service given the vagaries of economic cycles.

How gearing works

Table 8.1 shows an example of a business that is assumed to need 60,000 of capital to generate 10,000 operating profits. Four different capital structures are considered. They range from all share capital (no gearing) at one end to nearly all loan capital at the other. The loan capital has to be 'serviced', that is, interest of 12 per cent has to be paid. The loan itself can be relatively indefinite, simply being replaced by another one at market interest rates when the first loan expires.

TABLE 8.1   The effect of gearing on shareholders' returns

	No gearing	Average gearing	High gearing	Very high gearing
	N/A	1:1	2:1	3:1
Capital structure				
Share capital	60,000	30,000	20,000	15,000
Loan capital (at 12%)	–	30,000	40,000	45,000
Total capital	60,000	60,000	60,000	60,000
Profits				
Operating profit	10,000	10,000	10,000	10,000
Less interest on loan	None	3,600	4,800	5,400
Net profit	10,000	6,400	5,200	4,600
Return on share capital	10,000	6,400	5,200	4,400
	60,000	30,000	15,000	15,000
As percentage	16.6%	21.3%	26%	30.7%
Times interest earned	N/A	10,000	10,000	10,000
		3,600	4,800	5,400
	N/A	2.8 times	2.1 times	1.8 times

Following the table through you can see that return on the shareholders' money (arrived at by dividing the profit by the shareholders' investment and multiplying by 100 to get a percentage) grows from 16.6 to 30.7 per cent by virtue of the changed gearing. If the interest on the loan were lower, the ROSC, or return on shareholders' capital, would be even more improved by high gearing, and the higher the interest, the lower the relative improvement in ROSC. So in times of low interest rates, businesses tend to go for increased borrowings rather than raising more equity, that is money from shareholders.

At first sight this looks like a perpetual profit-growth machine. Naturally shareholders and those managing a business whose bonus depends on shareholders' returns would rather have someone else 'lend' them the money for the business than ask shareholders for more money, especially if by doing so they increase the return investment. The problem comes if the business does not produce the £10,000 operating profits shown in the table. Very often a drop in sales of 20 per cent means profits are halved. If profits were halved in this example, the business could not meet the interest payments on its loan. That would make the business insolvent, and so not in a 'sound financial position'; in other words, failing to meet one of the two primary business objectives.

What is an acceptable level of gearing?

Bankers tend to favour 1:1 gearing as the maximum for a business, although they have been known to go much higher. As well as looking at the gearing, lenders will study the business's capacity to pay interest. They do this by using another ratio called 'times interest earned'. This is calculated by dividing the operating profit by the loan interest. It shows how many times the loan interest is covered, and gives the lender some idea of the safety margin. The ratio for this example is given at the end of Table 8.1. Once again rules are hard to make, but much less than 3 × interest earned is unlikely to give lenders confidence. (See Chapter 3 for a comprehensive explanation of the use of ratios.)

Any decisions about gearing levels have to be taken with the level of business risk involved. Certain categories of venture are intrinsically more risky than others. Businesses selling staple food products where little innovation is required are generally less prone to facing financial difficulties than, say, internet start-ups, where the technology may be unproven with a short shelf-life and the markets themselves uncertain; see Figure 8.2.

FIGURE 8.2   Risk and gearing

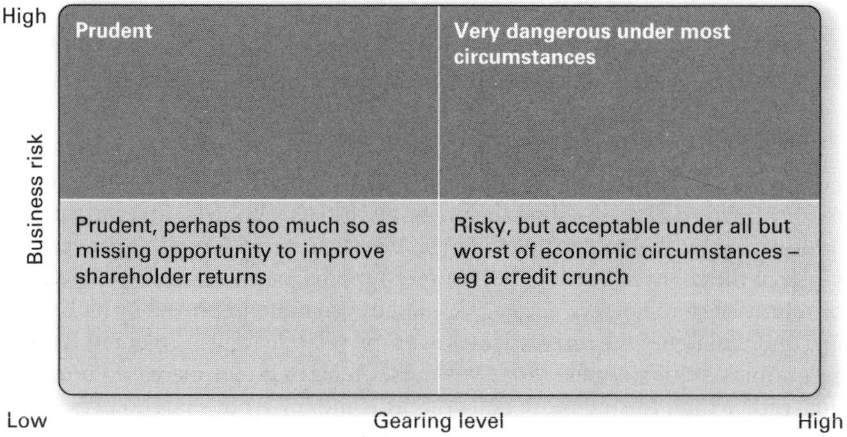

Off balance sheet activity

High gearing levels upset investors, who think their dividend stream will be threatened, and lenders, worried that their loans won't get serviced or repaid. So it's hardly surprising that financial whiz-kids are always looking for smoke and mirrors techniques to get liabilities either off the balance sheet or at least massaged favourably. The crucial date for any activity is the year end, and if that were, say, 31 March, whisking anything damaging out of the way on 30 March only to have it reappear on 1 April would render that item effectively invisible to anyone outside of the enterprise. As long as the auditors will sign off the accounts, assuming they spot it, then all will be well.

So how does this work? Suppose a company has offices bought for £100 million, with £80 million of that provided by way of a commercial mortgage. That £80 million will form part of the company's borrowings and so serve to push up its gearing level. If, using the year end above, the offices could be 'sold' to a third party on 30 March for at least £100 million, both the asset (the office) and the liability (the £80 million mortgage loan) would not show up in the year-end balance sheet. The net effect would be to artificially reduce the company's gearing, which in turn would reassure investors and make lenders more susceptible to approaches for more borrowings. On 1 April, an appropriate date as it happens, both asset and liability re-appear only to be banished again the following year. In reality the company carries the liability (and asset) throughout. No one, save perhaps the board of directors, the CFO and the auditors, will be any the wiser.

This was the technique, known in the trade as Repo 105, used by Lehman Brothers and approved by their auditors, Ernst and Young (E&Y). The sums made invisible in this way while Lehman was in its death throes exceeded $50 billion, sufficient to flatter even the most over-geared balance sheet. Although Repo 105 and similar techniques are in line with internationally acceptable accounting standards, their effect is to mislead. E&Y's annual fees earned from Lehman Brothers were $31 million and they and other financial magicians are often worth paying if the other option is failure.

Customer default

The sale process is not complete until, as one particularly cautious sales director put it: 'the customer has paid, used your product and not died as a consequence'. Although there are theoretically regulations to ensure that big firms pay small businesses promptly there is little evidence they do. Visit Payment League Tables (**www.paymentscorer.com**), a site maintained daily by the Institute of Credit Management and The Credit Management Research Centre. There you can see which sectors and firms are good or getting better, and bad or getting worse when it comes to paying their bills.

One of the top three reasons that businesses run into cash flow problems or in the worst cases fail is that a customer doesn't pay up in full or on time. You can take some steps to make sure this doesn't happen to your firm by setting prudent terms of trade and making sure the customers are creditworthy before you sell to them.

Set your terms of trade

You need to decide on your terms and conditions of sale and ensure they are printed on your order acceptance stationery. Terms should include when and how you require to be paid and under what conditions you will accept cancellations or offer refunds. The websites of the Office of Fair Trading (**www.oft.gov.uk**) and Trading Standards Central (**www.tradingstandards. gov.uk**) contain information on most aspects of trading relationships.

Check creditworthiness

There is a wealth of information on credit status for both individuals and businesses of varying complexity, so there is no need to trade unknowingly with individuals or businesses that pose a credit risk. The major agencies that compile and sell business credit histories include Experian (**www. UKexperian.com**), Dun & Bradstreet (**www.dnb.com**), Creditgate.com (**www. creditgate.com**) and Credit Reporting (**www.creditreporting.co.uk/b2b**). Between them they offer a comprehensive range of credit reports instantly online, including advice on credit limits and CCJs (County Court Judgments). Figure 8.3 shows part of a 16-page credit report that culminates in a specific score, giving the user some idea of the likelihood of getting paid, and an indication of how much credit should be extended to the company.

Get credit insurance

If your company can get a factoring company or invoice discounter to take on your clients, most of the risk of default will be covered by them. In return for a fee they will even take on responsibility for collecting money owed and pursue late payers. A recent independent research study of 2,000 businesses in 10 European economies by the Credit Management Research Centre at Leeds University Business School indicates that bad debts represent on average of 0.74 per cent for non-insured companies against 0.38 per cent for companies using credit insurance. While that may not sound too dramatic, when you consider that most companies make less than 10 per cent profit, losing 0.36 per cent through lack of insurance (0.74 − 0.38) is a hefty slice – around 3.6 per cent of potential extra gains.

Credit insurers' business proposition rests simply on the fact that they have better information – the big ones track the performance of over 40 million companies worldwide. Also, they don't have to base their credit decisions on short-term risks solely on the basis of an 18-month old P&L and balance sheet and a rough credit score. Regional risk offices established in the major cities are in charge of making direct contact with buyers (the clients of their clients) and of obtaining the most up-to-date information on their financial position. You can read more on this subject in Chapter 6 in the section on discounting and factoring.

FIGURE 8.3 Part of a credit report

Risk Score

Today's:	59
Previous:	27 until (28/06/2008)

Historical Trend

56 until (28/06/2008)
54 until (30/06/2007)
42 until (24/06/2006)
43 until (25/06/2005)

Score Key

0–35	Caution, High risk potential.
36–50	Caution, Moderate risk. Measured exposure.
51–60	Normal, Limited risk potential, Normal terms.
61–100	Confidence, Low risk potential.

Credit Limit (GBP)

Today's:	430,000
Previous:	100,000 until (28/06/2008)
Contract Limit (GBP):	6,000,000

There was a very significant Increase in Sales from £49,359,000 to £68,142,000 for the period ending 28/06/08.

The latest Accounts show an increase in Pre-tax Profits from £3,175,000 to £3,874,000.

Shareholders Funds increased from £1,247,000 to £5,584,000, while Total Assets Increased from £23,342,000 to £30,246,000.

The percentage of Profit in each unit of sales of 5.69 is above the industry average of 3.30.

The business activity in which this company is involved contains a higher amount of insolvencies compared to total population averages.

The company has been established for more than 13 years.

County Court Judgments Summary:	Number of exact unsatisfied CCJs: None
	Number of probable unsatisfied CCJs: None
	Number of possible unsatisfied CCJs: None

Do your own due diligence

There may be occasions when even the most creditworthy customers can't get credit insurance. The credit crunch of 2008–10 is a good recent example, but that of 1973–74 was severe also. So a company may have to make its own judgement on whether to risk supplying a customer. First off you will have to read the accounts. The important measures will be those that affect liquidity (a company's ability to meet short-term obligations) and solvency (the current level of borrowed money compared to the owners' investment).

Use the knowledge acquired in Chapter 3 to decide whether or not to supply to EAT Ltd on credit, based on the information in the company's accounts (see Figures 8.4 and 8.5; source: **www.thesmehub.com** – register for free then go to Member Services, Company Accounts Lookup and enter name).

The first slightly worrying observation is that while turnover is up – £75,544,025 compared to £68,141,924, profits are down – £2,110,808 compared to £4,336,980. Still, this is hardly surprising given the seriously difficult trading conditions during the worst recession the UK has experienced since the Second World War.

FIGURE 8.4   EAT Ltd profit and loss account for the years to June 2008 and June 2009

Profit and loss account	Period from 29 Jun 08 to 27 Jun 09 £	Period from 1 Jul 07 to 28 Jun 08 £
Turnover	75,544,025	68,141,924
Cost of sales	29,418,496	26,698,725
Gross profit	46,125,529	41,443,199
Distribution and administrative costs	43,425,803	37,682,701
Operating profit	2,699,726	3,760,498
Interest receivable	36,968	113,209
Profit on ordinary activities before taxation	2,736,694	3,873,707
Tax on profit on ordinary activities	(625,886)	463,273
Profit for the financial period	2,110,808	4,336,980

FIGURE 8.5 EAT Ltd balance sheets for June 2008 and June 2009

	27 Jun 09 £	28 Jun 08 £
Fixed assets		
Tangible assets	19,430,664	19,243,215
Current assets		
Stocks	649,140	644,978
Debtors	5,149,512	4,932,339
Cash at bank and in hand	6,227,386	5,425,881
	12,026,038	11,003,198
Creditors: amounts falling due within one year	11,284,968	12,147,727
Net current assets/(liabilities)	741,070	(1,144,529)
Total assets less current liabilities	20,171,734	18,098,686
Creditors: amounts falling due after more than one year	12,476,344	12,514,104
	7,695,390	5,584,582
Capital and reserves		
Called-up share capital	4,400,368	4,400,368
Share premium account	1,438,315	1,438,315
Profit and loss account	1,856,707	(254,101)
	7,695,390	5,584,582

There are, however, three pieces of positive information. First, the company has a lot more cash in 2009 (£6,227,385) compared to 2008 (£5,425,881). Also it is paying its creditors (which will include us if we decide to supply) faster, in 54.52 days (£11,284,968/£75,544,025 × 355) compared to 65.07 days in 2008 (£12,147,727/£68,141,924 × 365). Finally, although it is heavily geared – 1.62:1 (£12,476,344/£7,695,390) that is a lot lower gearing than in the previous year, which was 2.24:1 (£12,514,104/£5,584,582). The EAT case study gives the company's own analysis of the situation.

CASE STUDY EAT – an in-house credit risk assessment study

EAT was founded by Niall MacArthur (49), son of a Scottish Tory MP and his Canadian wife Faith (47). He took an MBA at City University Business School, then for the next 13 years worked in investment banking at Bankers Trust. The first EAT opened beside London's Charing Cross station in 1996 and today there are more than 80 branches, some 20 of them outside London.

EAT's strategy is based on MacArthur's first-hand experience of the shortening of City workers' 'lunch hour' to less than half that time and recognizing that the break from the office was very important: 'It had to be open-ended, fun, sexy and rewarding.' His competitive edge on Prêt a Manger (making sandwiches fresh onsite every day) is where they pride themselves: EAT makes all its own food – sandwiches, sushi, salad and soup – in its 15,000 sq ft (1,394 sq m) kitchen in Wembley. That in turn means they can serve faster food.

The board comprises managing director, founder and main shareholder Niall Mac-Arthur, owning more than 35 per cent of the company, who is mainly concerned with property acquisitions and funding of the chain. His wife Faith is the company's brand director and the power behind EAT's shop design and menu. Also on the board are retail director Colin Hughes, formerly of Prêt a Manger and Marks & Spencer; finance director Fraser Hall, who cut his teeth at pharmaceutical chain McCarthy and restaurant chain Pizzaland; and Stephen Lynn, the non-executive director who came in when 3i bankrolled the company six years ago. In August 2005, 3i sold its stake to private equity firm Penta Capital in a refinancing of the business.

In June 2008 it was announced that MacArthur planned to sell EAT inspired by the successful £345 ($552/€407) million sale of rival fast-food group Prêt a Manger to Bridgepoint. The company and its shareholders appointed advisers at PricewaterhouseCoopers (PWC) to carry out a strategic review of the business to facilitate the sale. No sale has yet gone through and this seems to have been parked until the economic climate has improved significantly.

The last five audited years' accounts are all listed as 'clean' and show sales growing at a compound rate of 21.5 per cent per annum to the current level of circa £70 ($112/€82.6) million. The last year's post-tax profit as filed was £4.3 ($6.9/€5.1) million, up from £3.3 ($5.3/€3.9) million in the preceding year.

The gross margin is 60 per cent, there is no debt, either long or short term, the net worth is about £6 ($9.6/€7) million with some £5.4 ($8.6/€6.4) million of cash in the bank. Although not able to match its current assets to its current liabilities, the litmus test of sound liquidity, its position is fast improving. Over the past five years the current ratio has improved each year, moving from 0.29 to 0.82 (greater than 1 is the optimal ratio). Normally a business selling food to retail customers for cash while taking around 40 days to settle its bills would be highly liquid, but EAT has used all the cash it can get to fuel its growth.

As far as credit rating is concerned the position is improving. Until 2007 it was ranked as being *moderately risky*; since then it has moved well into the *normal risk* bracket as its current score of 59 puts it just two points away from the score of 61 that is required to move into the lowest risk bracket. The company's total assets exceed £30 ($48/€35) million, up from £23 ($37/€27) million last year, and it is significantly more profitable than the average for the sector (EAT makes 5.69 per cent net profit compared to the industry average of 3.3 per cent).

So why won't credit insurers cover them? The main problems seem to be that the sector contains a much higher than average rate of insolvencies, so insurers will err on the side of caution; and the company has used supplier credit to fuel its fast growth, in effect using that money instead of providing more share capital *or* taking on any borrowings. This means suppliers have become bankers and investors, without any of the security that bankers would normally expect, or any of the upside that would accrue to shareholders from the businesses success. That in turn makes credit insurers wary as they too are carrying more risk than they would like.

Should we supply EAT without credit insurance cover?

The question hinges on EAT's capacity to survive and prosper in the present economic climate. In its favour is its relatively low price point, meaning it is still affordable, despite the fact that there are fewer people in jobs and more of them are bringing in their own lunches. Also, the company is very profitable, has a strong board of directors with both the expertise and track record to raise outside funds, and it has the capacity to take on borrowings if necessary. If EAT is one of the very few customers being supplied without insurance it would seem a risk worth taking on a measured basis.

Keep track of aged debtors

An important responsibility of management is to track how those who owe money for services and products comply with their obligations. Figure 8.6 shows that 14 per cent of debtors have exceeded the due date. As well as having the overall picture, a print out of the individual picture, account by account, will enable management to pursue debtors with the appropriate vigour. Not all late payers will become delinquent. In some cases the inflexibility of their payment systems is to blame. For example, some companies have cheque runs once a month only, so if an invoice comes in just after that date it could be close to eight weeks before it would have any chance of being paid. Creditor policies calling for payment in 30 days would register such cases as being in default, so clearly some oversight of the system is required.

FIGURE 8.6   Age analysis of debtors' invoices

Duration from invoice date	% of total debtors	Cumulative total %	Number of accounts
0–14 days	28	28	264
15–28 days	25	53	205
29–42 days	19	72	147
43–56 days Due date	14	86	82 Due date
57–70 days	7	93	38
71–84 days	4	97	16
85–98 days	2	99	20
99+ days	1	100	7

Warning signals that creditors are getting into financial difficulties include:

- cheques bouncing;
- partial payments being offered;
- post-dated payments being offered;
- claims that payments have been lost in the post;
- claims that the necessary signatories or payment approvers are away.

Dealing with delinquents

It usually falls to the finance department to deal with any problems relating to late or non-payment of accounts. However prudent your terms of trade and rigorous your credit checks, you will end up with late payers and at worst non-payers. There are ways to deal with them, but experience shows that once something starts to go wrong it usually gets worse. There is an old investment saying: 'the first loss is the best loss' that applies here.

Chasing debtors

The most cost-effective and successful method of keeping late payers in line is to let them know you know. Nine out of 10 small businesses do not routinely send out reminder letters advising customers that they have missed the payment date. Send out a polite reminder to arrive the day after payment is due, addressed to the person responsible for payments, almost invariably someone in the accounts department if you are dealing with a big organization. Follow this up within five days with a phone call, keeping the pressure on steadily until you are paid.

If you are polite and professional, consistently reminding them of your terms of trade, there is no reason your relationship will be impaired. In any event, the person you sell to may not be the person you chase for payment.

If you still have difficulty consider using a debt collection agency. You can find a directory of registered agents on the Credit Service Agency Website (**www.csa-uk.com/csa**>Members list).

Resorting to law

There are a number of ways in which you can use the courts in a cost-effective manner to recover money owed, short of appointing your own lawyers:

- *The Small Claims Court* is for people whose claim is for relatively small sums that would not be worth pursuing if you had to hire lawyers. Be warned, however, even if you win in the Small Claims Court you can still have problems enforcing the judgement and getting bad debtors to pay up. You can find information on the Small Claims Court at **www.courtservice.gov.uk**.

- *Money Claim Online* (**www.moneyclaim.gov.uk/csmco2/index.jsp**) is a service where those with claims of up to £100,000 can sue through the internet at any time, day or night. If the claim is undefended, the money can be recovered without anyone having to go to court.

- *Arbitration*, which involves an independent person listening to the arguments of both sides and making a commonsense decision, is a less expensive, faster and less threatening way of getting disputes resolved. You have to agree to be bound by the decision and as with any other 'judgement', you still have to get the loser to pay up. But at least there is no dispute that the money is owed you. The Chartered Institute of Arbitrators (**www.arbitrators.org**) and its European Branch (**www.european-arbitrators.org**) have information on the arbitration process and a database of professional arbitrators.

Before you resort to law

You should take one last precautionary measure before you chase debtors too hard. Make sure you are legally entitled to payment. Nothing will get as much egg on an MBA's face as discovering after a lengthy and expensive exercise in trying to force payment that the customer has a 'get out of gaol card' tucked away.

Customers buying products are entitled to expect that the goods are 'fit for purpose' in that they can do what they claim and, if the customer has informed you of a particular need, that they are suitable for that purpose. The goods also have to be of 'satisfactory quality', ie durable and without defects that would affect performance or prevent their enjoyment. For services you must carry the work out with reasonable skill and care and provide it within a reasonable amount of time. The word 'reasonable' is not defined and is applied in relation to each type of service. So, for example, repairing a shoe might reasonably be expected to take a week, while three months would be unreasonable.

If goods or services don't meet these conditions customers can claim a refund. If they have waited an excessive amount of time before complaining or have indicated in any other way that they have 'accepted' they may not be entitled to a refund, but may still be able to claim some money back for a period of up to six years. Trading Standards (**www.tradingstandards.gov.uk**> For business>guidance leaflets>A Trader's Guide to the Civil Law Relating to the Sale and Supply of Goods and Services) provides a summarized guide to the relevant laws in clear plain English.

Online and distance trading

The fastest growing and potentially the most complex area of business is selling by mail order via the internet, television, radio, telephone, fax or catalogue. Such activities require that you comply with some additional rules over and above those concerning the sale of goods and services described above. In summary, you have to provide written information, an order confirmation, and the chance to cancel the contract. During the 'cooling off period' customers have the unconditional right to cancel within seven working days, provided they have informed you in writing by letter, fax or e-mail.

There are, however, a wide range of exemptions to the right to cancel including accommodation, transport, food, newspapers, audio or video recordings and goods made to a customer's specification. The Office of Fair Trading (**www.oft.gov.uk**>Advice and resources>Advice for businesses> Selling at a distance) publishes a guide for businesses on distance selling.

Foreign exchange

It is almost inconceivable that an MBA will be working in a company that has no dealings with either overseas customers or foreign suppliers. This in turn means handling money in at least two currencies, your own and the country you will trade in or with. Many countries have their own currency, but not all currencies are equally stable. The less stable the currency the more cost and risk is involved in any transaction.

Key factors to consider about foreign currencies

There are four types of foreign currencies and each have very different risk profiles and need to be managed accordingly:

1 *Not fully convertible*, which means that the government of the country concerned exercises political and economic control over the exchange rate and the amount of its currency that can be moved in or out. China and India are amongst many countries that fall into

this category. These currencies can be very volatile and you will need permission to repatriate money.

2 *Pegged* is the most favourable way to obtain currency stability; it means the local currency is 'pegged' to a major convertible currency, such as the euro or dollar. While the local currency may move up and down against all other world currencies, it will remain or at least attempt to remain stable against the one it is pegged against.

3 *Dollarized* is a slight misnomer as the term is used to describe a country that abandons its own currency and adopts the exclusive use of the US dollar or another major international currency, such as the euro.

4 *Fully convertible* is a currency that stands on its own two feet and fluctuates as the country in question and its economy succeeds or fails. Russia, for example, lifted currency controls in July 2006 as a sign of economic confidence, making the rouble fully convertible.

Types of foreign exchange risk to be managed

A business has two distinct types of foreign exchange risk to consider when it comes to considering which, if any, risk management strategy to pursue.

1. Transaction exposure

Transaction exposure occurs when a business incurs costs or generates revenues in any currency other than the one shown in its filed accounts. Two types of event can lead to an exchange rate risk: a mismatch between cost of sales (manufacturing, etc) incurred in one currency and the actual sales income generated in another; and any time lag between setting the selling price in one currency and the date the customer actually pays up. As it is unlikely that there will have been no movement in exchange rates, transaction risk is real and potentially could have serious consequences.

2. Translation exposure

Translation exposure refers to the effects of movements in the exchange rate on the balance sheet and profit and loss account that occur between reporting dates on assets and liabilities denominated in foreign currencies. In practice any company that has assets or liabilities denominated in a currency other than the currency shown on its reported accounts will have to 'translate' them back into the company's reporting currency when the consolidated accounts are produced. This could be up to four times a year for major trading businesses. Any changes in the foreign exchange rate between the countries involved will cause movements in the accounts that have nothing to do with the underlying economic performance of the company.

Take the case of a UK-based company buying a US company when the exchange rate was £1 to $1.20. The abbreviated balance sheet of the US company (see Figure 8.7) shows that translating at the time of purchase back into £ results in a £ balance sheet total of £200. The following year,

FIGURE 8.7   Foreign exchange translation exposure in millions

Assets	USD	GBP 1.20	GBP 1.50	Liabilities	USD	GBP 1.20	GBP 1.50
Cash	30	24	20	Creditors	190	158	126
Investments	40	34	26	Bank loans	14	12	10
Debtors	130	108	88				
Fixed Assets	40	34	26	Shareholder			
				Funds	36	30	24
	240	200	160		240	200	160

however, the dollar has weakened, resulting in an exchange of $1.50 to £1. This is reflected in the second GBP column, with £ totals of 160. This has the wholly unwelcome effect of showing shareholders' funds reduced by £6 million – but actually the effect is entirely due to translation and might be reversed if the exchange rates move in the dollar's favour at a later date. Nevertheless, a company may feel obliged to manage its way out of the exchange rate effect if, for example, the result was an acceptable debt to equity ratio.

Help with managing foreign exchange risk

These organizations can help an MBA keep on top of foreign exchange matters.

The Reuters Forex Poll ranks HiFX plc within the top three most accurate foreign exchange forecasters globally, beating many of the world's leading banks. As well as carrying out all the functions of dealing in foreign exchange and having the near-ubiquitous currency converter on its website, there is some further information useful to the property investor.

OANDA (**www.oanda.com**) was first to market in making comprehensive currency exchange information available over the internet, and now licenses out to hotels and airlines providing exchange rate information on their websites. From the left-hand menu bar you will find an extensive range of valuable tools including Select FXConverter (Foreign Exchange Currency Converter) to access the multilingual Currency Converter with up-to-date exchange rates covering any of the 164 currencies used around the world. The date function is a neat addition as you can see what rate you would have got in the past. For example, £1 sterling would have bought only $1.41 in 1985, while it bought $1.89 in September 2006, a sizeable 34 per cent appreciation.

The Financial Markets Association website (**www.aciforex.com**>National Associations) has links to the websites of some 90 country-affiliated associations, listed by continent. The country associations contain directories of members.

Business tax and reporting procedures

09

- Tax principles
- The role of auditors
- Filing company reports
- Protecting investors
- Responsibilities of directors
- Ethics and enterprise

One reason a business produces accounts and reports is to enable internal staff to keep track of performance, but while that is an important reason it is not the only one or the most important. It is the parties external to the business, shareholders and government authorities in particular, that have specific expectations and requirements that must be adhered to. Furthermore it's the responsibility of the directors, and by extension their advisers – accountants, MBAs and legal staff – to keep the business on the straight and narrow.

Some business schools take tax and reporting very seriously indeed. California State University, Northridge (CSUN) has offered a Master's of Science in Taxation since the Fall of 2007, consisting of eight courses aiming to provide students with in-depth knowledge of all the key areas of taxation. The University of Southern Maine's MBA Program offers a number of specializations in taxation including Advanced Business Taxation, as well as providing the opportunity for an internship in taxation.

Principles of taxation

Tax in its various forms can account for up to half of a business's turnover. Taxes constitute the largest single creditor, the most likely event to cause a business to fold and ranks first in the pecking order when it comes to the disposal of assets in such an event. These two judgements against the Inland Revenue Commissioner gave the spur to the 'inventive' approach taken to the subject of tax by many businesses and their accountants:

> Every man is entitled if he can to order his affairs so as that the tax attaching under the appropriate Acts is less than it otherwise would be. If he succeeds in ordering them so as to secure the result, then, however unappreciative the Commissioners of Inland Revenue or his fellow taxpayer may be of his ingenuity, he cannot be compelled to pay an increased tax. (Lord Tomkin – IRC v Duke of Westminster, 1936)

> No man in this country is under the smallest obligation, moral or other, so to arrange his legal relations to his business or his property as to enable the Inland Revenue to put the largest possible shovel into his stores. (Lord Clyde – Ayrshire Pullman Motor Services and Ritchie v IRC, 1929)

For business people the justification for tax minimization is overwhelming. No other activity can enhance net profits so dramatically. Every pound, dollar or euro in tax saved drops straight to the bottom line.

Tax evasion, avoidance and mitigation

The opportunities are endless, from the seemingly prudent – Marks & Spencer seeking to obtain group tax relief in respect of losses incurred by certain European subsidiary companies in Belgium, France and Germany – to the plain criminal – stuffing the business with false invoices. China has the dubious distinction of being the world capital of false invoicing. In 2007/8 police there investigated 3,511 cases involving issuing false or tax-offsetting invoices, arrested 2,979 suspects, confiscated 10,510,000 fake invoices, smashed 101 illegal invoice-printing operations and retrieved 9.2 billion yuan in under-declared taxes.

The challenge for directors and managers is to recognize the distinction between different types of behaviour when it comes to tax law:

- *Tax fraud*, often called tax evasion to soften the underlying meaning, involves the intentional behaviour or actual knowledge of the wrongdoing, for example reducing the tax burden by underreporting income, overstating deductions, or using illegal tax shelters; this is a criminal matter.

- *Tax mitigation* involves the taxpayer taking advantage of a fiscally attractive option afforded by the tax legislation and 'genuinely suffers the economic consequences that Parliament intended to be suffered by those taking advantage of the option', as one Law Lord summed up the subject. For example, if a business is allowed to offset the cost of an asset against tax, then so long as it actually buys the asset it is mitigating its tax position.

● *Tax avoidance* lies in the blurred line between tax mitigation and tax fraud and is usually defined by the test of whether your dominant purpose – or your sole purpose – was to reduce or eliminate tax liability.

Tax types

As a business you are responsible for paying a number of taxes and other dues to the government of the day, both on your own behalf and for any employees you may have as well as being an unpaid tax collector required to account for end-consumers' expenditure.

There are penalties for misdemeanours and you are required to keep your accounts for six years, so at any point should tax authorities become suspicious they can dig into the past even after they have agreed your figures. In the case of suspected fraud there is no limit to how far back the digging can go.

Corporation tax

Companies pay tax on their profits at varying rates depending on their size and the amount of profit made. Small companies, currently pay tax at 20 per cent. The rest pay at 28 per cent. Both these tax rates and the break point used to define what constitutes a small company can be adjusted each year in the Budget. The current rates are published on the HM Revenue & Customs website (**www.hmrc.gov.uk/rates/corp.htm**). Corporation tax in many other countries is much lower. Bulgaria, for example, at the time of writing charges 10 per cent, the lowest in the EU.

Corporation tax covers the profit made in an accounting period, usually of one-year duration; it can be shorter under special circumstances, but never longer. Companies are responsibly for working out their own tax liability, paying the tax due and filing their tax return no later than 12 months after the end of the accounting period.

Capital allowances

The purchase of capital items such as plant, machinery and equipment, buildings and any such long-term assets are treated for tax purposes in a particular manner. In the profit and loss account these costs are usually shown as an item of depreciation spread over the working life of the asset(s) concerned. For tax purposes, however, depreciation is not an allowable expense; it is replaced with a 'writing down allowance' the amount of which varies according to the policies favoured by the government of the day. HM Revenue & Customs (**www.hmrc.gov.uk/capital_allowances/ investmentschemes.htm**) publishes the current rules and rates.

Capital gains tax

Any asset a business disposes of other than the goods it normally trades in is liable, in the event of there being a profit, to pay capital gains tax (CGT). Once that tax was complicated and subject to tapers and indexing depending on the type of asset and how long it was owned. Now in the UK as in many other countries a single rate of tax, in the case of the UK 18 per cent, is applied. As tax on income is 10 per cent higher there is much effort devoted to trying hard to switch profits made from one category to the other. Mostly these efforts are illegal or at best dubious and most fail the avoidance test in that the primary, often only, purpose of such schemes is to avoid tax and not the normal pursuit of business activities. HMRC (**www. hmrc.gov.uk/cgt/index.htm**) provides the latest information on these taxes.

Capital losses

Many sales of assets, old vehicles, computers and so forth, involve a loss rather than a gain. Subject to offsetting any tax relief already claimed from writing down allowances during the asset's life, such losses are usually offset against gains made on the sale of other assets within a set time period, usually several years.

Pay as you earn (PAYE)

Employers are responsible for deducting income tax from employee's pay and making the relevant payment to HMRC. If you trade as a limited company, as a director any salary you receive will be subject to PAYE. You will need to work out the tax due. HMRC gives details on PAYE in an Employers Pack (**www.hmrc.gov.uk/employers/employers-pack.htm**). This is a complex area as no two employees are likely to have the same tax circumstances due to the myriad tax credits on offer for various circumstances.

Subcontractors

Companies often seek to circumvent the complexities of PAYE and employment law by using subcontractors. This is particularly so in industries such as construction, but there are strict and precise rules. Subcontractors must hold either a Registration Card or a Subcontractors Tax Certificate. Where a subcontractor holds a Registration Card, the 'employer' must make a deduction for the subcontractor's tax and National Insurance Contribution (NIC) liability. Where the subcontractor holds a Subcontractors Tax Certificate, the contractor will pay salary gross leaving the tax to be paid by them. At the end of the day if tax is not paid there is every likelihood that the employer will be pursued by the tax authorities.

National Insurance Contributions (NIC)

Almost everyone who works has to pay a separate tax, NIC, collected by HMRC that, in theory at least, goes towards the state pension and other benefits. NIC are paid at different rates and self-employed people pay Class 4 contributions calculated each year on the self-assessment tax form.

The amount of NIC paid depends on a mass of different factors; marital status for women, volunteer development workers, share fishermen, self-employment and small earnings are all factors that attract NIC rates of between 1 per cent and 12 per cent. HMRC (**www.hmrc.gov.uk**>Library>Rates & Allowances>National Insurance Contributions) provides tables showing the current contribution rates; elsewhere on the site (**www.hmrc.gov.uk**> employers>National Insurance) you can download an Employers Annual Pack with all the complexities of NIC paperwork.

Value Added Tax (VAT)

VAT, a tax common throughout Europe though charged at different rates, is a tax on consumer spending, collected by businesses. Basically it is a game of pass the parcel, with businesses that are registered charging each other VAT and deducting VAT charged. At the end of each accounting period the amount of VAT you have paid out is deducted from the amount you have charged out and the balance is paid over to HMRC. In the UK the standard rate is 20 per cent, while some types of businesses charge lower rates and some are exempt altogether. In the UK businesses should register for VAT if their sales are expected to reach around £65,000 ($104,000/€77,000).

The way VAT is handled on goods and services sold to and bought from other European countries is subject to another set of rules and procedures. HMRC (**www.hmrc.gov.uk**>Businesses and Corporations>VAT) publishes a series of guides such as 'Should you be registered for VAT?' and a 'General Guide'.

VAT is a legal minefield with fine judgements being the order of the day, as Marks & Spencer can confirm. For decades it was obliged to pay VAT on its chocolate teacakes as HMRC categorized them as a biscuit, a luxury rather than a 'food' and hence liable to VAT. M&S has persuaded the European Advocate General that HMRC was wrong and so were awarded a refund running into millions.

Help and advice with international tax

These two information sources, between them, contain most of what an MBA needs to know to keep abreast of international tax matters.

Doing Business (**www.doingbusiness.org**). From the left-hand vertical menu bar select 'Paying Taxes'. From there you will find the taxes that a small to medium-sized business must pay or withhold in a given year, as well as measures of the administrative burden in paying taxes. The opening table in this section shows the total number of taxes paid, the time it takes to prepare, file and pay (or withhold) the relevant tax, the VAT and social security contributions (in hours per year), and total amount of taxes payable by the business, except for labour taxes. To see the full details of the tax regime for a specific country, use the dropdown box on the top right of the screen or click on the relevant country link on that page. By clicking on the column headers you can sort the relevant data to show, for example, which country has the highest or lowest taxes, requires the most or least time to deal with or involve the most or fewest separate tax payments.

Worldwide Tax (**www.worldwide-tax.com**). From the central menu on the homepage select 'Tax Rates Around the World – Comparison' to find a quick summary of income and corporate tax levels as well as VAT for all the countries covered. From the vertical menu bar on the left of the home page select from the 'Shortcut to countries' section the countries you are interested in researching. Once in the country page, scroll down to the country taxes menu in the centre of the page and from there select the appropriate tax from the menu offered. At the bottom of that menu you can select 'Tax News 20__' where you will find the latest changes in tax rules for the country in question.

Auditors – the gatekeepers

All companies of any size – in the UK that is with a turnover in excess of £5 million and in the United States above $5 million – are required to have their accounts audited, as do most companies with money invested by external shareholders. The audit is carried out annually by a qualified accountant appointed by the directors and approved by the shareholders, to examine evidence and give an opinion about the financial statements. To do so they carry out these main tasks:

- Evaluate the design and operating dependability of the business's accounting system and procedures.

- Evaluate and test the business's internal accounting controls that are established to deter and detect errors and fraud.

- Identify and critically examine the business's accounting methods to ensure they conform to the generally accepted accounting principles of the country in which the company is registered.

- Inspect documentary and physical evidence for the business's revenues, expenses, assets and liabilities, and owners' equities. This can involve carrying out a physical stock check, albeit on a sample basis, checking the condition of that stock, and confirming bank account balances.

The goal of all the audit work is to provide a convincing basis for expressing an opinion on the business's financial statements, and being able to confirm whether or not the company's financial statements and any directly supporting tables and schedules can be relied on. The auditor puts that opinion in the auditor's report.

Most audit reports give the business a clean bill of health, stating that the accounts give a true and fair view. In the case of relatively minor problems matters are usually cleared up before the accounts are filed. Just the threat of an adverse opinion almost always motivates a business to give way to the auditor and change its accounting methods for the figures to be reported. An adverse audit opinion, if it were actually given, indicates that the financial statements of the business are misleading, and by implication possibly fraudulent. The LSE and the SEC do not tolerate adverse opinions and would stop trading in the company's shares on an adverse opinion from its auditor.

The Companies Act 2006 has introduced some tough rules on how auditors, amongst others, should report on company accounts. MBAs, unless they are also accountants, don't get involved in doing audits, but they are expected to know who's who in the auditing world; *Accountancy Age* (**www.accountancyage.com/resource/top50**) will keep you informed.

The examples below are extracts from the auditors' reports for Tesco and Google; they give a fair appreciation of what such reports are likely to contain.

CASE STUDY Extracts of auditors reports on Tesco plc and Google Inc

Tesco plc Auditor's Report for year ending 28 February 2009

Basis of audit opinion

We conducted our audit in accordance with International Standards on Auditing (UK and Ireland) issued by the Auditing Practices Board. An audit includes examination, on a test basis, of evidence relevant to the amounts and disclosures in the parent company financial statements and the part of the Directors' Remuneration Report to be audited. It also includes an assessment of the significant estimates and judgements made by the Directors in the preparation of the parent company financial statements, and of whether the accounting policies are appropriate to the parent company's circumstances, consistently applied and adequately disclosed. We planned and performed our audit so as to obtain all the information and explanations which we considered necessary in order to provide us with sufficient evidence to give reasonable assurance that the parent company financial statements and the part of the Directors' Remuneration Report to be audited are free from material misstatement, whether caused by fraud or other irregularity or error. In forming our opinion we also evaluated the overall adequacy of the presentation of information in the parent company financial statements and the part of the Directors' Remuneration Report to be audited.

Opinion

In our opinion: the parent company financial statements give a true and fair view, in accordance with United Kingdom Generally Accepted Accounting Practice, of the state of the parent company's affairs as at 28 February 2009; the parent company financial statements and the part of the Directors' Remuneration Report to be audited have been properly prepared in accordance with the Companies Act 1985; and the information given in the Report of the Directors is consistent with the parent company financial statements.

PricewaterhouseCoopers LLP
Chartered Accountants and Registered Auditors
London 1 May 2009

Report of Independent Registered Public Accounting Firm, The Board of Directors and Stockholders Google Inc

We have audited the accompanying consolidated balance sheets of Google Inc as of December 31, 2006 and 2007 and the related consolidated statements of income, stockholders' equity, and cash flows for each of the three years in the period ended December 31, 2007. Our audits also included the financial statement schedule listed in the Index at item 15 (a) 2. These financial statements and schedule are the responsibility of the company's management.

Our responsibility is to express an opinion on these financial statements and schedule based on our audits. We have conducted our audits in accordance with the standards of the Public Company Accounting Oversight Board (United States). Those standards require that we plan and perform the audit to obtain reasonable assurances about whether the financial statements are free of material misstatement. An audit includes examining, on a test basis, evidence supporting the amounts and disclosures in the financial statements.

An audit also includes assessing the accounting principles used and significant estimates made by the management, as well as evaluating the overall financial statement presentation. We believe that our audits provide a reasonable basis for our opinion. In our opinion, the financial statements referred to above present fairly, in all material respects, the consolidated financial position of Google Inc at December 31, 2006 and 2007, and the consolidated results of its operations and its cash flows for each of the three years in the period ended December 31, 2007, in conformity with US generally accepted accounting principles. Also, in our opinion, the related financial statement schedule, when considered in relation to the basic financial statements taken as a whole, present fairly in all material respects the information set forth therein.

We have also audited, in accordance with the standards of the Public Company Accounting Oversight Board (United States), the effectiveness of Google Inc's internal control over financial reporting as of December 31, 2007, based on criteria established in Internal Control – Integrated Framework issued by the Committee of Sponsoring Organisations of the Treadway Commission and our report dated February 14, 2008, expressed an unqualified opinion thereon.

Ernst & Young LLP
San Jose, California
February 14, 2008

What auditors may uncover

Having an audit of a business's financial statements does not guarantee that all fraud, embezzlement, theft and dishonesty will be detected. Audits have to be cost-effective; auditors can't examine every transaction that occurred during the year. Instead, auditors carefully evaluate businesses' internal controls relying on sampling. That in turn means that some problems may remain undetected.

The auditors may uncover some or all of the following in their examination of a business's accounting records:

- *Errors in recording transactions:* these honest mistakes happen from time to time either through lack of experience or failure to pay attention to details. In such cases there is no indication of theft or fraud and all that management wants is the errors corrected and to be confident it won't happen again.

- *Theft, embezzlement and fraud:* this involves staff either alone or in collusion with others taking advantage of weak internal controls to remove cash, product or other assets.

- *Accounting fraud* (also called *financial fraud* or *financial reporting fraud*): this refers to top-level managers who know about and approve the use of misleading and invalid accounting methods with the objective of concealing the business's financial problems or artificially inflating profit. This is usually done for the benefit that accrues, say, by propping up the market price of the company's shares to make the stock options more valuable.

- *Management fraud:* in such cases managers may accept kickbacks or bribes from customers or suppliers.

Going concern – or perhaps not!

A *going concern* is a business that has sufficient financial wherewithal and momentum to continue its normal operations into the foreseeable future and would be able to absorb a bad turn of events without having to default on its liabilities. A business could be under some financial distress, but overall still be judged a going concern. Unless there is evidence to the contrary, the auditor assumes that the business is a going concern.

In some cases the auditor may see unmistakable signs that a business may not be able to convince its creditors and lenders to give it time to work itself out of its present financial difficulties. The creditors and lenders may force the business into involuntary bankruptcy, or the business may make a pre-emptive move and take itself into voluntary bankruptcy. (See Chapter 8 for more on handling the risk associated with business failure.)

Filing accounts

A company's financial affairs are in the public domain. As well as keeping HMRC informed, companies have to file their accounts with Companies House (**www.companieshouse.gov.uk/about/gbhtml/gb3.shtml**). Accounts should be filed within 10 months of the company's financial year-end. Small businesses can file abbreviated accounts that include only very limited balance sheet and profit and loss account information and these do not need to be audited. Businesses can be fined for filing accounts late.

You can find the report and accounts for all companies listed on UK stock markets at Free Company Report and Accounts (**www.fcreports.com**). US company accounts can be obtained from The Securities Exchange Commission (**www.sec.gov**). The Investor Relations Society (**www.irs.org.uk>** IR Best Practice) makes an award each year to the company producing the best set of report and accounts.

Typical content of the annual report and accounts

The contents of the annual report and accounts for a listed company quoted on a stock exchange (see Chapter 7 for more on stock markets) is more comprehensive than the requirements of private companies, which reduce in line with their size. Disclosure requirements for any substantial business come from three sources:

1 statutory law embodied in Companies Acts;

2 accounting standards as laid down in FRSs and SSAPs (Statements of Standard Accounting Practice);

3 if the business is listed on a stock market, the regulations specified by that market will apply.

The following main items are disclosed in the annual report and accounts:

Chairman's statement – a broad review of progress, changes in strategy and management and a guide to future prospects. For large organizations this may be supplemented by a CEO's (chief executive officers) review of each individual business's performance.

Operating and financial review – a detailed commentary on the financial results and influential factors.

List of directors – details of service, responsibilities and other directorships

Directors' report – a formal report on specific required items, eg dividend declaration, principal activities, share capital and substantial shareholdings, political and charitable contributions, directors' shareholdings, employment policy, creditor payment policy, close company status (a company with no more than five controlling parties) and appointment of auditors.

Report of the remuneration committee – policy statement on how the total remuneration package of executive and non-executive directors is set.

Corporate governance – a statement of compliance, or otherwise, with the Code of Best Practice on board structure and directors' remuneration.

Auditors' report – a statement of auditors' responsibility and their report on whether or not the financial statements give a true and fair view of the state of affairs.

Financial statements – comprising consolidated profit and loss account, balance sheet, cash flow statement, statement of total recognized gains and losses and parent company balance sheet only.

Notes to the financial statements – additional breakdown and analysis of figures appearing in the main financial statements.

Historic record of financial performance – a 10-year summary of the main financial figures and ratios reflecting profitability, dividends and shareholders' funds.

Notice of meeting – notice of the time and venue of the annual general meeting and the business to be conducted.

The Investor Relations Society (**www.irs.org.uk**>IR Best Practice) makes an award each year to the company producing the best set of report and accounts.

Directors' responsibilities and duties

Any MBA worth his or her salt is either a director of the company he or she works for, or aspires to become one. Be warned, however: a director also has to cope with some technical, more detailed requirements, for example sending in the accounts to Companies House, appointing an auditor if required, holding regular board meetings and keeping shareholders informed. More onerous than just signing them, a director is expected and required in law to understand the significance of the balance sheet, profit and loss account and cash flow statement.

A director's duties, responsibilities and potential liabilities include:

- To act in good faith in the interests of the company; this includes carrying out duties diligently and honestly.

- Not to carry on the business of the company with intent to defraud creditors or for any fraudulent purpose.

- Not knowingly to allow the company to trade while insolvent ('wrongful trading'); directors who do so may have to pay for the debts incurred by the company while insolvent.

- Not to deceive shareholders.
- To have a regard for the interests of employees in general.
- To comply with the requirements of the Companies Acts, such as providing what is needed in accounting records, appointing auditors and filing accounts. You can read the key points of the act on the Companies House (**http://www.companieshouse.gov.uk/ companiesAct/podcastArchive.shtml**) website; at this link you can hear a summary podcast.
- Appoint a company secretary, who for a public company must be appropriately qualified.

Companies House (**www.companies-house.com**>Guidance booklets> Directors and Secretaries Guide) is a comprehensive guide to secretaries' (and directors) duties and the 200 or so forms they may have to file at Companies House. The equivalent information on US corporations can be found on the Business.Gov website (**www.business.gov/finance/taxes/**).

Holding board meetings

Board meetings have to be held sufficiently regularly to allow the directors to 'discharge their duties effectively'. On average the boards of public companies meet eight to nine times a year and smaller companies once a quarter. The purposes of board meetings are to take major decisions and to keep everyone informed of events affecting business performance. Having regular board meetings ensures that important matters are properly considered and the various views and outcomes are recorded. Guidelines for successful board meetings are:

- Have as small a number of directors as possible, bearing in mind the size of the business. The amount of useful work a board can do is in inverse proportion to its size.
- Hold meetings regularly and set a timetable a year ahead, updated at the half year. This is vital if there are non-executive directors.
- Have an agenda, and stick to it. Start with the minutes of the previous meeting, get them accepted, move through the agenda and finish with AOB (any other business), and confirm the date and venue for the next meeting.
- Take and circulate minutes of the meeting.
- Have a board chairman whose role is to keep the board meeting on track.

Non-executive directors

Despite the comforting sound of the prefix in this title, 'non-executive' directors carry all the responsibilities of full-time directors, but are rarely close enough to the business to know exactly what the true financial position is. Big companies like to have them, usually to chair the remuneration committee that determines board salaries and bonuses and to provide further safeguards for shareholders. For small companies having a heavyweight outsider can sometimes lend extra credibility to a business proposition.

Organizations such as Venture Investment Partners (**www.ventureip.co.uk**) and the Independent Director Initiative (**www.independentdirector.co.uk**), a joint venture between Ernst & Young and the Institute of Directors, help in finding suitable non-executive directors for private businesses. Big businesses tend to recruit from within a network of recently retired directors of major quoted businesses.

Directors' misdemeanours

There are three types of activities that directors need to steer clear of if they don't want to join the several thousand or so directors on both sides of the Atlantic who are disqualified and fined each year, or the rather smaller number who end up in prison. Disqualification means that not only can't you run a company but if you issue your orders through others, having them act as a director in your place, you will leave them personally liable. You will be in breach of a disqualification order that can in turn lead to imprisonment and fines. In addition, you can be made personally liable for the debts and liabilities of any company in which you are involved.

Trading while insolvent occurs when your liabilities exceed your assets. At this point the shareholders' equity in the business has effectively ceased to exist and when shareholder equity is negative, directors are personally at risk and owe a duty of care to creditors – not shareholders. If you find yourself even approaching this area you need the prompt advice of an insolvency practitioner. Directors who act properly will not be penalized, and will live to fight another day.

The two areas most likely to lead disqualification are, 1) wrongful trading, which can apply if, after a company goes into insolvent liquidation, the liquidator believes that the directors (or those acting as such) ought to have concluded earlier that the company had no realistic chance of survival. In these circumstances the courts can remove the shelter of limited liabilities and make directors personally liable for the company's debts; 2) fraudulent trading, which is rather more serious than wrongful trading. Here the proposition is that the director(s) were knowingly party to fraud on their creditors. The full shelter of Limited Liability can be removed in these circumstances.

Values and the accounting reports

Values are the ethical concepts of right and wrong behaviour that govern the way in which we discharge our responsibilities. While many responsibilities lie within the scope of the law – shareholder protection, discrimination at work, misleading advertising and so forth – in those areas and the grey area that surrounds them lies the province of ethics and social responsibility. Right and wrong in themselves are often not too difficult to separate out. The problem usually stems from competing 'rights' – giving shareholders a better return vs saving the planet for example.

The owner, operating alone in a small business, or the board of directors are the custodians of the moral tone and in setting standards of behaviour towards everyone the business has dealings with. They are in some ways encouraged by legal constraints placed on them to take a narrow view of those responsibilities. They are required 'to act in good faith in the interests of the company', 'not to deceive shareholders and to appoint auditors to oversee the accounting records', 'not to carry on the business of the company with intent to defraud creditors or for any fraudulent purpose' and 'to have regard for the interests of employees in general'.

Directors and managers also have responsibilities to protect their customers when using their products or services or when visiting company premises, and to follow rules inhibiting pollution in the operating processes. But it is only relatively recently that companies have been required to take a wider view of their responsibilities to other 'stakeholder' groups. Enlightened managers, or those who are particularly astute depending on your level of cynicism, have often taken on broader responsibilities, sponsoring charities, funding social amenities such as play areas or providing low-cost housing. These initiatives are often spurred on by enlightened self-interest, say to help with recruiting and retaining employees, with getting favourable PR or in the case of low-cost housing, providing amenities that are a usual requirement in getting planning consent for a property development or a site for, say, a supermarket. All such activities are reported in the company annual report and accounts.

CASE STUDY   Unilever – Embedding Ethics
(www.unilever.com/ourvalues)

In 1887 William Hesketh Lever, already a highly successful soap manufacturer, was looking for a new site for his factory to allow him to expand. The site needed to be near to a river for importing raw materials, and a railway line for transporting the finished products. The 56 acres of unused marshy land at the site that became Port Sunlight, named after his soap, was far more than he needed simply for manufacturing purposes. Lever had something more all-embracing in mind. His stated aims were to create an environment that allowed his workers 'to socialise and Christianise business relations and get back to that close family brotherhood that existed in the good old days of hand labour'. His intention was to extend his responsibilities beyond making money for himself and to share that, albeit on his own terms, with everyone who worked for him. Between 1899 and 1914 Lever built some

800 houses, taking an active part in the design. The community's population of 3,500 shared allotments, public buildings including the Lady Lever Art Gallery, schools, a concert hall, open air swimming pool, church and a temperance hotel. His cottage hospital, built in 1907, continued until the introduction of the National Health Service in 1948. He also introduced schemes for welfare, education and the entertainment of his workers, and encouraged recreation and organizations that promoted art, literature, science or music.

Unilever, as the company is now known, has carried on the Lever values and vision in corporate life. The company's behaviour in all affairs is governed by a set of clear, stated and communicated guidelines. Starting with its core value, 'As a multi-local multinational we aim to play our part in addressing global environmental and social concerns through our own actions, and working in partnership with stakeholders at local, national and international levels', the company has developed this set of principles to guide its behaviour in all aspects of its work:

- Our corporate purpose states that to succeed requires 'the highest standards of corporate behaviour towards everyone we work with, the communities we touch, and the environment on which we have an impact'.

- Always working with integrity. Conducting our operations with integrity and with respect for the many people, organizations and environments our business touches has always been at the heart of our corporate responsibility.

- Positive impact. We aim to make a positive impact in many ways: through our brands, our commercial operations and relationships, through voluntary contributions, and through the various other ways in which we engage with society.

- Continuous commitment. We're also committed to continuously improving the way we manage our environmental impacts and are working towards our longer-term goal of developing a sustainable business.

- Setting out our aspirations. Our corporate purpose sets out our aspirations in running our business. It's underpinned by our code of business principles which describes the operational standards that everyone at Unilever follows, wherever they are in the world. The code also supports our approach to governance and corporate responsibility.

- Working with others. We want to work with suppliers who have values similar to our own and work to the same standards we do. Our business partner code, aligned to our own code of business principles, comprises ten principles covering business integrity and responsibilities relating to employees, consumers and the environment.

10

Mergers and acquisitions

- Why most mergers miscarry – and why some don't
- Planning an acquisition strategy
- Valuing businesses
- Rules of takeovers

Acquisitions and mergers are areas that an MBA is almost certain to encounter early in his or her career. On some MBA programmes there may well be some unique content contained in specialized electives. For example, at the London Business School there is an elective on Financial Analysis of Mergers, Acquisitions and Other Complex Corporate Restructurings, or the partially related subject, Dealing with Financial Crime on offer at Cass Business School.

Although M&A are popular with CEOs the research literature produces, at best, inconclusive evidence to support the hypothesis that M&As generally create increased shareholder value for the owners of the acquiring firm. Since Kitching's seminal work 'Why do mergers miscarry?' (*Harvard Business Review* November–December, 84–101) there has been a big question mark over the subject of acquisitions and shareholder value. Porter ('From competitive advantage to corporate strategy', *Harvard Business Review*, 65 (3), 43–59, 1987) concluded that 'acquisitions have been largely unsuccessful when one considers that over half were subsequently divested'. A clear majority of the academic studies published over the past 50 years come down on the side of the doubters.

So why, you might wonder, do acquisitions capture so much of top management's attention? That arrogance plays a major part in this process is supported by the way that most corporate acquisitions are carried by relatively inexperienced individuals operating almost alone. This quotation from *The Wall Street Journal*, 'a struggle between a few ambitious men using public companies in which they owned a fractional share, for their own gain', captures the dominance of ego and arrogance in the merger process. A light-hearted but statistically sound study was conducted by two academics from Columbia University. They found a way of confirming what we all knew already: there is a link between the premiums paid by bosses and their own inflated self-esteem. They measured such factors as the boss's salary relative to his peers and the acres of flattering press coverage and proved that the higher the self-esteem the higher the premium they paid to acquire the business and consequently the less likely it was that they would create additional value for their shareholders.

The other factor that draws top management to M&A is the immediacy of the apparent reward. Most business strategies present few opportunities to produce clear winners and losers in a very short time frame. But with an acquisition strategy the successful bidder is declared the 'winner' by employees, middle management, competitors, their industry and the financial community at large, all within a matter of weeks. And even if the bid fails, the business community sees the management as a virile aggressor. The consequences of failure take years, even decades to emerge. Time Warner's acquisition of AOL and eBay's of Skype are two such examples where nothing of much value to the acquirers has arisen save copious positive press coverage in the early weeks after the event.

Of course the protagonists are invariably cheered on by their professional advisers who stand to make a healthy profit whatever the outcome. There are, however a number of conditions that research shows are more likely to lead to success.

1. Size matters

Deals between equals in terms of size are more likely to work well than not. The converse is also true. Where the acquired business is much smaller the chances of success are low.

2. Experience counts

For example, M&A is viewed as a cornerstone of the strategy of Cisco, whose top management have made such a study of the subject that management consultants from around the globe take their advice. In the United States, which has the greatest experience base of every type of M&A, buyers are more sophisticated and are less likely to overpay for their acquisitions than are Europeans, for example. In the United States, the medium control premium paid for a public company has been dropping steadily over the past decade from 58 per cent to just 26 per cent. In Europe by contrast, the average premium increased from 31 to 37 per cent.

3. Cash is king

One much vaunted reason for medium-sized firms to go public is the opportunity to use paper to fund acquisitions. But much academic research suggests that both bidders and targets lose in stock-financed deals, as opposed to those financed by cash. The reasons for this are:

- Cash deals are quicker and less costly to implement than share deals.
- A stock offer opens up the bidding to a wider group (ie any firm with or without cash). This in turn increases the competitiveness, which tends to be a disadvantage to the bidder.
- Issuing new stock can be viewed negatively by the capital markets, leading to a drop in the share price of the bidder. This in turn can make the deal more expensive for the acquiring firm.

Avoid firms where the management owns a large slice of the business. It seems reasonable to assume that increased managerial share ownership, through options and the like, encourages managers to maximize shareholder value rather than simply to pursue aggrandisement strategies for their own sake. Giving managers a share of ownership requires them to bear a higher part of the cost of poor decisions. At the same time, greater ownership gives company managers greater control of the company, a power that can be used to resist acquisitions. Managers often resist bids, even when the bid looks likely to create greater shareholder value. Research bears these views out conclusively.

4. Cross-border deals work well

It seems that when firms expand into a new geographic market the shareholders of the acquiring firm are highly likely to experience significant increases in shareholder wealth, but not if they try to repeat the process in the same market. One interesting study (Doukas, J and Travlos, N G, 1988, 'The effects of corporate multinationalism on shareholder's wealth: Evidence from international acquisitions', *Journal of Finance* 43, 1161–75) found that US bidders going abroad for the first time made significant positive abnormal gains. Those making further acquisitions in the overseas countries in which they were operating did not fare so well. They made either zero or insignificant gains from second and subsequent acquisitions.

Going on the acquisition trail

M&A strategies are often messy, and in hostile bids there can be blood on the carpet. But just because they may end up messy – that is almost inevitable in corporate warfare – they don't have to start off that way. Getting information on public companies is relatively easy. They are required by the rules of the stock exchange they are listed on to provide comprehensive and current – usually quarterly – information on performance. If any major event occurs, for example a serious profit warning, a legal dispute or anything that could materially affect the current profit forecast, that will have to be disclosed immediately. Searching out private companies will call for a bit more digging.

Onesource (**www.onesource.com/global-business-information.aspx**), for example, is a comprehensive source for global information on companies, industries and executives that comes in four regional editions covering North America, the United Kingdom, Europe and Asia Pacific. Onesource provides summarized profit and loss accounts and balance sheet data, a four-year trend, key performance ratios, growth rates and relative performance, sector by sector. Appendix 1 lists key financial information resources.

These are some steps you can advise to be taken in improve the chances of making a successful acquisition, merger or joint venture.

Know why you want to buy

Ideally the reasons to buy a business need to be practical and down-to-earth and embedded in the firm's core strategy. Sound reasons for acquisitions include the following:

- to increase market share and eliminate a troublesome competitor;
- to broaden your product range or give you access to new markets;
- to diversify into new markets, acquiring the necessary management, marketing or technical skills to enable you to capture a reasonable slice of the market relatively quickly;
- to get into another country or region;
- to protect an important source of supply that could be under threat from a competitor;
- to acquire additional staff, factory space, warehousing or distribution channels, or to get access to additional major customers more quickly than by starting up yourself.

Your company should produce a written statement explaining the rationale behind your reason to buy – before you start looking for companies to buy – otherwise you could end up pursuing a bargain just because it seems cheap, that has absolutely nothing to do with your previously defined commercial goals. It is also worth remembering that companies available at knockdown prices are likely to need drastic surgery. So unless you fancy your chances as a company doctor, stay well away.

Decide what you want to buy

It can take over one person-year of work, on average, to find and buy a business. The more accurately you describe your ideal purchase the simpler, quicker and cheaper your search will be. Just imagine trying to buy a house without any idea where you wanted to live, how much you wanted to spend, how many bedrooms you needed, whether you wanted a new house or a listed building, or if you wanted a garden. The search would be near impossible to organize, it could take forever, and the resultant purchase would almost certainly please no one. The same problems arise when buying a company. The definition of what you want to buy should explain:

- the business area/products/service the company is in;
- the location;
- the price range and the cash you have available;
- the management depth and the management style you are looking for;
- the minimum profitability and return on capital employed you could accept. It is worth remembering that if the company you plan to buy only makes 1 per cent profit while you make 5 per cent, and you are of equal size, the resultant profit will be 3 per cent: $(5 + 1)/2$;
- the image compatibility between your company and any target;
- scope for integration and cost savings;
- the tax status – for example a business nursing a substantial loss could be worth looking at if that can be offset against your company's profits, so reducing tax due.

Outside of the factors listed above, you may have vital reasons that, if not met, would make the acquisition a poor bet. For example, if you want to iron out major cash flow or plant capacity cycles, there is little point in going for a business similar to your own. That will only make the peaks and troughs more pronounced.

Investigate and approach

Once you have your shopping list of prospective purchases you need to arm yourself with everything you can find out about them. Get their literature, get samples, copies of their advertising, press comment and, of course, their accounts. Then get out and see their premises and as much of their operation as possible. If you cannot get in, get one of your salespeople in to look over the business for you. This investigation will help you both to shorten your shopping list and to put it into order of priority. Now you are ready for the approach. Although you are technically buying, psychologically you would be well advised to think of acquiring a company as a selling job. As such you cannot afford to have any approach rejected either too early or without a determined effort.

You have three options as to how to make the initial approach and each has its merits. You can telephone, giving only the broadest reason for your approach – saying, perhaps, that you wish to discuss areas of common interest. You could write and be a little more specific about your purpose, following that up with a phone call to arrange a meeting, perhaps over lunch. Finally, you could use a third party such as an accountant or consultant (reasons of secrecy could make this method desirable) or a corporate finance house: if executive time is at a premium, there may be no other practicable way.

The first meeting is crucial and you need to achieve two objectives. First, you must establish mutual respect, trust and rapport. Nothing worthwhile will follow without these. Then you need to establish in principle that both parties are seriously interested. Time scale, price, methods of integration, etc can all be side-stepped until later, except in the most general sense.

Valuing a target

There are two special situations that make an initial valuation relatively easy, at least in theory.

1. Share price

First, if your target is already floated on a stock market its value is measured by buyers and sellers every day, or perhaps more often in turbulent times. For example, during the banking meltdown in the autumn of 2008 HBOS's shares oscillated by as much as 40 per cent on an almost daily basis. It was not alone in seeing violent swings and indeed some stock markets, most prominently the Russian main market, actually had to shut down as the volume of selling orders and the spread of prices were too great to comprehend yet alone manage. Nevertheless, the market sets the value of every business on a stock exchange for every transaction. This market price is not necessarily the price that the owners will get for their shares, but in more normal times it is a reasonably close approximation.

2. Asset value

Ongoing businesses are all valued by some measure of future expected profits. In fact the accounts don't even attempt to put a value on the assets. Fixed assets, except for freehold property, are recorded as the cost at date of purchase, reduced by a notional depreciation amount that's sole purpose is to allocate costs over an asset's working life. The asset itself could be of virtually no value at all, such as, say, second-hand office furniture. But that would not be revealed in the balance sheet, whose purpose in this respect is only to show where money has come from and what has been done with that money. The exception to this rule is if a business is not going to continue trading, for example if no buyer can be found. In those circumstances the assets now all have to be valued and sold off piecemeal.

Price/earnings rules

The simplest and most usual way for businesses to be valued is using a formula known as the price/earnings ratio. The P/E ratio is calculated by dividing the share price into the amount of profit earned for each share. For example, if a business makes £100,000 profit and has 1,000 shares, the profit per share is £100. If the share price of that company is £10, then its P/E ratio is 10 (£100/10). So much for the science, now for the art. P/E ratios vary with the business sector and the current market sentiment for that sector. For example, the high tech sector may have a P/E ratio of 30 or more at times – Google had a P/E of 100 at one point. That means that shareholders were prepared to pay $100 for every $1 of profit the company was making. For Barclays Bank, however, they were only paying £10 for every £1 of profits and in the market mayhem of 2008 the banking sector slipped well below that. The market as a whole trades with P/Es between 10 and 20.

You can check out the P/E for your business sector either by looking in the *Financial Times*, or if you can't wait until morning check out ProShare's website (**www.proshareclubs.co.uk**>Research Centre>Performance Tables> Chose a Sector). There you can see the current P/E ratio for every company in your sector, as long as they are listed on the London Stock Exchange. If you want to see how much interest there is in your business sector right now visit Interactive Investor (**www.iii.co.uk**>markets>sectors). There you can see the sector whose shares have been bought and sold the most over the past day, month and year.

However, private companies don't trade on as high a P/E multiple as their big brothers on the stock market do. So if a public company in your sector is on a P/E of 12, as a private company your prospective P/E would be around 8, or a third less. Why? Good question. The simplest answer is that while shares in your business are hard to dispose of, you can unload a public company every business day by making a phone call to your broker. In other words, the premium is for liquidity.

BDO Stoy Hayward's Private Company Price Index (PCPI) tracks the relationship between the current FTSE P/E ratio and the P/Es currently being paid on the sale of private companies. Puts simply, the PCPI lets a company without a stock market listing get a reasonable idea of what it will actually sell for now (see **www.bdo.co.uk**>Publications – View by title>Private Company Price Index).

Discounting future earnings

A valuation technique popular with the venture capital community is to discount future earnings. We know intuitively that getting cash in sooner is better than getting it in later. In other words, a dollar received now is worth more than a dollar that will arrive in one, two or more years because of what we could do with that money ourselves, or because of what we ourselves have to pay out to have use of that money. So anyone buying your business will need to ascribe a value to a future stream of earnings to arrive at what is known as *the present value*. If we know we could earn 20 per cent on any money, we know the maximum we would be prepared to pay now for a £ coming to us in one year' time would be around 80p. If we were to pay £1 now to get £1 back in a year's time we would in effect be losing money.

TABLE 10.1 Discounting a stream of future earnings

£	Cash Flow A	Discount Factor at 15% B	Discounted Cash Flow A × B
Initial cash cost NOW (Year 0)	20,000	1.00	20,000
Net cash flows			
Year 1	1,000	0.8695	870
Year 2	4,000	0.7561	3,024
Year 3	8,000	0.6575	5,260
Year 4	7,000	0.5717	4,002
Year 5	5,000	0.4972	2,486
Total	25,000		15,642
Cash surplus	5,000	Net Present Value	(4,358)

The process used to handle this process is known as discounting and the technique is termed 'discounted cash flow' (DCF). The residual discounted cash is called the 'net present value'. The first column in Table 10.1 shows the simple cash flow implications of an investment proposition: a surplus of 5,000 comes after five years from putting 20,000 into a project. But if we accept the proposition that future cash is worth less than current cash, we need to know how much less. If we assume an investor wants to make at least a 15 per cent return on his or her investment then that is the discount rate selected (this doesn't matter too much as you will see in the section on internal rate of return).

The formula for calculating what a dollar received at some future date is worth is:

$$\text{Present Value (PV)} = \$P \times 1/(1 + r)^n$$

where $P is the initial cash cost, r is the interest rate expressed in decimals and n is the year in which the cash will arrive. So if we decide on a discount rate of 15 per cent the present value of a dollar received in one year's time is:

$$\text{Present Value} = \$1 \times 1/(1 + 0.15)^1$$
$$= 0.87 \text{ (rounded to two decimal places)}$$

So we can see that our 1,000 arriving at the end of year one has a present value of 870; the 4,000 in year two has a present value of 3,024 and by year five present value reduces cash flows to barely half their original figure. In fact far from having a real payback in year four and generating a cash surplus of 5,000, this project will make us 4,358 worse off than we had hoped to be if we needed to make a return of 15 per cent. The investment in buying this business fails to meet the criteria using DCF.

DCF is a useful starting point but does not give us any definitive information. For example, all we know about the above investment is that it doesn't make a return of 15 per cent. To know the actual rate of return we need to chose a discount rate that produces a net present value of the entire cash flow of 0, known as the 'internal rate of return'. The maths is time-consuming but Solutions Matrix Web site (**www.solutionmatrix.com**) has a tool for working out payback, discounted cash flow, internal rate of return, and a whole lot more calculations relating to capital budgeting. You have to register on the site first before downloading the free capital budgeting spreadsheet suite and tutorial. From the home page, click on 'Download Center' and 'Download Financial Metrics Lite for Microsoft Excel'. Using this spreadsheet you will see that the IRR for the project in question is slightly under 7 per cent, not much better than bank interest and certainly insufficient to warrant taking any risks for. Venture capital providers will be looking for an IRR of above 30 per cent.

Rules of thumb

Some business sectors have their own yardsticks for estimating the value of a business. For example, sales turnover is often used for computer maintenance and mail order businesses; the number of customers for a mobile phone airtime providers; the number of outlets for an estate agency, restaurant or pub chain; and grocery shops are valued partly on their turnover and partly on the value of the stock they hold. BizStats (**www.bizstats.com/rulesofthumb.htm**) has a nifty table giving a list of these rules.

CASE STUDY City Flyer Express

Robert Wright, a Cranfield MBA who started up his venture, Connectair, immediately after completing his MBA, sold out to Harry Goodman, late of International Leisure fame, for around £7 ($11/€8.3) million. Not bad for just under five years' work. However, negotiations with Goodman took nearly a year, and the opening offer was barely a seventh of that sum. In the end the deal was valued on a multiple of landing slots, as Goodman planned to use these for his fleet of much larger planes and so create value. Things didn't quite work out as planned and International Leisure went bust. Robert bought the business back from receivership for a nominal £1 and with venture capital from 3i built up the business again, this time under the name City Flyer Express. A decade later he sold the business to British Airways for a healthy £75 ($120/€88.5) million.

Multiple models

Some valuation techniques, particularly those used by business brokers that help sell private companies, involve using a number of adjustments to the basic P/E method. One such approach is based on the following formula:

$$\text{add-back profitability} \times \text{industry sector P/E} \\ + \text{adjustment for assets and liabilities}$$

The add-back profitability involves trying to arrive at what the profit might be in the hands of the acquiring company. In the case where the reported profit of a business for sale is say £500,000 it might be argued that the £50,000 of interest charges should be added back to the profits on the basis that new owners would finance the company in a different way and would have access to these funds as disposable profits. The same argument could be made for the two directors who are paying themselves a hefty £300,000 a year, when in fact the business could be run with a divisional manager by the acquirer paying around £100,000 including a performance-related bonus. That would add a further £200,000 to the profits available in the business. There could be deductions to profits too, if the acquiring firm doesn't expect to be able to retain the income stream post-purchase: specialist consultancy income from work done by one of the owners or the rental income arising from letting out part of the business premises, if that won't continue, for example. To carry our example on let's assume that amounts to a deduction of £100,000. So the business's continuing profits would be assessed as: £500,000 + £50,000 + £200,000 − £100,000 = £650,000. That figure would then be the basis on which to apply the P/E multiple. In the case where the sector P/E is 5, the value would be £3.25 million rather than the £2.5 million that would otherwise have been assumed.

There is one further adjustment made in this valuation approach: an adjustment for assets and liabilities by calculating the net assets, that is the surplus of assets over liabilities. The argument for this is that this represents the current value of the owner's stake in the business. The P/E approach gives the value of future earnings, so adding one to the other gives the 'real' value. In practice any valuation approach is just the starting point for negotiations.

Valuing minority shareholdings

If you are not buying an entire business but taking a minority stake, perhaps putting down a marker for a later bid or as part of a strategic alliance strategy, the rules on value are specialized. The value of your stake will not just be smaller because you have fewer shares, but a minority stake usually can neither force nor prevent the sale of a business. Discounts are applied to most share calculations for a lack of marketability. The HMRC website is useful for understanding this area; see **www.hmrc.gov.uk/manuals/svmanual/svm06000.htm**. It describes some ideas of how to value 50 per cent of a company. Further guidance on values greater than 50 per cent can be found at: **www.hmrc.gov.uk/manuals/svmanual/svm06120.htm**. Once the shareholding drops below 50 per cent details are less precise. The HMRC website does not give any details regarding minority shareholders and does not suggest that the discount should be greater.

Limit the risks

Buying a business will always be risky. If you have done your homework and got the price right, with any luck the risks will be less. Here are some other things you can do to lessen the risks:

- *Set conditional terms:* for example, you could make part of the price conditional on a certain level of profits being achieved.
- *Handcuff key employees:* if most of the assets you are buying are on two legs, get service contracts or consultancy arrangements in place before the deal is signed.
- *Non-competitive clauses:* make sure that neither the seller nor the key employees can set up in competition, taking all the goodwill you have just bought.

- *Tax clearances:* obviously you want to make sure any tax losses you are buying, or any tax implications in the purchase price, are approved by HMRC before committing yourself.

- *Warranties and indemnities:* if, after you have bought, you find there is a compulsory purchase order on the vendor's premises and the patent on its exciting new product is invalid, you would quite rightly be rather miffed. Warranties and indemnities set out the circumstances in which the seller will make good the buyer's financial loss, so you could try to include anything crucial that looks worrying under this heading. Not unnaturally, the seller will resist, but you need to be firm on key points.

Manage the acquisition

However well negotiated the deal, most acquisitions that go wrong do so because of the human factor, particularly in the first few weeks after the deal is made public. Some important rules to follow are listed below. Have an outline plan for how to handle the merger and be prepared to be flexible. (Interestingly enough, only one buyer in five has a detailed operational plan of how to manage their acquisition, but as 67 per cent of those being bought believe the buyer has such a plan, it is psychologically important.):

- Let business go on as usual for a few weeks as you learn more about the internal workings of the company. Then you can make informed judgements on who or what should go or remain in post. This rule is followed by 90 per cent of successful acquisitions.

- Hold management and staff meetings on day one to clear up as much misunderstanding as you can. This should be done by the CEO.

- Never announce takeovers on a Friday. Staff will have all weekend to spread rumours. Wednesdays are best: just enough time to clear up misunderstandings, followed by a useful weekend breathing space.

- Make cuts/redundancies a once-only affair. It is always best to cut deep, and then get on with running the business. Continuous sacking saps morale, and all the best people will leave, before it is their turn.

- Set limits of authority and reporting relationships and put all banking relationships in the hands of your own accounts department, as quickly as possible.

CASE STUDY

Furniture company IKEA was founded by Ingvar Kamprad an entrepreneur from the Småland province in southern Sweden, when he was just 17, having cut his teeth on selling matches to his nearby neighbours at the age of 5, followed by a spell selling flower seeds, greeting cards, Christmas decorations and eventually furniture. IKEA targets young white-collar workers as its prime customer segment, selling through 235 stores in more than 30 countries. It offers home furnishing products of good function and design at prices young people can afford. It achieves this by using simple cost-cutting solutions that do not affect the quality of the products. Worth £16 billion, Kamprad is the world's seventh richest man, but his only extravagance is buying businesses. The Swedish furniture giant made 11 acquisitions between 1991 and 2008, took stakes in four companies and divested itself of six. Kamprad himself lives more frugally. He lives in a bungalow, flies easyJet and drives a 15-year-old Volvo. When he arrived at a gala dinner recently to collect a business award, he was turned away by the security guard because they saw him getting off a bus. He and his wife Margaretha are often seen dining in cheap restaurants. He does his food shopping in the afternoon when prices are lower and even then haggles prices down.

City code on takeovers and mergers

Buying up a plc is a more complicated process than taking over a private company or business – The Take Over Panel (**www.thetakeoverpanel.org.uk**) rules on taking over another company quoted on a stock market run to 266 pages! In the first instance, shareholders in the business being acquired have to be offered the same deal. Family, directors and those with major blocks of shares can't be offered preferential treatment. The buying company must be able to fulfil the cash consideration involved before making any announcement. There are conditions under which a potential bidder must either make a formal offer or walk away from the target for at least six months. Once 90 per cent of a target company's shares have been acquired the remaining shareholders have to accept the deal.

Business plans and budgets

11

- Forecasting sales
- Monitoring economic cycles
- Preparing business plans
- Setting budgets
- Checking on performance

All management decisions have to be set out in a form that will ensure that they can be successfully implemented. For the business or enterprise as a whole that form is a business plan setting out in detail the role each part of the organization has to play for the next three to five years. That period is needed as recognizing an opportunity, developing a product or service to exploit that opportunity and bringing it to market all take time and the plan has to encompass all these stages to be of any value. The dichotomy here is that while strategy takes time for the results to show, the world in which the business is implementing its plans is changing. As one military strategist succinctly put it, all plans disintegrate on contact with the enemy. So three- to five-year business plans need to be reviewed fundamentally each year and progress monitored at least quarterly.

All aspects of preparing the business plan, the supporting forecasts, budgets and economic overview, are a tasks that MBAs are invariably expected to be able to carry out, or support line managers in doing so. It calls for a broad level of understanding of key aspects of the business – cash flow, profit margins, funding issues, marketing and selling and human resource issues – that few others in the organization are likely to have. It is an opportunity for an MBA to broaden and deepen his or her relationships with all key executives as well as the board of directors. Often tedious and always time-consuming, the task of preparing business plans should be welcomed as a career progression opportunity par excellence.

Forecasting

Sales drive much of a business's activities; they determine cash flow, stock levels, production capacity and ultimately how profitable or otherwise a business will be, so unsurprisingly much effort goes into attempting to predict future sales. A sales forecast is not the same as a sales objective. An objective is what you want to achieve and will shape a strategy to do so. A forecast is the most likely future outcome given what has happened in the past and the momentum that provides for the business.

Any forecast is made up of three components and to get an accurate forecast you need to decompose the historic data to better understand the impact of each on the end result:

1 *Underlying trend:* the general direction – up, flat or down – over the longer term, showing the rate of change.

2 *Cyclical factors:* the short-term influences that regularly superimpose themselves on the trend. For example, in the summer months you would expect sales of swimwear, ice cream and suntan lotion to be higher than in the winter. Ski equipment would probably follow a reverse pattern.

3 *Random movements:* irregular, random spikes, up or down, caused by unusual and unexplained factors.

Using averages

The simplest forecasting method is to assume that the future will be more or less the same as the recent past. The two most common techniques that use this approach are moving average and weighted moving average.

Moving average takes a series of data from the past, say the last six months' sales, adds them up, divides by the number of months and uses that figure as being the most likely forecast of what will happen in month seven. This method works well in a static, mature market where change happens slowly, if at all.

The *weighted moving average* method gives the most recent data more significance than the earlier data since it gives a better representation of current business conditions. So before adding up the series of data each figure is weighted by multiplying it by an increasingly higher factor as you get closer to the most recent data.

Exponential smoothing and advanced forecasting techniques

Exponential smoothing is a sophisticated averaging technique that gives exponentially decreasing weights as the data get older; conversely more recent data are given relatively more weight in making the forecasting. Double and triple exponential smoothing can be used to help with different types of trend.

More sophisticated still are Holt's and Brown's linear exponential smoothing and Box-Jenkins, named after those two statisticians, which applies auto-regressive moving average models to find the best fit of a time series.

Fortunately all an MBA needs to know is that these and other statistical forecasting methods exist. The choice of which is the best technique to use is usually down to trial and error. Various software programs will calculate the best-fitting forecast by applying each technique to the historic data you enter. See what actually happens and use the technique that's forecast is closest to the actual outcome. Professor Hossein Arsham of the University of Baltimore (**http://home.ubalt.edu/ntsbarsh/Business-stat/ otherapplets/ForecaSmo.htm#rmenu**) provides a useful tool that allows you to enter data and see how different forecasting techniques perform. Duke University's Fuqua School of Business, consistently ranked amongst the top 10 US business schools in every single functional area, provides this helpful link (**www.duke.edu/~rnau/411home.htm**) to all its lecture material on forecasting.

Causal relationships

Often when looking at data sets it will be apparent that there is a relationship between certain factors. Look at Figure 11.1, which is a chart showing the monthly sales of barbeques and the average temperature in the preceding month for the past eight months.

FIGURE 11.1   Scatter diagram example

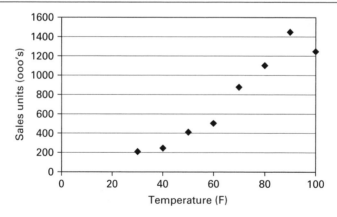

It's not too hard to see that there appears to be a relationship between temperature and sales – as we might expect. By drawing the line that most accurately represents the slope, called the line of best fit, we have a useful tool for estimating what sales might be next month, given the temperature that occurred this month; see Figure 11.2.

FIGURE 11.2 Scatter diagram – the line of best fit

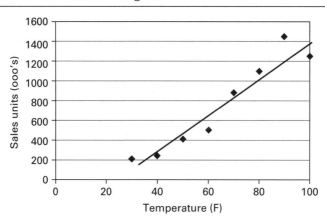

The example used is a simple one and the relationship obvious and strong. In real life there is likely to be much more data and it will be harder to see if there is a relationship between the 'independent variable', in this case temperature, and the 'dependent variable', sales volume. Fortunately there is an algebraic formula known as 'linear regression' that will calculate the line of best fit for you.

There are a couple of calculations then needed to test if the relationship is strong (it can be strongly positive; even if strongly negative it will still be useful for predictive purposes) and significant. The test are known as R-Squared and the Students t test, and all an MBA needs to know is that they exist and you can probably find the software to calculate them on your computer already. Otherwise you can use Web-Enabled Scientific Services & Applications (**www.wessa.net/slr.wasp**) software, which covers almost every type of statistic calculation. The software is free online and provided through a joint research project with KU Leuven Association, a network of 13 institutions of higher education in Flanders.

For help in understanding these statistical techniques, read Gerard E Dallal of Tufts book, *The Little Handbook of Statistical Practice*, available free online (**www.tufts.edu/~gdallal/LHSP.HTM**). At Princeton's website (**http://dss.princeton.edu/online_help/analysis/interpreting_regression.htm**) you can find a tutorial and lecture notes on the subject as taught to its Master of International Business students.

Economic cycles

The current stage of the economic cycle that the business finds itself in when making forecasts will have a significant bearing on decision making. While few MBAs will be expected to have detailed knowledge of economics, they will be required to have a passing appreciation of the subject. Economies tend to follow a cyclical pattern that moves from boom, when demand is strong, to slump – the economists' term for a downturn. The death of the cycle has often been claimed as politicians believe they have become better managers of demand, but the 'this time it's different' school of thinking has been proved wrong time and time again.

The cycle itself is caused by the collective behaviour of billions of people – the unfathomable 'animal spirits' of businesses and households. John Maynard Keynes explained animal spirits this way:

> Most, probably, of our decisions to do something positive, the full consequences of which will be drawn out over many days to come, can only be taken as the result of animal spirits – a spontaneous urge to action rather than inaction, and not as the outcome of a weighted average of quantitative benefits multiplied by quantitative probabilities.

Added to the urge to act is the equally inevitable herd-like behaviour that leads to excessive optimism and pessimism. Charles Mackay (*Extraordinary Popular Delusions and the Madness of Crowds*), Joseph De La Vega (*Confusión de Confusiones*) and the more recent *Irrational Exuberance* (Robert J Shiller, 2nd edn) between them provide a comprehensive insight into the capacity for collective over-reaction. From the tulip mania in 17th-century Holland and the South Sea Bubble (1711–1720) to the internet bubble in 1999 and the collapse in US real estate in 2008 the story behind each bubble has been uncomfortably familiar. Strong market demand for some commodity (gold, copper, oil, etc), currency, property or type of share leads the general public to believe the trend cannot end. Over-optimism leads the public at large to overextend itself in acquiring the object of the mania, while lenders fall over each other to fan the flames. Finally, either the money runs out or groups of investors become cautious. Fear turns to panic selling, so creating a vicious downward spiral that can take years to recover from.

Categories of cycle

Economics is the science, in so far as it can be considered one, of the indistinctly knowable rather than the exactly predictable. Though all cycles, even the one you are in, are difficult to understand or predict with much accuracy there are discernable patterns and some distinctive characteristics.

Figure 11.3 shows an elegant curve, which depicts the theoretical textbook cycle. Four phases typically occur in each textbook cycle:

U1, where demand is picking up and toeing the line of the long-term trend;

U2, where demand exceeds the long-term trend;

D1, where demand dips down to hit the long-term trend; and

D2, where demand slumps below the long-term trend.

FIGURE 11.3   Textbook economic cycle

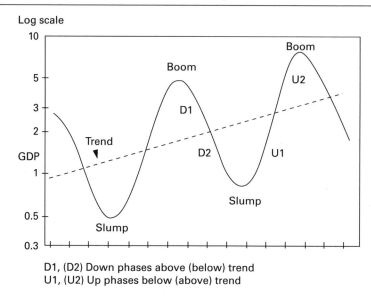

D1, (D2) Down phases above (below) trend
U1, (U2) Up phases below (above) trend

To make things more complicated there is not one cycle but at least four that operate, each with different characteristics yet interacting one with the others.

Kondratieff's long waves

Kondratieff (**www.kwaves.com/kond_overview.htm**), a Soviet economist who fell out with Russia's Marxist leaders and died in one of Stalin's prisons, advanced the theory that the advent of capitalism had created long wave economic cycles lasting around 50 years. His theories received a boost when the Great Depression (1929–33) hit world economies and resonated in Britain in 1980–81 when factory closures, high unemployment and crippling inflation devastated the country. The idea of a long wave is supported by evidence that major technologies from the first printing press to the internet take 50 years to yield full value, before themselves being overtaken.

Kuznet's cycle

US economist Simon Kuznet, a Nobel Laureate (1971) worked in the University of Pennsylvania and made a lifelong study of economic cycles. He identified a cycle of 15–25 years duration covering the period it takes to acquire land, get the necessary permissions, build property and sell. Also known as the 'building cycle' this has credibility as so much of economic life is influenced by property and the related purchases of furniture and associated professional charges, for example for lawyers, architects and surveyors.

Juglar cycle

Clement Juglar, a French economist, studied the rise and fall in interest rates and prices in the 1860s. He observed boom and bust waves of 9 to eleven years going through four phases in each cycle – prosperity, where investors piled into new and exciting ventures; crisis, when business failures started to rise; liquidation, when investors pull out of markets; and recession, when the consequences of these failures begin to be felt in the wider economy in terms of job losses and reduced consumption.

Kitchin cycle

In 1923, Joseph Kitchin published in the Harvard University Press an article entitled 'Review of economic statistics,' outlining his discovery of a 40-month cycle resulting from a study of US and UK statistics from 1890 to 1922. He observed a natural cyclical path caused, he believed, by movements in inventories. When demand appears to be stronger than it really is, companies build and carry too much inventory, leading people to over-estimate likely future growth. When that higher growth fails to materialize, inventories are reduced, often sharply, so inflicting a 'boom, bust' pressure on the economy.

Monitoring cycles

The National Bureau of Economic Research (**www.nber.org/cycles.htm**) provides a history of all US business cycle expansions and contractions since 1854. The Foundation for the Study of Cycles (**http://foundation-forthestudyofcycles.org**), an international research and educational institution established in 1941 by Harvard economist Edward R Dewey, provides a detailed explanation of different cycles. The Centre for Growth and Business Cycle Research based in the School of Social Sciences, The University of Manchester (**www.socialsciences.manchester.ac.uk/cgbcr**) provides details of current research, recent publications and downloadable discussion papers on all aspects of business cycles.

Business plans

The plan is in essence the route map from where the business is to where it wants to get and how it will go about getting there. It includes the roles and responsibilities of key players, the resources required in terms of money, people and materials, and so forth. While there is much debate about exactly what should go into the business plan and how it should be laid out, there is no doubt that it is the essential tool for ensuring that a well-thought-out strategy is executed successfully.

CASE STUDY   Boden

Johnnie Boden's first catalogue was hand-drawn by a friend with just eight items. That was back in 1991 and since then the business has gone from bedroom to boardroom by way of a near catastrophic lack of capital. The mail order company now competes with Gap, Marks & Spencer and John Lewis for a slice of the mainstream fashion market, with sales of £129.5 million, profits of £22.75 million, over 600 employees despatching over 3,000 orders every day from their warehouse.

Boden (**www.boden.co.uk**) has reason to feel pleased. But it very nearly wasn't the success story it undoubtedly is. In an interview with *Real Business* (**www.realbusiness. co.uk>ARTICLE**) Boden explained why for the first three years the mail order clothes company was losing money hand over fist. 'We kept on running out of cash,' says Boden. 'Although the concept was strong, I had no decent business plan.'

Below is the suggested general layout for a business plan as used on the MBA programme at Cranfield. From observations at international business plan competitions, it seems to be fairly universal.

Executive summary

This is the most important part of the plan and will form the heart of any presentation to the board, shareholders or prospective investors. Written last, it should be punchy, short – ideally one page but never more than two – and should enthuse any reader. Its primary purpose is to excite and inspire an audience to want to read the rest of the business plan.

The executive summary should start with a succinct table showing past performance in key areas and future objectives; see Table 11.1. This will give readers a clear view of the businesses capacity to perform as well as the scale of the task ahead.

Then the executive summary should continue with sections covering the following areas:

- What the primary products/services are and why they are better or different from what is around now.
- Which markets/customer groups will most need what you plan to offer and why.
- How close you are to being ready to sell your product/service and what if anything remains to be done.
- Why your organization has the skills and expertise to execute this strategy and, if new or additional people are required, who they are or how you will recruit them.

TABLE 11.1 Executive summary – history and projections

Last year	This year	Business area	Year 1	Year 2	Year 3 etc
		Sales turnover by product/service 1. 2. etc Total sales			
		Gross profit % Operating profit % Total staff nos			
		Sales staff nos Capital employed Return on capital employed %			

- Financial projections showing in summary the sales, profit, margins and cash position over the next three to five years.
- How the business will operate, sketching out the key steps from buying in any raw materials through to selling, delivering and getting paid.
- The physical resources – equipment, premises – the plan calls for.

The contents – putting flesh on the bones

Unlike the executive summary that is structured to reveal the essence of your business proposition, the plan itself should follow a logical sequence such as this:

- *Vision:* a vision's purpose is to stretch the organization's reach beyond its grasp. Generally, few people concerned with the company can now see how the vision is to be achieved, but all concerned agree that it would be great if it could be. Once your vision becomes reality it may be time for a new challenge, or perhaps even a new business.
- *Mission:* a mission statement explains concisely what you do, who you do it for and why you are better or different from others operating in your market. It should be narrow enough to give focus yet leave enough room for growth. Above all it should be believable to all concerned.
- *Objectives:* these are the big picture numbers such as market share, profit and return on investment that are to be achieved by successfully executing the chosen strategy.

- *Marketing:* this section provides information on the product/service on offer, customers and the size of the market, competitors, proposed pricing, promotion and selling method.

- *Operations:* this area covers any processes such as manufacture, assembly, purchasing, stock holding, delivery/fulfilment and website.

- *Financial projections:* detailed information on sales and cash flow for the period of the plan showing how much money is needed, for what, by when, and the most appropriate source of those funds: long- or short-term borrowings, equity, factoring or leasing finance for example.

- *Premises:* the space and equipment needed (if starting up from home, how the premises will comply with the law).

- *People:* the skills and experience you have on board that will help run this business and implement the chosen strategy; what other people you will need and where you will find them.

- *Administrative matters:* any IP (intellectual property) on your product or service; the insurance you need; the changes, if any, needed to the accounting, control and record systems.

- *Milestone timetable:* this should show the key actions you have still to take to be ready to achieve major objectives and the date these will be completed.

- *Appendices:* use these for any bulky information such as market studies, competitors' leaflets, customer endorsements, technical data, patents, CVs and the like that you refer to in your business plan.

Using business planning software

There are a number of free software packages that will help you through the process of writing a business plan. The ones listed below include some useful resources, spreadsheets and tips that may speed up the process, but are not substitutes for finding out the basic facts about your market, customers and competitors:

American Express (**http://home3.americanexpress.com/smallbusiness/ tool/biz_plan/index.asp**). American Express runs something it calls the Small Business Exchange Business Plan Workshop. This workshop will help you create a business plan to guide your business through the start-up or growth phase, or with a search for capital. Learning on their fictional plan, you will be ready to create one of your own.

BizPlanIt (**www.bizplanit.com/free.html**) has free resources including free business plan information, advice, articles, links and resources, and a free monthly newsletter, the *Virtual Business Plan* to pinpoint information.

Bplans.com (**www.bplans.com**), created by Palo Alto Software, offers thousands of pages of free sample plans, planning tools and expert advice to help you start and run your business. Their site has 60 free sample business plans on it and its software package, Business Plan Pro, has these plans plus a further 140. The sample business plans are tailored for every type of business, from aircraft rental to wedding gowns.

Royal Bank of Canada (**www.royalbank.com/sme/index.html**) has a wide range of useful help for entrepreneurs as well as its business plan writer package and three sample business plans.

Budgets and variances

Budgeting is the principle interface between the operating business units and the finance department. As a staff function the finance department or anyone with MBA skills will be expected to assist managers in preparing a detailed budget for the year ahead for every area of the organization and is in effect the first year of the business plan. MBAs are invariably expected to play a role in facilitating the process within their department. Budgets are usually reviewed at least halfway through the year and often quarterly. At that review a further quarter or half-year can be added to the budget to maintain a one-year budget horizon. This is known as a 'rolling quarterly (half-yearly) budget'.

Budget guidelines

Budgets should adhere to the following general principles:

- The budget must be based on realistic but challenging goals. Those goals are arrived at by both a top-down 'aspiration' of senior management and a bottom-up forecast of what the department concerned see as possible.
- The budget should be prepared by those responsible for delivering the results – the salespeople should prepare the sales budget and the production people the production budget. Senior managers must maintain open communication so that everyone knows what other parties are planning for.
- Agreement to the budget should be explicit. During the budgeting process, several versions of a particular budget should be discussed. For example, the boss may want a sales figure of £2 million, but the sales team's initial forecast is for £1.75 million. After some debate, £1.9 million may be the figure agreed upon. Once a figure is agreed, a virtual contract exists that declares a commitment from employees to achieve the target and commitments from the employer to be satisfied with the target and to supply resources to achieve it. It makes sense for this contract to be in writing.

- The budget needs to be finalized at least a month before the start of the year and not weeks or months into the year.
- The budget should undergo fundamental reviews periodically throughout the year to make sure all the basic assumptions that underpin it still hold good.
- Accurate information to review performance against budgets should be available seven to 10 working days before the month's end.

Variance analysis

Explaining variances is also an MBA-type task so performance needs to be carefully monitored and compared against the budget as the year proceeds, and corrective action must be taken where necessary. This has to be done on a monthly basis (or using shorter time intervals if required), showing both the company's performance during the month in question and throughout the year so far.

Looking at Table 11.2 we can see at a glance that the business is behind on sales for this month, but ahead on the yearly target. The convention is to put all unfavourable variations in brackets. Hence, a higher-than-budgeted sales figure does not have brackets, while a higher materials cost does. We can also see that while profit is running ahead of budget, the profit margin is slightly behind (−0.30 per cent). This is partly because other direct costs, such as labour and distribution in this example, are running well ahead of budget.

TABLE 11.2   The fixed budget

Heading	Month			Year to date		
	Budget	Actual	Variance	Budget	Actual	Variance
Sales	805*	753	(52)	6,358	7,314	956
Materials	627	567	60	4,942	5,704	(762)
Materials margin	178	186	8	1,416	1,610	194
Direct costs	74	79	(5)	595	689	(94)
Gross profit	104	107	3	820	921	101
Percentage	**12.92**	**14.21**	**1.29**	**12.90**	**12.60**	**(0.30)**

* Figures indicate thousands of pounds

Flexing the budget

A budget is based on a particular set of sales goals, few of which are likely to be exactly met in practice. Table 11.2 shows a company that has used 762,000 more materials than budgeted. As more has been sold, this is hardly surprising. The way to manage this situation is to flex the budget to show what, given the sales that actually occurred, would be expected to happen to expenses. Applying the budget ratios to the actual data does this. For example, materials were planned to be 22.11 per cent of sales in the budget. By applying that to the actual month's sales, a materials cost of 587,000 is arrived at.

TABLE 11.3   The flexed budget

Heading	Month			Year to date		
	Budget	Actual	Variance	Budget	Actual	Variance
Sales	753*	753	–	7,314	7,314	–
Materials	587	567	20	5,685	5,704	(19)
Materials margin	166	186	20	1,629	1,610	(19)
Direct costs	69	79	(10)	685	689	(4)
Gross profit	97	107	10	944	921	(23)
Percentage	**12.92**	**14.21**	**1.29**	**12.90**	**12.60**	**(0.30)**

* Figures indicate thousands of pounds

Looking at the flexed budget in Table 11.3, we can see that the company has spent £19,000 more than expected on materials, given the level of sales actually achieved, rather than the 762,000 overspend shown in the fixed budget.

The same principle holds for other direct costs, which appear to be running £94,000 over budget for the year. When we take into account the extra sales shown in the flexed budget, we can see that the company has actually spent £4,000 over budget on direct costs. While this is serious, it is not as serious as the fixed budget suggests. The flexed budget allows you to concentrate your efforts on dealing with true variances in performance.

The SCORE website (**www.score.org**>Business Tools>Template Gallery> Sales Forecast) has a downloadable Excel spreadsheet from which you can make sales and cost projections on a trial and error basis. Once you are satisfied with your projection, use the profit and loss projection (**www. score.org**>Business Tools>Template Gallery>Profit and Loss Projection (3 Years)) to complete your budget.

Seasonality and trends

The figures shown for each period of the budget are not the same. For example, a sales budget of 1.2 million for the year does not translate to 100,000 a month. The exact figure depends on two factors: 1) The projected trend may forecast that, while sales at the start of the year are 80,000 a month, they will change to 120,000 a month by the end of the year; the average would be 100,000. 2) By virtue of seasonal factors, each month may also be adjusted up or down from the underlying trend. You could expect the sales of heating oil, for example, to peak in the autumn and tail off in the late spring.

The core

12

- Understanding markets
- Getting to grips with people
- Shaping organizational structures
- Strategic options
- Tools of strategic analysis

Every MBA student, whether he or she takes a general programme or one that specializes in a particular disciple, as this book does, will be required to study the four core disciples. These contain the basic tools that an MBA will use or need to refer to more or less every working day, and comprise:

1 *Finance and accounting.* The subjects covered in this book.

2 *Marketing.* The outward face of a business is addressed to its customers and its success or failure is the measure of how well it performs in the market. Markets have to be identified, product attributes assessed, competitors understood and advertising messages developed to reach chosen markets. Marketing is perhaps the discipline with the largest number of misunderstood and misapplied business tools of all.

3 *Organizational behaviour.* Organizing, inspiring, motivating, rewarding and managing both individuals and teams is the enduring challenge in organizations as they grow and develop. Often people are the defining advantage that one organization has and can sustain over its competitors.

4 *Strategy.* This is the unifying discipline, often called 'business strategy'. It deals with the core purpose of an enterprise and how it should respond to the challenges of a fast-changing environment. It centres not just on how strategy is shaped, for example using Porter's Five Forces, but with the recognition that no organization can be truly great in the absence of shared goals, values and a sense of purpose – a shared picture of the future of the enterprise.

This chapter contains the essential tools within each of those disciples to enable a business finance student to bring his or her skills to bear and to play a more rounded role in shaping and implementing the direction of the organization he or she works in but is inhibited by a lack of fundamental business knowledge.

Marketing

Business schools didn't invent marketing but they certainly ensured its pre-eminence as an academic discipline. *Principles of Marketing* and *Marketing Management*, seminal books on the subject by Philip Kotler *et al* of Kellogg School of Management at Northwestern University, have been core reading on management programmes the world over for decades. The schools' Marketing Department has rated at the top in all national and international ranking surveys conducted during the past 15 years. (You can see Kotler lecture at **www.anaheim.ed**>CEO Webcast.)

Marketing is defined as the process that ensures the right products and services get to the right markets at the right time and at the right price. The devil in that sentence lies in the use of the word 'right'. The deal has to work for customers, because if they don't want what you have to offer the game is over before you begin. You have to offer value and satisfaction otherwise people will either choose an apparently superior competitor, or if they do buy from you and are dissatisfied they won't buy again. Worse still, they may bad-mouth you to a lot of other people. For marketers, being right means there have to be enough people wanting the product or service to make the venture profitable; and ideally those numbers should be getting bigger rather than smaller.

So inevitably marketing is something of a voyage of discovery for both supplier and consumer from which both parties learn something and hopefully improve. The boundaries of marketing stretch from inside the mind of the customers, perhaps uncovering emotions they were barely aware of, out to the logistic support systems that get the product or service into customers' hands. Each part of the value chain from company to consumer has the potential to add value or kill the deal. For example, at the heart of the Amazon business proposition are a superlatively efficient warehousing and delivery system and a simple zero-cost way for customers to return products they don't want and get immediate refunds. These factors are every bit as important as elements of Amazon's marketing strategy as are its product range, website structure, Google placement or its competitive pricing.

Marketing is also a circuitous activity. As you explore the topics below you will see that you need the answers to some questions before you can move on, and indeed once you have some answers you may have to go back a step to review an earlier stage.

Market research

The purpose of market research is to ensure you have sufficient information on customers, competitors and markets to be reasonably confident enough people want to buy what you want to sell at a price that will give you a viable business proposition.

You do not have to launch a product or enter a market to prove there are *no* customers for your goods or services. Frequently even some modest market research beforehand can give clear guidance as to whether your venture will succeed or not.

While big businesses may employ market research agencies to design and execute their research, an MBA should understand the process and be able to carry out elementary research quickly and on a low budget.

The importance of market share

The market you operate in will be shared by various competing businesses in different proportions. Typically there will be a market leader, a couple of market followers and a host of businesses trailing in their wake. The slice each competitor has of a market is its 'market share'. You will find that marketing people are fixated on market share, perhaps even more so than on absolute sales. That may seem little more than a rational desire to beat the 'enemy' and appear higher in rankings, but it has a much more deep-seated and profound logic.

Back in the 1960s a firm of US management consultants observed a consistent relationship between the cost of producing an item (or delivering a service) and the total quantity produced over the life of the product concerned. They noticed that total unit costs (labour and materials) fell by between 20 and 30 per cent for every doubling of the cumulative quantity produced.

So any company capturing a sizeable market share will have an implied cost advantage over any competitor with a smaller market share. That cost advantage can be used to make more profit, lower prices and compete for an even greater share of the market, or to invest in making the product better and so stealing a march on competitors.

Competitive position

It follows that if market share and relative size are important marketing goals, you need to assess the positions of your products and services relative to the competition in your relevant market. The technique most often used to carry out this analysis is SWOT.

Strengths, Weakness, Opportunities and Threats (SWOT)

This is a general-purpose tool developed in the late 1960s at Harvard by Learned, Christensen, Andrews and Guth, and published in their seminal

FIGURE 12.1   Example SWOT chart for a hypothetical Cobra Beer competitor

Strengths	*Weaknesses*
1. Beginning to get brand recognition 2. Established strongly in Indian restaurants	1. Don't have own production 2. Need more equity finance to be able to advertise more strongly
Opportunities	*Threats*
1. We could capitalize more on our relationships in Indian restaurants 2. We are only in the UK – so have the world to go for	1. We are vulnerable to a big player targeting our niche 2. Our sector looks like being the target of major tax rises which could reduce overall demand

book, *Business Policy, Text and Cases* (Richard D Irwin, 1969). The SWOT framework consists of a cross with space in each quadrant to summarize your observations; see Figure 12.1.

In this example the SWOT analysis is restricted to a handful of areas, though in practice the list might run to a dozen or more areas within each of the four quadrants. The purpose of the SWOT analysis is to suggest possible ways to improve the competitive position and hence market share while minimizing the dangers of perceived threats. A strategy that this SWOT would suggest as being worth pursuing could be to launch a low-alcohol product (and sidestep the tax threat) that would appeal to all restaurants, rather than just Indian (widen the market). The company could also start selling in India using the international cachet of being a UK brand. That would open up the market still further and limit the damage that larger UK competitors could inflict.

Market segmentation

Different customers can have different needs of much the same product or service. The classic marketing case is that of the different benefits toothpaste users expect, with one group preoccupied with whiteness and another only interested in fighting tooth decay. Tackling these different needs means that we have to organize our marketing effort to address them individually – but trying to satisfy everyone may mean that we end up satisfying no one fully. The marketing process that helps us deal with this seemingly impossible task is 'market segmentation'. This is the process whereby customers and potential customers are organized into clusters or groups of 'similar' types.

For example, a carpet/upholstery cleaning business has private individuals and business clients running restaurants and guest-houses. These two segments are fundamentally different, with one segment being more focused on cost and the other more concerned that the work is carried out with the least disruption to their business. Each of these customer groups is motivated to buy for different reasons and your marketing message has to be modified accordingly.

The marketing mix

The term 'marketing mix' has a pedigree going back to the late 1940s when marketing managers referred to mixing ingredients to create strategies. The concept was formalized by E Jerome McCarthy, a Marketing Professor at Michigan State University in 1960. The mix of ingredients with which marketing strategy can be developed and implemented are price, product (or/and service), promotion and place. A fifth 'P', people, is often added. Just as with cooking, taking the same or similar ingredients in different proportions can result in very different 'products'. A change in the way these elements are put together can produce an offering tailored to meet the needs of a specific market segment.

The ingredients in the marketing mix only represent the elements that are largely, though not entirely, within a firm's control. Uncontrollable ingredients include the state of the economy, changes in legislation, new and powerful market entrants and rapid changes in technology.

Understanding customer needs

The founder of a successful cosmetics firm, when asked what he did, replied: 'In the factories we make perfume, in the shops we sell dreams.' Those of us in business usually start out defining our business in physical terms. Customers on the other hand see businesses having as their primary value the ability to satisfy their needs. Even firms that adopt 'customer satisfaction' or 'customer delight' as their stated maxim often find it a more complex goal than it at first appears. Take Blooming Marvellous, a business making fashionable maternity wear. It makes clothes for mothers to be, sure enough: but the primary customer need it is aiming to satisfy is not to preserve their modesty or to keep them warm. The need it was aiming for was much higher: it was ensuring its customers would feel fashionably dressed, which is about the way people interact with each other and how they feel about themselves. Just splashing, say, a Tog rating showing the thermal properties of the fabric, as you would with a duvet, would cut no ice with Blooming Marvellous's potential market.

Until you have clearly defined the needs of your market(s) you cannot begin to assemble a product or service to satisfy them. Fortunately help is at hand. A US psychologist, Abraham Maslow, who taught at Brandeis University, Boston and whose International Business School now ranks highly in *The Economist's* survey of top business schools (see Appendix 2 (online) for more on business school rankings) demonstrated in his research that 'all customers are goal seekers who gratify their needs by purchase and consumption'. He then went a bit further and classified consumer needs into a five-stage pyramid he called the 'hierarchy of needs', starting with physiological needs, such as for air, water, sleep and food, which are all absolutely essential to sustain life. Then comes safety: the need of consumers is to feel safe and secure. Social needs are concerned with the need to belong – associations, friendships and other groupings. Until these basic needs are satisfied, higher needs such as esteem and self-actualization will not be considered. These last two are about the need to be respected by others and to be happy and content in yourself.

You can read more about Maslow's needs hierarchy and how to take it into account in understanding customers on the Net MBA website (**www.netmba.com**>Management>Maslow's Hierarchy of Needs).

Promotion and advertising

The answers to these five questions underpin all advertising and promotional strategies:

1 What do you want to happen?
2 If that happens how much is it worth?
3 What message will make it happen?
4 What media will work best?
5 How will you measure the effectiveness of your effort and expense?

1. What do you want to happen?

Do you want prospective customers to visit your website, phone, write or e-mail you, return a card, or to send an order in the post? Do you expect them to have an immediate need to which you want them to respond now, or do you want them to remember you at some future date when they have a need for whatever it is you are selling?

The more you are able to identify a specific response in terms of orders, visits, phone calls or requests for literature, the better your promotional effort will be tailored to achieve your objective, and the more clearly you will be able to assess the effectiveness of your promotion and its cost versus its yield.

2. How much is that worth to you?

Once you know what you want a particular promotional activity to achieve, it becomes a little easier to estimate its cost. Suppose a £1,000 advertisement is expected to generate 100 enquiries for your product. If experience tells you that on average 10 per cent of enquiries result in orders, and your profit margin is £200 per product, then you can expect an extra £2,000 profit. That 'benefit' is much greater than the £1,000 cost of the advertisement, so it seems a worthwhile investment. With your target in mind you can decide how much to spend on advertising each month, revising that figure in the light of experience.

3. Deciding the message

Your promotional message must be built on facts about the company and about the product. The stress here is on the word 'facts', and while there may be many types of fact relating to you and your products, your customers are only interested in two: the facts that influence their buying decisions, and the ways in which your business and its products stand out from the competition.

These facts must take account of customer needs. There is an assumption sometimes that everyone buys for obvious, logical reasons only, when we all know of innumerable examples showing this is not so. Do people only buy new clothes when the old ones are worn out? Do bosses have desks that are bigger than their subordinates because they have more papers to put on them?

4. Choosing the media

Your market research should produce a clear understanding of who your potential customer group are which in turn will provide pointers as to how to reach them. But even when you know who you want to reach with your advertising message it's not always plain sailing. *The Fishing Times*, for example, will be effective at reaching fishermen but less so at reaching their partners who might be persuaded to buy them fishing tackle for Christmas or birthdays. Also, *The Fishing Times* will be jam-packed with competitors. It might just be worth considering a web ad on a page giving tide tables to avoid going head-to-head with competitors, or getting into a gift catalogue to grab that market's attention.

If consumers already know what they want to buy and are just looking for a supplier then, according to statistics, around 60 per cent will look at the print edition of *Yellow Pages* (or similar); 12 per cent will use a search engine; 11 per cent will use telephone directory enquiries and 7 per cent online *Yellow Pages*. Only 3 per cent will turn to a friend. But if you are trying to persuade consumers to think about buying a product or service at a particular time, then a leaflet or flyer may be a better option. Once again it's back to your objectives in advertising. The more explicit they are the easier it will be to choose media.

5. Measuring results

Judy Lever, co-founder of Blooming Marvellous, the maternity-wear company mentioned earlier, believes strongly not only in evaluating the results of advertising, but in monitoring a particular media capacity to reach her customers:

> We start off with one-sixteenth of a page ads in the specialist press, then once the medium has proved itself we progress gradually to half a page, which

experience shows to be our optimum size. On average there are 700,000 pregnancies a year, but the circulation of specialist magazines is only around the 300,000 mark. We have yet to discover a way of reaching all our potential customers at the right time – in other words, early on in their pregnancies.

Place

Place' is the fourth 'P' in the marketing mix. This aspect of marketing strategy is about how products and services are actually got into customer's hands.

If you are a retailer, restaurant or hotel chain, for example, your customers will come to you. Here, your physical location will most probably be the key to success. For businesses in the manufacturing field it is more likely that you will go out to 'find' customers. In this case it will be your channels of distribution that are the vital link. For many businesses delivering a service, the internet will be both the ordering and fulfilment vehicle.

Organizational behaviour

Organizational behaviour, usually shortened to OB, is the whole rather amorphous area that deals with people, why they behave the way they do and how to create and manage an organization that can achieve the goals set for the business. As one cynical CEO summarized the task, 'to get people to do what I want them to do because they want to do it'.

The single most prevalent reason for a strategy failing lies in its implementation; the analysis and planning behind a proposed course of action are rarely the root of the problem. That is more likely to lie in the selection of the people to implement the strategy, their management, motivation, rewards and the way in which they are organized and led. Stated like that it sounds a fairly simple task.

Unfortunately people both individually and collectively are rarely malleable and infinitely variable in their likely responses to situations. The famous German military strategist Moltke's statement that, 'No campaign plan survives first contact with the enemy' applies here if the word 'enemy' is replaced by 'organization'. However, by understanding and applying a number of principles and concepts on the typical MBA syllabus you can improve an organization's chances of achieving its objectives.

Strategy vs structure, people and systems

This is the 'which came first' question akin to that of the chicken and the egg. Unless you are starting up an organization on a greenfield site with no people other than yourself and only a pile of cash, every business situation involves some compromise between the ideal and the possible when it comes to people and structures.

FIGURE 12.2 A framework for understanding organizational behaviour

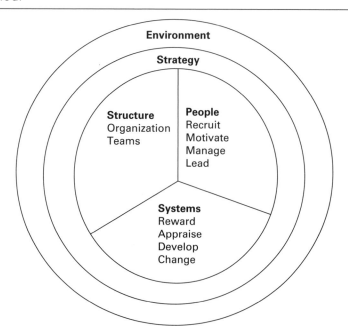

The theory is clear. An organization's strategy, itself a product of its business environment, determines the shape of the organization structure, the sort of people it will employ and how they will be managed, controlled and rewarded. But in the real world the business environment is constantly changing as the economy fluctuates, competitors come and go and consumer needs, desires and aspirations alter. In any event a business is limited in its freedom of action. However violent and essential a change in strategy, a business will rarely be free to hire and fire staff at will simply to change direction. The exception is in the case of a complete closure or withdrawal from an activity such as that of Marks & Spencer's controversial closure of its French outlets in 2001. This move was considered vital to the survival of the whole business, and despite May Day protests in France the company's shares rose 7 per cent on the announcement.

Figure 12.2 is a useful aide to understanding how to approach OB. The concentric circles are a metaphor to remind us of the circular nature of the subject. You can't just tackle one area without having an impact on others.

Organizational charts

Pictorial methods of describing how organizations work have been around for centuries. Both the Roman and Prussian armies had descriptions of their hierarchical structures, and the latter incorporated line and staff relationships. There is also some evidence that the ancient Egyptians documented their methods for organizing and dividing workers on major projects such as the pyramids. However, Daniel C McCallum is generally credited with developing the first systematic set of organizational charts in 1855 to organize railroad building on an efficient basis. The trigger for his innovation was the discovery that the building costs per mile of track did not drop with the length of line being built, contrary to logic. The inefficiencies were being caused by poor organization.

Basic hierarchical organization

The simple structure shown in Figure 12.3 has every person or part of the organization reporting in to one person. It works well when the organization is small, decisions are simple or routine and communications are easy.

FIGURE 12.3 Basic hierarchical organization chart

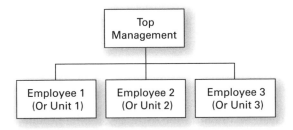

This basic structure can be based on one of several groupings including:

- functions such as marketing or manufacturing;
- geography such as country or region;
- product;
- customer or market segment such as trade, consumers, new accounts or key accounts.

Span of control

The number of people a manager can have reporting to him or her in a hierarchy is governed by the span of control. Few people reporting and the span of control is narrow; more is wide.

A narrow span of control means any one manager has fewer people reporting to him or her so communication should be better and control easier. However, as the organization grows that usually means creating more and more layers of management, so negating any earlier efficiency.

A wide span of control, also known as a flat management structure, involves having many people or units reporting to one person. This usually means having fewer layers of management, but it calls for a greater level of skill from those doing the managing. The nature of the tasks being carried out by subordinates will limit the capacity to run a flat organization. For example, a regional manager responsible for identical units such as branches of a supermarket chain, supported by good and well-developed control systems, may be able to have 10 or more direct reports. But if the organization comprises very different types of unit, for example retail outlets, central bakeries, garages, factories, accounts departments and sales teams, the ability of any one manager to handle that diversity will be limited.

A further factor to take into account is the skill level of both managers and managed. A higher skilled workforce can operate with a wider span of control as they will need less supervision, and a higher skilled manager can control a greater number of staff.

Line and staff organization

One way to keep an organization structure flat as the enterprise gets bigger and more complex is to introduce staff functions that take over some of the common duties of unit managers. For example, production managers could probably handle their own recruitment, selection and training of staff while they have a dozen or so people in their domain. Once that expands to hundreds, and if growth is also impacting on other management areas such as sales and marketing, then it may be more efficient to create a specialist HR unit to support the line managers.

Staff positions support line managers by providing knowledge and expertise, but the buck ultimately stops with the line manager. Three types of authority are created in a line and staff organization (see Figure 12.4), and alongside some efficiencies there is the possibility for conflict:

1 *Line authority* goes down the chain of command, giving those further up the right and responsibility to instruct those below them to carry out specific tasks.

2 *Staff authority* is the right and responsibility to advise line managers in certain areas. For example, an HR staffer will advise a line manager on redundancy terms, conditions of employment and disciplinary issues.

3 *Functional authority* or limited line authority gives a staff member the ultimate sanction over particular functions such as safety or financial reporting. There are possibilities for conflict in the relationship between line and staff but these can be minimized in two ways. In the first instance staff people report to their own superiors who have line authority over them. Second, line and staff personnel can be organized into teams with shared goals and objectives.

FIGURE 12.4   Line and staff organization chart

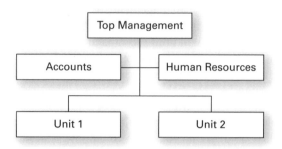

Functional organization

In a functional organization the staff and line managers all report to a common senior manager (see Figure 12.5). This places more of a burden on the senior manager, who has a wider span of control and a greater variety of tasks to take responsibility for. However, this structure concentrates all responsibility in one person and so minimizes the potential for conflict. It may also deny an organization the high level of expertise that comes with having a professional staff function. For example, this would leave the onus for being fully conversant with current employment law on a production manager, rather than giving him or her access to staff advice. He or she can of course read up on the law, but that is not quite as good as having it as a part of an everyday skill and experience base.

FIGURE 12.5   Functional organization chart

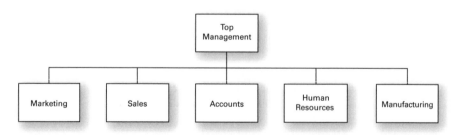

Matrix organization

A matrix organization gives two people line authority for interlocking areas of responsibility. In Figure 12.6 you can see that a manager is responsible for sales of product group 1 in both Europe and Asia. However, a manager is also responsible for the sales of all product groups within his or her continent.

The aim of a matrix structure is to ensure all key areas in an organization have a line manager responsible for championing them. There is still the possibility for conflict of interest. For example, the person responsible for product group 2 may try to get more attention for his or her product in a particular market than it really warrants. In theory the managers in matrix organizations are senior enough to iron out their differences. That is not always the case in practice and their mutual boss has to resolve the issue.

FIGURE 12.6   Matrix organization chart

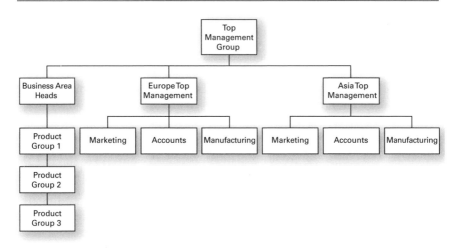

Strategic business unit (SBU)

SBUs (see Figure 12.7) are in effect separate enterprises with full responsibility for their own profit or loss. They may be organized in any one of the above structures. If they don't have their own specialist staff function they may buy it in from the parent company when required. This maintains the concept of full profit accountability.

SBUs are further divided into those that simply have control over current revenue and expenditure and those 'investment centres' that can make capital expenditure decisions such as setting up a new plant, investing in research and development or buying up competitors.

FIGURE 12.7 Strategic business unit organization chart

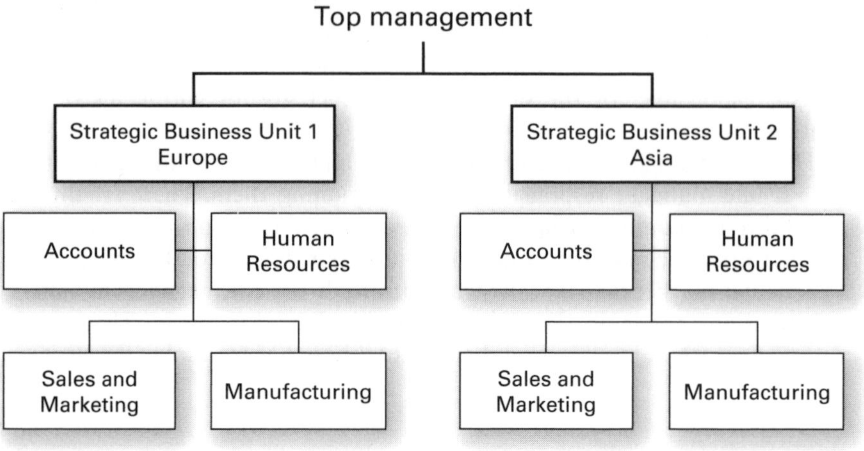

Motivation

As a subject for serious study, motivation is a relatively new 'science'. Thomas Hobbes, a 17th-century English philosopher, suggested that human nature could best be understood as self-interested cooperation. He claimed motivation could be summarized as choices revolving around pain or pleasure. Sigmund Freud was equally frugal in suggesting only two basic needs: the life and the death instinct. These ideas were the first to seriously challenge the time-honoured 'carrot and stick' method of motivation that pervaded every aspect of organizational life from armies at war to weavers in Britain during the Industrial Revolution.

The first hint, in the business world that there might be more to motivation than rewards and redundancy came with Harvard Business School Professor Elton Mayo's renowned Hawthorne Studies. These were conducted between 1927 and 1932 at the Western Electric Hawthorne Works in Chicago. Starting out to see what effect illumination had on productivity, Mayo moved on to see how fatigue and monotony fitted into the equation by varying rest breaks, temperature, humidity and work hours, even providing a free meal at one point. Working with a team of six women, Mayo changed every parameter he could think of including increasing and decreasing working hours and rest breaks, then finally returning to the original conditions. Every change resulted in an improvement in productivity, except when two 10-minute pauses morning and afternoon were expanded to six 5-minute pauses. These frequent work pauses, they felt, upset their work rhythm.

Mayo's conclusion was that showing' someone upstairs cares' and engendering a sense of ownership and responsibility were important motivators that could be harnessed by management. After Mayo came a flurry of theories on motivation. William McDougall in his book, *The Energies of Men* (1932, Methuen) listed 18 basic needs that he referred to as 'instincts' (eg, curiosity, sell-assertions, submission). H A Murray, Assistant Director of the Harvard Psychological Clinic, catalogued 20 core psychological needs including achievement, affiliation and power. The motivation theories most studied and applied by business school graduates are those espoused by Maslow (see earlier in this chapter) and the following.

Theory X and Theory Y

Douglas McGregor, an American social psychologist who taught at two top schools, Harvard and the Massachusetts Institute of Technology (MIT), developed these theories to try to explain the assumptions about human behaviour that underlies management action.

Theory X makes the following assumptions. The average person has an inherent dislike of work and will avoid it if possible, so management needs to put the emphasis on productivity, incentive schemes and the idea of a 'fair day's work'. Because of this dislike of work, most people must be coerced, controlled, directed and threatened with punishment to get them to achieve the company's goals. People prefer to be directed, want to avoid responsibility, have little ambition and really want a secure life above all.

While Theory X does explain some human behaviour, it does not provide a framework for understanding behaviour in the best businesses. McGregor, and others, have proposed an alternative.

Theory Y has as its basis the belief that physical or mental effort at work is as natural as either rest or play. Under the right conditions, hard work can be source of great satisfaction. Under the wrong conditions it can be a drudge, which will inspire little effort and less thought from those forced to participate. Once committed to a goal, most people at work are capable of a high degree of self-management. Job satisfaction and personal recognition are the highest 'rewards' that can be given, and will result in the greatest level of commitment to the task in hand. Under the right conditions most people will accept responsibility and even welcome more of it. Few people in business are being 'used' to anything like their capacity, nor are they contributing creatively towards solving problems.

Typical Theory X bosses are likely to keep away from their employees as much as possible. However small the business, for example, they may make sure they have an office to themselves, and its door is kept tightly shut. Contact with others will be confined to giving instructions about work and complaining about poor performance. A Theory Y approach will involve collaborating over decisions rather than issuing orders, and sharing feedback so everyone can learn from both success and failures, rather than just reprimanding when things go wrong.

Hygiene and motivation theory

Frederick Hertzberg, Professor of Psychology at Case Western Reserve University in Cleveland, discovered that some distinct factors were the cause of job satisfaction and dissatisfaction. His research revealed that five factors stood out as strong determinants of job satisfaction:

1 *Achievement.* People want to succeed, so if you can set goals that people can reach and better, they will be much more satisfied than if they are constantly missing targets.

2 *Recognition.* Everyone likes his or her hard work to be acknowledged. Not everyone wants that recognition made in the same way, however.

3 *Responsibility.* People like the opportunity to take responsibility for their own work and for the whole task. This helps them grow as individuals.

4 *Advancement.* Promotion or at any rate progress are key motivators. In a small firm, providing career prospects for key staff can be a fundamental reason for growth.

5 *The attractiveness of work itself (job interest).* There is no reason why a job should be dull. You need to make people's jobs interesting and give them a say in how their work is done. That will encourage new ideas on how things can be done better.

When the reasons for dissatisfaction were analysed, they were found to be concerned with a different range of factors:

- *Company policy:* rules, formal and informal, such as start and finish times, meal breaks, dress code.
- *Supervision:* the extent to which employees are allowed to get on with the job, or have someone looking over their shoulder all day.
- *Administration:* whether things work well, or paperwork in a muddle and supplies always come in late.
- *Salary:* whether employees getting at least the going rate and benefits comparable with others.
- *Working conditions:* whether people are expected to work in substandard conditions with poor equipment and little job security.
- *Interpersonal relationships:* whether the atmosphere at work is good or people are at daggers drawn.

Hertzberg called these causes of dissatisfaction 'hygiene factors'. He reasoned that the lack of hygiene will cause disease, but the presence of hygienic conditions will not, of itself, produce good health. So the lack of adequate 'job hygiene' will cause dissatisfaction but hygienic conditions alone will not bring about job satisfaction; to do that you have to work on the determinants of job satisfaction.

Strategy

Joseph Lampel, Professor of Strategy at Cass Business School and author of *Strategy Bites Back* (2005, Financial Times-Prentice Hall) tells the story of when he received an urgent request from one of his MBA students: 'Could I please provide a clear and easy-to-use definition of strategy?' 'My career,' wrote the student, 'may depend on it,' and 'besides I would like to start the course with a better idea of what I am supposed to be looking out for.' Lampel goes on to explain that he was less surprised by the request than by the fact that it came before the course had even begun. He was used to being approached at the end of the course by students confessing that they still do not know exactly what strategy is.

Strategy, though a core subject in every business school, is less an academic discipline that an ever-shifting appraisal of how an organization should position itself to best meet the challenges it faces. Rather like the quote attributed to one Governor of the Bank of England who said that the true meaning of Christmas would not be apparent until Easter, when it comes to estimating retail sales, successful strategies are really only recognizable after the event.

The three generic strategies

Credit for devising the most succinct and usable way to get a handle on the big picture has to be given to Michael E Porter, who trained as an economist at Princeton, taking an MBA (1971) and PhD (1973) at Harvard Business School where he is now a professor. His book, *Competitive Strategy: Techniques for analyzing industries and competitors* (1980, Free Press), in its 63rd printing and translated into 19 languages, sets out the now accepted methodology for devising strategy. As well as being essential reading in most business schools, courses based on Porter's work are taught in partnership with more than 80 other universities around the world using curriculum, video content and instructor support developed at Harvard.

Porter's first observation was that two factors above all influenced a business's chances of making superior profits. First, there was the attractiveness or otherwise of the industry in which it primarily operated. Second, and in terms of an organization's sphere of influence more important, was how the business positions itself within that industry. In that respect a business could only have a cost advantage in that it could make product or deliver service for less than others. Or it could different in a way that mattered to consumers, so that its offers would be unique, or at least relatively so. He added a further twist to his prescription. Businesses could follow either a cost advantage path or a differentiation path industry wide, or they could take a third path – they could concentrate on a narrow specific segment (see earlier in this chapter for more on market segments), either with cost advantage or differentiation. This he termed 'focus' strategy.

Cost leadership

Low cost should not be confused with low price. A business with low costs may or may not pass on those savings to customers. They could use that position alongside tight cost controls and low margins to create an effective barrier to others considering either entering or extending their penetration of that market. Low cost strategies are most likely to be achievable in large markets, requiring large-scale capital investment, where production or service volumes are high and economies of scale can be achieved from long runs.

Low costs are not a lucky accident; they can be achieved through the following main activities.

Operating efficiencies

These include new processes, methods of working or less costly ways of working. Ryanair and easyJet are examples where analysing every component of the business made it possible to strip out major elements of cost – meals, free baggage and allocated seating for example – while leaving the essential proposition – we will fly you from A to B – intact.

Product redesign

This involves fundamentally rethinking a product or service to look for more efficient ways to work or cheaper substitute materials to work with. The motor industry has adopted this approach with 'platform sharing', where major players including Citroen, Peugeot and Toyota have rethought their entry car models to share major components.

Product standardization

A wide range of product and service offers claiming to extend customer choice invariably leads to higher costs. The challenge is to be sure that proliferation gives real choice and adds value. In 2008 the UK railway network took a long hard look at its dozens of different fare structures and scores of names, often for identical price structures, that had remained largely unchanged since the 1960s, and reduced them to three basic product propositions. Adopting this and other common standards across the rail network aimed to substantially reduce the excessively transaction costs of selling tickets.

Economies of scale

This can be achieved only by being big or bold. The same head office, warehousing network and distribution chain can support Tesco's 3,263 stores as it can, say, the 997 that Somerfield has. The former will have a lower cost base by virtue of having more outlets to spread its costs over as well as having more purchasing power.

The experience (or learning) curve

The fact that costs decline as the output volume of a product or service increased, though well known earlier, was first developed in 1936 as a usable accounting process by T P Wright, a US aeronautical engineer. His process became known as the 'Cumulative average model' or Wright's Model. Subsequently models were developed by a team of researchers at Stanford known as the Unit Time Model or Crawford's Model, and The Boston Consulting Group (BCG) popularized the process with its Experience Curve showing that each time the cumulative volume of doing something – either making a product or delivering a service – doubled, the unit cost dropped by constant and predictable amounts. The reasons for the cost drop include:

- Repetition makes people more familiar with tasks and consequently faster.
- More efficient materials and equipment becomes available from suppliers as their own costs go down through the experience curve effect.
- Organization, management and control procedures improve.
- Engineering and production problems are solved.

BCG was founded in 1963 by Bruce D Henderson, a former Bible salesman and engineering graduate from Vanderbilt University, who left the Harvard Business School 90 days before graduation to work for Westinghouse Corporation. From there he went on to head Arthur D Little's management services unit before joining the Boston Safe Deposit and Trust Company to start a consulting arm for the bank. Naming this the Experience Curve, it was the strategy tool that put BCG on the path to success and has served it well ever since.

The value of the experience curve (shown in Figure 12.8) as a strategic process is that it helps a business predict future unit costs and gives a signal

FIGURE 12.8   The experience curve

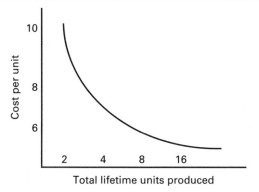

Total lifetime units produced

when costs fail to drop at the historic rate, both vital pieces of information for firms pursuing a cost leadership strategy. Every industry has a different experience curve that itself varies over time. You can find out more about how to calculate the curve for your industry on the Management and Accounting website (**http://maaw.info/LearningCurveSummary.htm**). The National Aeronautics and Space Agency (**http://cost.jsc.nasa.gov/learn.html**) provides a learning curve calculator.

Differentiation

The key to differentiation is a deep understanding of what customers really want and need and, more important, what they are prepared to pay more for. Apple's opening strategy was a 'fun' operating system based on icons, rather than the dull MS-DOS. This belief came from their understanding that computer users were mostly young and wanted an intuitive command system and the 'graphical user interface' delivered just that. Apple has continued its differentiation strategy, but adds design and fashion to ease of control in the way it delivers extra value. Sony and BMW and are also examples of differentiators. Both have distinctive and desirable differences in their products and neither they nor Apple offers the lowest price in their respective industries; customers are willing to pay extra for the idiosyncratic and prized differences embedded in their products.

Differentiation doesn't have to be confined to just the marketing arena, nor does it always lead to success if the subject of that differentiation goes out of fashion without much warning. Northern Rock, the failed bank that had to be nationalized to stay in business, thought its strategy of raising most of the money it lent out in mortgages through the money markets was a sure winner. It allowed the bank to grow faster than its competitors, which placed more reliance on depositors for their funds. As long as interest rates were low and the money market functioned smoothly it worked, but once the differentiators that fuelled Northern Rock's growth were reversed, its business model failed.

Focus

Focused strategy involves concentrating on serving a particular market or a defined geographic region. IKEA, for, example, targets young, white-collar workers as its prime customer segment, selling through 235 stores in more than 30 countries. Ingvar Kamprad, an entrepreneur from the Småland province in southern Sweden, who founded the business in the late 1940s, offers home furnishing products of good function and design at prices young people can afford. He achieves this by using simple cost-cutting solutions that do not affect the quality of products.

Warren Buffett, the world's richest man, who knows a thing or two about focus, combined with Mars to buy US chewing gum manufacturer Wrigley for \$23 (£14.3/€17) billion in May 2008. Chicago-based Wrigley, which launched its Spearmint and Juicy Fruit gums in the 1890s, has specialized in chewing gum ever since and consistently outperformed its more diversified competitors. Wrigley is the only major consumer products company to grow comfortably faster than the population in its markets and above the rate of inflation. Over the past decade or so, for example, other consumer products companies have diversified. Gillette moved into batteries used to drive many of its products by acquiring Duracell. Nestlé bought Ralston Purina, Dreyer's, Ice Cream Partners and Chef America. Both have trailed Wrigley's performance.

Businesses often lose their focus over time and periodically have to rediscover their core strategic purpose. Procter & Gamble (P&G) is an example of a business that had to refocus to cure weak growth. In 2000, the company was losing share in seven of its top nine categories, and had lowered earnings expectations four times in two quarters. This prompted the company to restructure and refocus on its core business: big brands, big customers and big countries. It sold off non-core businesses, establishing five global business units with a closely focused product portfolio.

First to market fallacy

Gaining 'first mover advantage' are words used like a mantra to justify high expenditure and a headlong rush into new strategic areas. This concept is one of the most enduring in business theory and practice. Entrepreneurs and established giants are always in a race to be first. Research from the 1980s that shows that market pioneers have enduring advantages in distribution, product-line breadth, product quality and especially market share, underscores this principle.

Beguiling though the theory of first mover advantage is, it is probably wrong. Gerard Tellis, of the University of Southern California, and Peter Golder, of New York University's Stern Business School, argued in their book *Will and Vision: How latecomers grow to dominate markets* (2001, McGraw-Hill) and subsequent research that previous studies on the subject were deeply flawed.

In the first instance earlier studies were based on surveys of surviving companies and brands, excluding all the pioneers that failed. This helps some companies to look as though they were first to market even when they were not. P&G boasts that it created the United States' disposable-nappy (diaper) business. In fact a company called Chux launched its product quarter of a century before P&G entered the market in 1961.

Also, the questions used to gather much of the data in earlier research were at best ambiguous, and perhaps dangerously so. For example the term, 'one of the pioneers in first developing such products or services' was used as a proxy for 'first to market'. The authors emphasize their point by listing popular misconceptions of who were the real pioneers across the 66 markets they analysed:

online book sales – Amazon (wrong), Books.com (right)

copiers – Xerox (wrong), IBM (right)

PCs – IBM/Apple (both wrong), Micro Instrumentation Telemetry Systems (MITS) introduced its PC, the Altair, a $400 kit, in 1974 followed by Tandy Corporation (Radio Shack), in 1977.

In fact the most compelling evidence from all the research was that nearly half of all firms pursuing a first to market strategy were fated to fail, while those following fairly close behind were three times as likely to succeed. Tellis and Golder claim the best strategy is to enter the market 19 years after pioneers learn from their mistakes, benefit from their product and market development, and be more certain about customer preferences.

Shaping strategy – tools and techniques

While Porter's five forces approach to strategy formulation is, as far as business schools are concerned at least, the standard starting point, there are a number of other tools that an MBA needs to be familiar with. Some pre-date Porter, some overlap, and others home in on specific issues. Like many such tools they overlap with those used in marketing. Below are the main tools and techniques an MBA will be expected to know and understand.

Ansoff's Growth Matrix

Igor Ansoff, while Professor of Industrial Administration in the Graduate School at Carnegie Mellon University, published his landmark book, *Corporate Strategy* (1965, McGraw-Hill), where he explained a way of categorizing strategies as an aid to understanding the nature of the risks involved. He invited his students to consider growth options as a square matrix divided into four segments (see Figure 12.9). The axes are labelled with products and services running along the 'x' axis, starting with 'existing' and 'new'; and markets up the 'y' axis similarly labelled.

FIGURE 12.9   Ansoff's Growth Matrix

	Existing products	**New products**
Existing markets	**Market penetration**	**Product development**
New markets	**Market development**	**Diversification** Horizontal Vertical Concentric Conglomerate

Ansoff then went on to assign titles to each type of strategy, in an ascending scale of risk (you can find out more about the matrix at **www.strategy-vectormodel.com**>Theories>Ansoff Matrix):

- *Market penetration*, which involves selling more of your existing products and services to existing customers – the lowest risk strategy.

- *Product/service development*, which involves creating extensions to your existing products or new products to sell to your existing customer base. This is more risky than market penetration, but less risky than entering a new market where you will face new competitors and may not understand the customers as well as you do your current ones.

- *Market development* involves entering new market segments or completely new markets either in your home country or abroad.

- *Diversification* is selling new products into new markets, the most risky strategy as both are relative unknowns. Avoid unless all other strategies have been exhausted. Diversification can be further subdivided into four categories of increasing risk profile: 1) horizontal diversification (entirely new product into current market); 2) vertical diversification (move backwards into firm's supplier's or forwards into customer's business); 3) concentric diversification (new product closely related to current products either in terms of technology or marketing presence but into a new market); 4) conglomerate diversification (completely new product into a new market).

2. Boston Matrix

Developed in 1969 by the Boston Consulting Group, this tool can be used in conjunction with the lifecycle concept to plan a portfolio of product/service offers. The thinking behind the matrix, shown in Figure 12.10, is that a company's products and services should be classified according to their cash generating or consumption ability against two dimensions: the market growth rate and the company's market share. Cash is used as the measure rather than profit, as that is the real resource used to invest in new offers. The objective is to use the positive cash flow generated from 'cash cows', usually mature products that no longer need heavy marketing support budgets, to invest in 'stars', that is fast growing, usually newer products, positioned in markets in which the company already has a high market share – usually newer markets. 'Dogs' should be disinvested and 'question marks' limited in number and watched carefully to see if they are more likely to become stars or dogs.

Strategic purpose

Business leaders, ably supported by their MBAs have three major tasks: to determine the direction, chart the course and set the goals. The direction of

FIGURE 12.10   The Boston Matrix

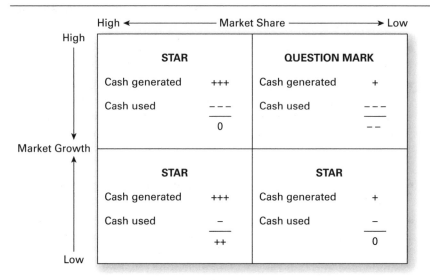

FIGURE 12.11   The purpose pyramid

a business has a number of components that can be best understood if thought of as being parts of a pyramid; see Figure 12.11.

Vision

A vision is about stretching the organization's reach beyond its grasp. Few now can see how the vision can be achieved, but they can see that it would be great if it could be.

Microsoft's vision of a computer in every home, formed when few offices had one, is one example of a vision that has nearly been reached. As a mission statement in 1990 it might have raised a wry smile. After all it was only a few decades earlier that IBM had estimated the entire world demand for its computers as seven!

NASDAQ, the entrepreneurs' stock market, has as its vision to build the world's first truly global securities market: 'A world-wide market of markets built on a world-wide network of network linking pools of liquidity and connecting investors from all over the world thus assuring the best possible price for securities at the lowest possible costs.' That certainly points to beyond the horizon envisaged by business today.

Having a vision will make it easier to get employees to buy into a long-term commitment to a business, seeing they could have career opportunities and progression in an organization that knows where it is going.

Mission

A mission is a direction statement, intended to focus your attention on the essentials that encapsulate your specific competence(s) in relation to the market/customers you plan to serve. First, the mission should be narrow enough to give direction and guidance to everyone in the business. This concentration is the key to business success because it is only by focusing on specific needs that a small business can differentiate itself from its larger competitors. Nothing kills off a business faster than trying to do too many different things too soon. Second, the mission should open up a large enough market to allow the business to grow and realize its potential. You can always add a bit on later. In summary, the mission statement should explain:

- What business you are in and your purpose.
- What you want to achieve over the next one to three years, ie your strategic goal.
- How, ie your ethics, values and standards.

Above all, mission statements must be realistic, achievable – and brief.

Objectives

The milestones on the way to realizing the vision and mission are measured by the achievement of business objectives. These objectives 'cascade' through the organization from the top where they are measures of profit, through to measures such as output, quality, reject rates, absenteeism and so forth.

Objective-setting is a primary process in which clear performance measures are agreed with every employee. The achievement of specific objectives is the ultimate measure of effective leadership.

CASE STUDY

Judy Lever and Vivienne Pringle started Blooming Marvellous over 20 years ago when they were both pregnant. After searching for the kind of fashionable clothes they used to wear and drawing a blank, they guessed they had found a gap in the market. They stated their purpose and goals as follows:

> Arising out of our experiences, we intend to design, make and market a range of clothes for mothers-to-be that will make them feel they can still be fashionably dressed. We aim to serve a niche missed out by Mothercare, Marks & Spencer, etc, and so become a significant force in the mail order fashion for the mothers-to-be market.
>
> We are aiming for a 5 per cent share of this market in the Southeast, and a 25 per cent return on assets employed within three years of starting up. We believe we will need about £25,000 start-up capital to finance stock, a mail order catalogue and an advertising campaign.

They kept on their day jobs and would meet after work every day at Judy's house to answer enquiries, send out leaflets and dispatch products in the post every day. They outsourced work to a pattern cutter, a small factory, some fabric suppliers and eventually to a small distribution centre. After a year or so of modest sales they felt confident enough to set up their first business premises – a 1,200 sq ft warehouse on a business park staffed by four of the women who had been working in their distribution centre.

The company now employs 150 people, has 14 shops and has extended its range to include nursery products, toys, themed bedroom accessories and a separate brand called Mini Marvellous that caters for children aged 2–8 years old. Over a third of sales come directly via its website (**www.bloomingmarvellous.co.uk**).

Balanced scorecard

The balanced scorecard (see Figure 12.12), developed by Robert Kaplan and David Norton and published in a *Harvard Business Review* article in 1992, is a management process that sets out to align business activities to the vision and strategy of the organization, improve internal and external communication, and monitor organization performance against strategic goals. Its uniqueness was to add non-financial performance measures to traditional financial targets to give managers and directors a more 'balanced' view of organizational performance.

Although Kaplan and Norton are credited with coining the phrase, the idea of a balanced scorecard originated with General Electric's work on performance measurement reporting in the 1950s, and the work of French process engineers (who created the *tableau de bord* – literally, a 'dashboard' of performance measures) in the early part of the 20th century.

Four perspectives are included in the management process, which in effect extends the range of management by objectives and value-based

FIGURE 12.12   The balanced scorecard

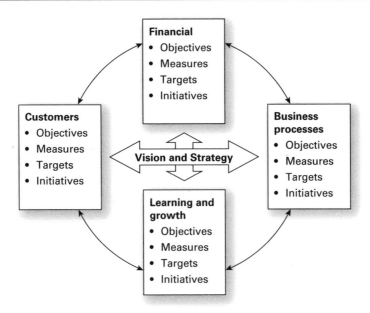

management into areas beyond purely financial target setting. A number of objectives, measures, targets and initiatives can be set to achieve specific Key Performance Indicators (KPIs) for each perspective:

1 *Financial:* these include KPIs for return on investment, cash flow, profit margins and shareholder value.

2 *Customers:* here the KPIs can be for customer retention rates, satisfaction levels, referrals and complaints.

3 *Internal business processes:* these can include stock turn, accident rates, defects in production, reduction in the number of processes and improvements in communication.

4 *Learning and growth:* employee turnover, morale levels, training and development achievements and internal promotions vs new recruits are all KPIs to use here.

The four perspectives are linked by a double feedback loop, the purpose of which is to ensure that KPIs are not in conflict with one another. For example, if customer satisfaction could be achieved by improving delivery times, achieving that by, say, increasing stock levels might conflict with a financial target of improving return on capital employed.

INDEX

Abrams, Neill 79 *see also* Ocado
Academy of Management Journal 90
Accountancy Age 165
accountants 1, 7, 12, 31–32, 36, 66, 109,
    126–27, 131, 159–60, 165, 179
accounting
    basic 16
    branches 11
    conventions 31, 35
    financial 11
    firms 131
    formula 61
    fraud 167
    function 12
    invalid 167
    knowledge 2
    methods 164
    package 16
    period 17, 38, 161, 163
    policies 165
    principles, accepted 164, 166
    records 14–15, 31, 170, 172
    skills 2
    standards 26, 128, 147, 168
Accounting Standards Board 29, 37
acquisitions 2–5, 26–27, 125–26, 129,
    141, 174–79, 181, 183, 185–86
adopters, early 137
advertising 18–19, 22, 98, 172, 178, 201,
    206–7
adviser, nominated 128
advisers 52, 127, 144, 159
AEX (Amsterdam Exchange) 131
Alternative Investment Market (AIM) 128
Amazon 67, 120
American Accounting Association 66
American Nickel Company 1
amortization 27 *see also* depreciation
analysts 90
animal spirits 191
annual report 12, 168, 172
Apple 50, 61, 78, 220
arbitration 155
arrogance 174–75
Ashridge 121
Asset Based Finance Association 112
asset *see also* fixed asset
    classes 140
    financing 4

security 102
    stripping 125
    utilization 11
    value 179
assumptions 17, 24, 68, 94, 107, 207, 215
Aston (Business School) 5
audit
    opinion 165
    reports 128
auditors 4, 7, 34, 52, 128, 147, 159,
    164–65, 167–69, 172

Babson 94
balance sheet
    activity 146
    data 177
    items 52
    reports 7
    statements 40
    structure 25–26
    values 82
balanced score card 226
Balon, Adam 122
Bangor Business School 2
bank *see also* merchant bank
    accounts 103, 116
    borrowings 51, 103
    debt 126
    finance 100, 103
    loans 18, 23, 42, 80, 107, 115, 139, 158
    overdraft 24, 43, 46
Bank of England 102, 217
bankers 12, 17, 19, 24, 32, 41, 43, 52, 79,
    100–2, 128, 131, 146, 153
Bankers Trust 152
bankruptcy 122
Barclays Bank 180
Barclays Private Equity 129
BBC 106
BCG (Boston Consulting Group) 219
BDO Stoy Hayward 180
Bebo 119, 137
behaviour 2, 69, 71, 100, 138, 160,
    171–73, 191
BEP (break-even point) 72–74, 76–7
Best Social Accounts 139
beta factor 81–82
Bethlehem Steel Corporation 1
Bezos, Jeff 120

Bilimoria, Lord   109
bills   4, 35, 43, 45, 59, 62, 91, 111–12, 134,
      147, 152
Birch, Michael   119, 137
Blackwell, James   120
BMW   220
Board
   chairman   170
   meetings   170
   of directors   78, 122, 147, 172, 187
   salaries   171
   strong   153
   structure   169
Boden, Johnnie   194
bonds   4, 80, 91, 100, 106–7, 124
bonus   145
bookkeeping
   basic   16
   double-entry   14, 34
   process   9
   record   28, 33
   single-entry   13–14
   software packages   16
borrowings   24, 100, 104–5, 147, 153
Boston Consulting Group (BCG)   219
Boston Safe Deposit and Trust Company
      219
Box-Jenkins   189
Brandeis University   205
brands   173, 221
Brink, Nina   132
British Airways   183
British Business Angels Association   118
British Standards Institution   88
British Venture Capital Association   120
      see also venture capital associations
Brown, Jill   87
browsers   60
BSE (Bombay Stock Exchange)   134
budget guidelines   197
budget model   4
budget ratios   199
Budgeting   197
budgets
   fixed   199
   flexed   199
Buffett, Warren   220
business
   angels   4, 91, 117–19, 124, 136
   award   186
   best   215
   brokers   183
   closure   4
   competitions   139
   core   221

cycles   4, 193
   ethical   139
   growing   109, 119
   incubators   4, 91
   insurance   126
   international   36
   mature   51
   merged   4
   model   67, 104, 123, 137, 220
   new   50, 87, 102, 111, 121, 195
   performance, improving   38, 56
   plan   102, 105–6, 187, 193–94, 196–97
   private   89, 171
   quoted   171
   ratios   49, 52
   reports   3
   risk   96, 136, 141, 146
   schools   1, 5–6, 94, 121, 159, 189, 202,
      217
   sound   19

California State University   159
Cameron, Duncan   137
capital
   allowances   12, 161
   asset pricing model see CAPM
   budgeting   5, 86, 182
   cost of   12, 79, 82–84, 107
   expenditure   33
   owner's   25, 44, 144
   permanent   102
   public   117, 125
   rationing   83
   structure   12, 125, 144–45
   weighted average cost of   83, 85
capitalism   192
CAPM (Capital asset pricing model)   80–81
career   3, 174
Carli, Luiss Guido   131
Carphone Warehouse   122
cash
   balance   19
   borrowed   107
   high   51
   insufficient   17
   lifesaving   59
   movements   19, 21
   raising   79
   unused   90
cash flow
   deficit   17
   difficulties   59
   discounted   84, 86, 181–82
   forecasts   9, 17
   spreadsheet   19

Cass Business School 3, 174, 217
Centre for Growth and Business Cycle
  Research 193
chairman 79, 122 *see also* board
Chief Executive Officer 79
Chief Financial Officer 79
Cisco 121, 175
Citigroup 133
Citroen 218
City University Business School 152
Clarke, Jeff 133
Cobra 109
Coca-Cola 78, 122
code, city 98, 186
Columbia University 175
Commissioners of Inland Revenue 160
Companies House 51, 58, 95, 99, 168–70
company
  accounts 38, 41, 51, 165, 168
  doctor 177
  dynamic 128
  factoring 111, 148
  large 12
  listed 52, 130, 168
  multinational 12
  ownership 113
  performance 43
  reports 159
  secrets 88
  start-up 119
  surviving 221
competence 120
competition 26, 94, 130, 184, 203, 207
competitive
  advantage 174
  pressures 143
  pricing 202
competitors 2, 11, 31, 38–40, 58, 72, 83,
    129, 132, 175, 177, 196, 201, 203,
    207, 209
computers 17–19, 24–25, 44, 57, 61, 69,
    111, 162, 190
concepts 2–3, 21, 32, 35–6, 51, 97, 105,
    194, 205, 208, 213, 221
confidentiality 109
conflict 211–13
conservatism 33, 35–36
consistency 31, 35–36
consolidated accounts 157
consultant 179
contribution 64–65, 76, 163
control 5, 10–11, 42, 59, 87–9, 126, 134,
    140, 156, 166, 176, 196, 210–13,
    219–220
conventions 35–36, 43, 59–60, 198

Copenhagen Business School 130
core
  competency 89
  disciplines 5
cost *see also* fixed costs, operating costs *and*
    variable costs
  advantage 72, 203, 217
  analysis 71
  basis 125
  concept 32
  leadership 218
  model 69–73
  of sales 23, 39, 56, 150
  administrative 150
  direct 198–9
  marginal 64, 77
  nominal 82
  semi-variable 71
Cranfield School of Management 2, 5, 183,
    194
Crawford's Model 219
credit
  acceptance 4
  agencies 10
  analysis 102
  cards 120
  crunch 146, 150
  decisions 148
  history 102
  insurance 148, 150, 153
  score 52, 148
Credit Management Research Centre
    147–48
  creditors 24–25, 40, 44, 49–50, 57, 95,
    97, 116, 151, 154, 158, 167, 171
creditworthiness 10, 148
crisis 193
CSUN (California State University,
    Northridge) 159
currencies 101, 108, 156–58, 191 *see also*
    exchange rate
  convertible 157
  foreign 12, 156–57
  handling 36
  international 157
  local 157
currency stability 157
current liabilities 26, 39, 43, 45–46, 50, 57,
    152 *see also* liabilities
customer
  choice 218
  endorsements 196
  groups 194, 205
  relations 89
  segment 186, 220

Dallal, Gerard E   190
Debenhams   106
debentures   80, 106–7, 144
debt
    bad   148
    capital   4, 82, 102, 104, 144
    collection agency   155
    covenants   4
    instruments   91
    private   95
    short-term   43
debtors   19, 21, 25–26, 30, 39, 44–45,
        49–50, 57, 108, 112, 151, 153–54,
        158
deficit   17–18
depreciation *see also* amortisation
    annual   48
    charges   22
    expense   22
    methods   28–29, 33
derivatives   4
Deutsche Bank   121, 133
Deutsche Stock Exchange   134
differentiation   217, 220
directors
    company's   127
    fellow   123
    full-time   170
    independent   90
    retired   171
disclosure requirements   168
discount   60, 85, 101, 180, 184
discounted cash flow   181–82
discovery   140, 193, 202, 210
discrimination   172
distribution   125, 150, 198, 208, 221
dividend
    declaration   168
    deductions   43
    payments   19, 46, 138
    stream   146
    yield   52
due diligence   124, 132, 150
Duke University's Fuqua School   189
Dun & Bradstreet   10, 148
Dunstone, Charles   122
duties   7, 12–13, 169–71

earnings   47, 84, 163, 180–81, 184
easyJet   186, 218
economics   123, 190–91
effectiveness   47, 166, 206
employees
    despatching   194
    interests of   170, 172

    potential   133
    senior   58
employment policy   168
Enron   37
Enterprise Finance Guarantee Scheme   91,
        103
entrepreneurs   65, 97, 104, 121, 133,
        135–37, 143, 186, 197, 220–21
environnent   105, 172–73, 209
EOQ (Economic Order Quantity)   61
equity
    capital   80, 82, 95
    cost of   80–82
    investors   4
    private   117, 121, 124, 126, 152
    ratio   2, 46, 158
Ernst & Young   171
European Business Angels Network   118
European Founders Capital (EFC)   119
European Observatory for SME Research   144
European Union Grant Adviser   138
European Venture Capital Association   120
exchange rate *see also* currencies
    effect   158
    fluctuations   141
    information   158
expenses   17, 22–23, 30, 35, 39, 53, 77, 87,
        161, 164, 199, 206
Experian   148
experience curve   219–20

failure   49, 109, 138, 144, 147, 167, 193,
        201, 215
failure curve   143
FAME (Financial Accounting Made
        EASY)   52
FASB (Financial Accounting Standards
        Board)   37
FIFO (First In First Out)   28 *see also* stock
Financial Accounting Standards Board
        (FASB)   37
financial
    appraisal   83
    crime   3, 174
    difficulties   146, 154, 167
    financial reports   3, 38
    financial risk   4, 94, 108, 144
    financial statements   7, 11, 38, 49, 51,
        102, 164–67, 169
    jeopardy   95
    magicians   147
Financial Markets Association   158
financing
    activities   20–1
    asset usage   111

business   3, 91, 93, 95, 97, 99, 111
costs   22, 42
methods   115, 138
spectrum   101
strategic   10
strategy   3, 107, 127, 140
Five Forces   201 *see also* Porter, Michael E
fixed assets   24–27, 29–30, 32, 36, 39, 44,
47, 57, 108, 113, 151, 158, 179 *see
also* asset
fixed costs   63–5, 69–77, 87–88 *see also*
costs *and* variable costs
floating   89, 115, 128, 130
forecasting   5, 188–89
The Foundation for the Study of Cycles   193
Fox , Martha Lane   119

GAAP (Generally Accepted Accounting
Practices)   36
GDP (Gross Domestic Product)   192
gearing   4, 46, 78, 108, 133, 144–46
see also leverage
George Washington University   94
Golder, Peter   221
Goldman Sachs   78–9, 124, 132
Goodman, Harry   183
goods, cost of   23, 28, 42, 57
Goodsell, Andrew   127
goodwill   24, 26, 33, 37, 184
Google   116, 137, 165, 180
Google Foundation   53
governance   173
Grade, Michael   79, 113
Graebner, Melissa   90
grants   101, 104, 138
Great Depression   192
gross profit   22–23, 30, 39, 41–42, 56–57,
62, 77, 150, 195, 198–99
growth
expected annual   80
fast   153
healthy   57, 59, 62
phase   196
rapid   122, 128–29
rates   177
ratios   46
strategies   58, 62
unprofitable   56
weak   221

Hale, Victoria   139
Hammurabi's code   100
Harvard Business Review   174
Harvard Business School   1, 52, 77, 131,
214, 217, 219

HBOS   110
hedge funds   5
Henderson, Bruce D   219
Hertzberg, Frederick   216
hierarchy of needs   206
HM Revenue and Customs   121, 162
Hobbes, Thomas   214
HSBC   109, 139
HSBC's Start-up Stars Awards   139
hygiene factors   216

IAB (International Association of
Bookkeepers)   16
IASB (International Accounting Standards
Board)   37
IBM   86, 113, 121
IKEA   186, 220
Imperial College London   5, 137
income
match   35
non-operating   22
rental   183
statement   3, 7, 21, 26, 38
stream   183
taxes   23, 54
underreporting   160
incorporation   98
indemnities   4, 185
Independent Directors Initiative   171
inflation   40, 50, 62, 221
information
external   2
financial   3, 9–10, 31, 36, 95
global   177
internal   2
information memorandum   108
initial public offering *see* IPO
Innocent   122
innovation   94, 135, 138, 146, 210
insolvencies   149, 153
Institute of Certified Bookkeepers   16
Institute of Chartered Accountants   37
Institute of Credit Management   147
Institute of Directors   171
intangible assets   20, 27
intellectual property   24, 26, 27, 88, 196
see also patents
interest
common   179
paying   109
vested   11
interest charges   183
interest payments   12, 46, 101, 103, 144–5
interest rates   41, 46, 80, 85, 102–3, 107,
182, 193, 220

International Accounting Standards   36
internet   18, 22, 58, 117, 137, 155–6, 158,
      192, 208
inventories   26, 61, 108, 193
investment banks   78, 124
investment centres   213
investment decisions   10, 83
investment terms   122
Investor Relations Society   169
investors
      institutional   132–3
      potential   128, 132
invoices   4, 15, 34, 59, 89, 91, 110–12,
      153–54
IPO (initial public offering)   78–79, 121,
      125–26, 130–33
Irrational Exuberance   191
Irwin   204
Richard D

John Castaing   134
John Maynard Keynes   191
Jones
      Geoffrey   93
      Tony   114
Joseph De La Vega   191
Journal of Finance   176
JP Morgan Cazenove   78
Juglar cycle   193
Junk bonds   107

Kamprad, Ingvar Kamprad   186, 220
Kellogg School of Management   94, 202
Keynes, John Maynard   191
key performance indicators   227
Kirchoff, Bruce A   143
Kitchin, Joseph   193
Kondratieff's long waves   192
Kotler, Philip   202
KPMG   124
Kuznet's cycle   192

Lampel, Joseph   217
lastminute.com   119
law   34, 65, 94, 96, 100, 131, 143, 155–56,
      168–169, 172, 196, 212
leaseback   4, 91, 113–14
leasing   111, 113
Leeds University Business School   148
legal
      action   94
      constraints   172
      identity   26, 97
      relations   160
      structure   95, 97, 99, 135

Lehman Brothers   67, 122, 147
lenders   4, 7, 11, 40–1, 104, 108–9, 136,
      144, 146–47, 167, 191 see also banks
letters of credit   112
Levchin, Max   121
Lever, William Hesketh   172
leverage   4, 78, 144 see also gearing
Lewis, John   78, 194
liabilities see also current liabilities
      limited   96–97, 171
      long-term   46
      personal   95–96
      potential   169
      short-term   24, 26, 43
      understate   37
      unlimited   96
LIFO (Last In First Out)   28 see also FIFO
      (First In Last Out)
limited companies   10, 52, 96–97, 115,
      135, 162
linear regression   190
liquid   45, 89, 152
liquidation   125, 193
liquidity   33, 41, 43, 50, 130, 150, 180
listing   127, 130, 134, 221
Liverpool University   2
loan
      bilateral   108
      capital   40, 82, 144–45
      fixed-rate   103
      long-term   12, 22, 24, 46
      short-term   24
      syndicated   108
      variable   46
London Business School (LBS)   1, 2, 3, 5, 174
London School of Economics   123
London Stock Exchange   52, 128, 180
losses   3, 7, 15–16, 23, 38, 66, 79, 94–95,
      117, 124, 133, 154, 160, 162, 169,
      178, 185, 213
Lowe, Rachel   106
Lynn, Stephen   152

M&A strategies   176
MacArthur, Niall   152
Mackay, Charles   191
Madness of Crowds   191
mail order   156
management
      accounting   11
      buy-outs   119, 138
      consultants   175, 203
      layers of   210–11
      middle   175
      style   178

Manchester Business School 1
Marks & Spenser 209
market,
  conditions 102, 107
  fallacy 221
  large 218
  market
  price 28, 33, 47, 78, 167, 179
  research 203, 207
  share 72, 79, 130, 177, 195, 203–4,
    221
marketing 6, 53, 106, 120, 177, 187, 196,
  201–2, 205, 210–12, 214
marketing goals 203
marketing mix 205, 208
marketing strategy 3, 205, 208
Mars 220
Maslow, Abraham 205
Massachusetts Institute of Technology (MIT)
  2, 215
materiality 35–36
matrix organization 213
Mayo, Elton 214
MBA
  ambitious 41
  perspective 66
  role 75
  skills 197
  specialized 1
  syllabus 208
McCarthy, Jerome 205
McCallum, Daniel C 210
McDonald's 78, 121
McDougall, William 215
McGraw-Hill 221
McGregor, Douglass 215
Melinda Gates Foundation 140
merchant bank 127 see also banks
mergers 3–5, 98, 127, 141, 174–75, 177,
  179, 181, 183, 185–86
Metcalfe, Julian 121
Mezzanine financing 4
Michigan State University 205
Microsoft 116, 121
mission statement 195
MIT (Massachusetts Institute of Technology)
  2, 215
money
  borrowed 150
  cost-free 138
  family 126
  markets 3, 12, 220
  measurement 31
  raising 122–23
  repatriate 157

  short-term 102
  transfer 112
Money Supermarket 137
monopoly 106
Morgan Chase 9
Morrison 114
mortgages 82, 100, 106, 137, 220
motivation 208, 214–15
moving average 188 see also weighted
  moving average

National Bureau of Economic
  Research 193
National Computer Centre 129
National Venture Capital Association
  120
negotiations 17, 183–84
Nestlé 221
net asset 32, 140, 184
net cash flows 20, 84–5, 181
net income 23, 47, 54
network 13, 101, 117, 171, 190
New Jersey Institute of Technology 143
New York Stock Exchange 130
New York University's Stern Business
  School 221
Nokia Venture Partners (NVP) 121
non-profit organizations 98
Northern Rock 220
Northwestern University 202
Nottingham University 137
NVP (Nokia Venture Partners) 121

objectives 40, 179, 194–96, 207–8,
  211
Ocado 67, 78–79
Office of Fair Trading 148, 156
offsetting 113, 162
Onesource 177
Oneworld Health 139
online
  directories 118, 120
  spreadsheets 23, 77
  tools 29
operating costs 10, 113–14 see also cost
opportunity 47, 83, 115, 119, 121, 127,
  159, 176, 187, 216
option 107, 111, 114, 125, 138, 147, 160,
  207
outsourcing 86–89
overdrafts 4, 11–12, 19, 23, 25–26, 42,
  44, 49, 57, 59, 91, 102–4, 110
overhead spending 47
overtrading 17, 19, 41
Oxford (Business School) 5

Paccioli, Luca   14
Palm Pilot   121
Palo Alto Software   197
parent company   120–21, 165–66, 213
partners   5, 11, 95–97, 129, 140, 207
partnership
  agreement   96
  obligations   95
  structures   97
passive investors   96
patents   26–7, 140, 185, 196
    see also intellectual property
payback   83, 84, 86, 138, 182
payment in kind (PIK)   109
Payment League Tables   147
PayPal   121
PCPI (Private Company Price Index)   180
PE Ratio   47
PeaPod Inc   79
Penn State   94
performance
  firm's   132
  improving   59
personal development   6
Peugeot   218
Piasecki, Dave   61
Pizza Hut   118
plans   4, 6, 15–16, 68, 89–90, 105, 127,
    129, 131, 166, 178, 185, 187,
    193–97
PLUS   128–29
policy statement   169
Porter, Michael E   174, 201, 217
Prêt a Manger   121, 152
price   26, 28, 33, 40, 47, 62, 75–8, 87, 107,
    109, 124–25, 132–33, 135, 179–80,
    184, 186
price earnings ratio   47
PricewaterhouseCoopers LLP   166
Princeton   190, 217
private companies   51, 98, 140, 168, 177,
    180, 183, 186
Private Company Price Index (PCPI)   180
private equity providers   12
Procter & Gamble   221
products   2, 11, 34, 40–1, 61–65, 68,
    87–90, 101, 104, 111, 135–36,
    185–87, 1949–6, 202–10, 213,
    217–21
professional bodies   36
profit
  decisions   68
  forecast   177
  goals   66, 77

growth   59, 80
level   69
margins   21, 50, 58, 77–78, 187, 198,
    206
promotion   196, 205–6, 216
prospectus   111, 131–32
psychologists   1, 205
public companies   51–52, 89–90, 126,
    170, 175, 177, 180

quality   41, 87–88, 186

ratios   3, 7, 38–43, 45–52, 89, 125, 146,
    169, 180
Real Business   194
receivership   183
redundancies   69, 185, 214
refinancing   107, 152
Repo   105, 147
research   3, 53, 60, 87, 104, 121, 138,
    175–76, 193, 203, 205, 213, 216,
    221
resources   57–58, 120, 156, 193, 196,
    214
responsibilities   4, 7, 11, 96, 108, 111,
    115, 148, 153, 159, 166, 168–73,
    193, 211–13, 215–16
revenues   21, 23, 53, 56, 137, 157, 213
risk capital   117, 119, 128, 136
risk levels   82, 102
risk management   4–5, 143, 145, 147,
    151, 153, 155, 157
Royal Bank of Canada   197
R-Squared   190
Ryanair   218

safety margin   146
Sainsbury   79
sales
  absolute   203
  achieved   46
  cost of   23, 45, 157
  forecasting   187
  income   35, 38, 157
Salisbury, Katherine   139
Sarbanes-Oxley Act   37
Savoy Hotel Group   116
SBUs (Strategic business unit)   213
scatter diagram   189
School for Social Entrepreneurs   139
School of Social Sciences   193
SCORE   200
service agreements   129
service contracts   184

service mix   62
Stettler, Howard F   66
share
  buyback   90
  calculations   184
  capital   24, 40, 43, 46, 97, 116, 136,
    144–45, 151, 153, 168
  price   90, 125, 176, 179–80
shareholders
  deceive   170, 172
  external   164
  minority   184
  ordinary   116, 138
  pre-float   133
shares
  allotted   98
  fractional   175
  ordinary   47, 80–81, 116, 138
  owning   116
  preference   116, 138, 144
Shiller, Robert J   191
Sinclair Beecham   121
SITPRO   112
skills   2–3, 5–6, 56, 66, 69, 88, 95, 136,
    155, 194, 196, 202, 211
Skype   175
social entrepreneurs   139
social responsibilities   172
software   17, 190
span of control   210–11
spreadsheet   19, 52, 62, 86, 182, 196
staff   47, 58, 87, 105, 114, 118, 127, 133,
    167, 177, 185, 209, 211–12
staff functions   197, 211
    see also structures
stakeholders   173
Stanford   2, 219
Steering Wheel ratios   48 see also Tesco
Steiner, Tim   79
stock   14–15, 17, 19, 21, 24–26, 28, 30, 33,
    39, 43–46, 49, 57–58, 60–62, 104–6,
    132, 176
stock exchanges   80, 130, 134, 168, 177,
    179
stock warrant   55
Strategic business unit (SBUs)   213
strategy
  acquisition   5, 174–75
  company's   79
  cost leadership   220
  differentiation   220
  financial   86, 115
  focus   217
  generic   217

structures   3, 14, 22, 57, 91, 93, 208–10,
    212–13, 218
Student t test   190
SWOT analysis   204

takeovers   98, 116, 125, 174, 185–86
tax   12, 17, 19, 22–3, 26, 30, 42–43, 46,
    48, 56–57, 62, 65, 99, 125, 141,
    159–64
tax authorities   11, 33, 161–2
tax fraud   160–1
team   12, 88, 127, 131–32, 136, 140, 201,
    211, 214, 219
term sheet   108, 124–25
Tesco   47–48, 51, 79, 113–14, 165
Theory X and Theory Y   215
Toyota   218
track record   119, 127, 153
treasury   12
Tufts   190
turnover   20, 59, 67, 77, 79, 87, 101, 105,
    112, 129–30, 150, 164, 182

Unilever   172–73
University of Baltimore   189
University of Chicago Booth School of
    Business   2
University of Manchester   193
University of Pennsylvania   192
University of Southern California   221
University of Southern Maine   159

variable costs   63–64, 70–73, 75–77, 87
    see also cost
variance analysis   198
VAT (Value Added Tax)   11–12, 17, 26, 48,
    56, 95, 163–4
VCs (Venture capitalists)   118–20, 129,
    136, 138
venture capital   4, 91, 115, 118, 120–21,
    183
venture capital associations   120
    see also British Venture Capital
    Association
Venture Investment Partners   171

Waitrose   79
Wall Street Journal   175
warrant   86, 124, 182
warranties   4, 129, 185
Waterstone, Tim   60, 104, 136
websites   49, 58, 61, 101, 111, 118, 120,
    130–31, 148, 158, 170, 196, 206
weighted average cost of capital   82

weighted moving average   188 *see also* moving average
Westinghouse Corporation   219
Westphal, James   90
WH Smith   104–5, 120
Wharton   1
work-in-progress   24
working capital   25–26, 30, 39–40, 43–6, 49–50, 57, 59–60
World Wide-Tax.com   130
Wright, Jon   122

Wright, Robert   183
Wrigley   221
writing down allowance   161

Yahoo   52–53, 137
yardsticks   51, 182

Z-Score   49
Zeitlin, Jonathan   94
Zero coupon bonds   107
Zurich Insurance   137